CW01573309

PE
THE

Shashi Warrier turned

journalism and computing. He is the author of several books: *Hangman's Journal*, *Sniper*, *Night of the Krait*, *The Homecoming*, *Sally and the Warlocks and Other Stories* and *The Marblewood Forest*. He is a member of the adjunct faculty of BITS, Pilani, from where he completed his master's in economics in 1981.

In between bursts of writing and lecturing, he likes to listen to music, mostly Hindustani, and to ride motorcycles. He lives in Mangalore with his wife, Prita, and their two dachshunds.

THE ORPHAN DIARIES

Shashi Warrier

PENGUIN BOOKS

PENGUIN BOOKS
Published by the Penguin Group
Penguin Books India Pvt. Ltd, 11 Community Centre, Panchsheel Park, New Delhi 110017, India
Penguin Group (USA) Inc., 375 Hudson Street, New York, New York 10014, USA
Penguin Group (Canada), 90 Eglinton Avenue East, Suite 700, Toronto, Ontario, M4P 2Y3, Canada (a division of Pearson Penguin Canada Inc.)
Penguin Books Ltd, 80 Strand, London WC2R 0RL, England
Penguin Ireland, 25 St Stephen's Green, Dublin 2, Ireland (a division of Penguin Books Ltd)
Penguin Group (Australia), 250 Camberwell Road, Camberwell, Victoria 3124, Australia (a division of Pearson Australia Group Pty Ltd)
Penguin Group (NZ), 67 Apollo Drive, Rosedale, North Shore 0632, New Zealand (a division of Pearson New Zealand Ltd)
Penguin Group (South Africa) (Pty) Ltd, 24 Sturdee Avenue, Rosebank, Johannesburg 2196, South Africa

Penguin Books Ltd, Registered Offices: 80 Strand, London WC2R 0RL, England

First published by Penguin Books India 1998
This edition published by Penguin Books India 2009

Copyright © Shashi Warrier 1998, 2009

All rights reserved

10 9 8 7 6 5 4 3 2 1

This is a work of fiction. Names, characters, places and incidents are either the product of the author's imagination or are used fictitiously, and any resemblance to any actual person, living or dead, events or locales is entirely coincidental.

ISBN 9780143066187

Typeset in Perpetua by InoSoft Systems, Noida
Printed at De Unique Printers, New Delhi

This book is sold subject to the condition that it shall not, by way of trade or otherwise, be lent, resold, hired out, or otherwise circulated without the publisher's prior written consent in any form of binding or cover other than that in which it is published and without a similar condition including this condition being imposed on the subsequent purchaser and without limiting the rights under copyright reserved above, no part of this publication may be reproduced, stored in or introduced into a retrieval system, or transmitted in any form or by any means (electronic, mechanical, photocopying, recording or otherwise), without the prior written permission of both the copyright owner and the above-mentioned publisher of this book.

This book is for my parents

Acknowledgements

It's strange how far out of their way people will go to aid genuine endeavour. Many people helped out with this book, including: Suresh, Chitra and Aditya; Bharathi and Ghanashyam; Jayapriya and Harish; Dinesh and Satish; Biju; and Drs Deepa and S.K. Subramaniam. To all of them I'm grateful, as also to those who preferred not to be named here.

Thanks also to David and Ravi of Penguin, who did their best.

chapter one

The point man disappeared in front of my eyes. Then the crickets stopped chirping.

A torch came on thirty yards away, then another. 'I thought I heard something here.' It was a young man's voice, speaking to his companion in Urdu. I was safe, the two guards would never look into the ditch I occupied at the moment. The rest of the team, too, had taken cover behind me. But the point man, Hari, who had climbed out of the safety of the ditch, was out there somewhere, invisible amongst the trees of the deciduous forest. The moonlight was faint, thanks to the clouds that had gathered late in summer. Visibility was next to nil, and I'd lost Hari when he moved, his camouflage clothing blending in with the background. Then I caught the gleam of his eyes as he crouched motionless in a small clump of bushes.

We hadn't made any noise coming in. The guard would have heard not the sound of our approach but instead a silence where there should have been none. Any top-flight watchman attunes himself to the noises of the environment, to the rhythm of background noises. When the rhythm changes, he notices the change, as this youngster had just now. The silence of the crickets had given us away. I pulled the night-vision glasses out of my pack and strapped them on. In the green vision of the glasses, the torches, almost blindingly bright, came closer, sweeping from side to side as the guards scanned the gaps between the tall sal trees.

'Leave it, Aziz, you're imagining things. You haven't had enough sleep in the past two weeks.' From the sound of it, this second man seemed the older, more senior guard.

Aziz, the youngster, stopped, his torch settling in one direction at the base of an almond tree several yards away. In the pale wash of torchlight I saw him shake his head and draw away, his sub-machine gun—a British Sterling, probably, unusual in these parts where AK-47s and the newer AK-74s were much more common—pointing upward, ready for action.

'Hey, come and look at this!' called the older man, waving his torch. 'Look at the size of that snake!'

The younger man saw it too. 'Leave it alone!' he said. 'It's a cobra. It won't come near you unless you scare it. It'll go away on its own . . . must have caught a rat that made a noise.' They stood watching the snake for a while, then retreated towards the small collection of buildings they were guarding. The cobra had saved us.

In the shadows Hari waited for the guards to move out of range, took five quick steps forward, then dropped flat behind another clump of bushes. Inside the ditch, I straightened up and climbed slowly out, making no noise.

The remaining four men in the team followed softly behind. A few seconds later, we were all motionless again, some yards closer now to the group of huts that was our objective that night. We'd repeat this over and over, then strike quickly, and leave.

We could afford no mistakes. We were some thirty kilometres from Uri, in the southern end of Pakistan Occupied Kashmir, just inside the perimeter of the clearing outside a terrorist camp. Inside was an American tourist, kidnapped six weeks ago by this splinter group of the Hezbol Mujahiddeen. His captors wanted freedom for three terrorists captured four months earlier. The government had offered to negotiate. The kidnappers refused to budge. Stalemate.

We'd been lucky on this one. A former terrorist who had given himself up in exchange for an amnesty and a job had heard of the foreigner held captive in this area and warned us. A team of eleven Special Operations Force (SOF) men had crossed the border disguised as terrorists to investigate. We were all dressed in Khan suits, with waistcoats and smelly blankets. We had stopped bathing and brushing our teeth regularly three weeks earlier, and had just begun to get used to our own smells. We were all bearded, all thinner than we'd been when we began, and all used to hunger.

Eking out our meagre supplies with what we could trap in the forest, we had lived off the land for three weeks now, working out escape routes, looking for possible informers, getting the hang of the terrain, getting used to the thin air at this altitude, and, most important, waiting for permission to go.

The permission had come eight hours earlier, at three in the afternoon, from Major General Kelkar, Director of Special Operations. Brief as ever, all he'd told me during our last coded conversation on the VHF was, 'Go!' And here we were, all eleven of us, waiting for a chance to neutralize the guards before bursting into the wooden hut that held the hostage.

After so long undercover it was a relief to be on the way out. Even the rescue, the climax though it was of this operation, would be easier than living with the fear of discovery, maintaining strict radio silence except for my occasional contacts with Kelkar.

One of the guards lit a cigarette. They were relaxed again, and I could hear their soft conversation from fifty yards away. Sound carries far on silent nights in those valleys. A weak drizzle started, which was welcome: the rain would give us cover. I pulled a walkie-talkie out of the harness around my middle, under the kameez of the Khan suit, raised it to my face and said one word: 'Go!' Another team of five men, on the far side of the grounds around the buildings, was waiting for my signal. Their leader acknowledged immediately: 'Going!'—and in we went.

Hari took the older guard, and I took Aziz. I crept up behind him and was just a step away when he sensed something and turned his turbaned head, the bandanna about the lower half of his face flying. I'd been half-expecting something of the kind, knowing how he'd reacted to the silence of the crickets. I ducked under his Sterling and as he raised it to hit me I punched him in the larynx as hard as I could, feeling cartilage crack beneath my knuckles. He went down with a soft cough and I hit him again, just below the nose, to make sure he wouldn't raise an alarm. I caught him as he began to sink to the ground and lowered him gently, soundlessly. I felt for a pulse in his wrist, and found none. I pushed him to a side, off the path, out of the moonlight and into the shadows, then crept forward to join Hari.

There were three buildings ahead of us. To the left was a barn-like structure of wood, which we knew was their storage depot. They kept their arms and explosives in a cellar underneath, innocuous stuff like fuel and fodder for their sheep above. Straight ahead was where they lived, a two-storey hut, also of wood. The hostage was in a room upstairs, accessible only through a trapdoor in the wooden floor. We'd seen him a couple of times through binoculars from half a mile away, a tall, shambling figure who seemed to have adapted to the circumstances and made friends with his captors, for I'd seen them laugh together. To the right was another shed which served as a sort of conference room where they gathered for prayers as well.

A sudden chill breeze arose from the north, blowing the gathering clouds away. Smells are a whole lot more important in those parts than elsewhere, especially in the rains. The smell of water tends to camouflage other odours but you can still make out a man a hundred yards away, if your nose is sharp enough, from the smell of wool and sweat and dirt. We kept downwind.

The windows downstairs were barred, as we knew they would be. We'd come equipped for this. Each of us had a small quantity, wrapped carefully in plastic, of something called silly putty, a favourite with magicians. Silly putty softens iron, getting into the interstices to weaken the bond that holds the metal together. Hari went lightly up to the window, fixed a large rubber sucker on one of its panes and using a diamond-tipped cutter, cut a circle around it. When he pulled the sucker, it came away, bringing the circle of glass with it. He reached in, undid the latch inside the window, opened it wide. To the top and bottom of two adjacent bars he applied the putty, then ducked back to wait for a while.

He waited a few minutes, then straightened up again, and still as quiet as a wraith, bent the bars back wide enough to make an opening for a man to squeeze through, even a big man wrapped in winter clothes and hindered by a harness full of pockets containing the tools of stealth. I eased out from behind the bush and crept up to join him. As I moved beside him and hunkered into the shadow of the wall, he pulled himself upwards and into the house through the gap in the window, quiet as a cat, landing like a feather on his rubber-soled boots. I followed easily enough—Hari, at a shade over six feet, was nearly six inches taller—and saw him edge up to the door to the passageway which led to another bedroom on this floor.

We had to get to the bottom of the trapdoor without waking anyone, preferably finishing off anyone on this floor. There were three men at least here, and we didn't know where they were. We found out soon enough. One of the doors opened with a creak and in the dim lamplight we saw a man emerge, rubbing the sleep out of his eyes, on his way to urinate outside.

Hari took the sleepy man in four steps, creeping up behind him. I saw him lower the man to the floor and push him aside silently. He did a thumbs down to indicate that the man was dead, and headed for the door of the room from which his victim had come. I followed him.

In the moonlight streaming in through a window we saw two men huddled under their blankets. One lay on his back, snoring lightly, the other on his right side. I don't like to attack sleeping men but there was no choice. Hari took the snorer and I the other. We killed them with our knives. I don't know how Hari felt but I had to keep down a wave of nausea that threatened to overwhelm me.

The way to the top was clear. As best we could make out, there were five men inside the building, two outside. The two outside were gone, and so now were three of the five inside. That left two on the same floor as the hostage. I signalled the team to check the other rooms on the ground floor and headed for the base of the ladder which led to the trapdoor. It creaked when I put my weight on it, but I didn't hear a response so I kept climbing. There was a latch to a side of the trapdoor—there probably wasn't one on the other side, because if at all the hostage was to be kept there alone they wouldn't want him locking himself in. I slid the latch open without making a sound, then gently tried the door. It lifted an inch and then stuck. I pushed slightly harder but it stayed stuck. Sweating now, I pushed harder still and it opened with a crack like a pistol shot. Hari, standing below me on the ladder, gave me a boost the moment he heard the noise, and I found myself propelled up through the doorway, head and chest above floor level.

There were three men sleeping on mattresses on the wooden plank floor. One of the men stirred and sat up, reaching for a weapon by his side, but I didn't give him a chance. I shot him with the silenced pistol I'd drawn on the way up. I shot him twice, in quick succession, then hauled myself up through the door. By now the second man had sensed something wrong, and begun to rise. But Hari was through the doorway and onto him, spade in hand. In the SOF we'd learnt to use the infantryman's spade not just to dig trenches in which to take cover, but also as a weapon—to break through doors, to throw it reasonably accurately at a target, to hack dummies. Hari loved his spade. I turned away, not wanting to see what he was doing to the half-asleep man.

The third man was the hostage, still sound asleep, probably drugged. I shook him by the shoulder to wake him up, and he surfaced slowly. Too slowly for my liking. 'Wha . . . Whadyawan?' he mumbled, then brushed my hand off and turned over. I put a hand over his mouth and pinched him hard on the shoulder. That brought him surging up. I held him down easily—after all those weeks in captivity and with all that drugging he was weak as a kitten—and whispered, 'Shut up! We've come to get you out, so just come along without making a noise!' He blinked uncomprehendingly and I shone a torch in his face. His pupils were dilated, and I could see the pulse racing in his neck. The man was stoned out of his mind.

I heard a noise behind me. Even as I turned and rolled, the man who had crept silently up fired. The bullet stung my upper arm and then another man from my team was behind him, firing silently from the hip at a range of less than five feet.

I rose, grabbed the hostage by the collar of his kameez and hauled him to his feet. He came stumblingly up, and I dragged him to the trapdoor. 'Hey, man,' he whined, 'what's all this?'

'Get moving!' I told him, pointing through the trapdoor.

He looked around, his eyes adjusting to the light. 'Hey, man, you *killed* those guys,' he said, 'Majeed and Abdul! Who the *fuck* are you guys, man?'

He wouldn't come easily. Hari upper-cut him on the chin, knocking him out, and between the two of us we lowered him down to the rest of the team waiting below. They caught him, lowered him to the floor, and then we were off.

We had assembled here along six different routes, coming up in pairs. We had originally planned to split up into groups after taking the American, but now it looked like we'd need at least five people to take him along. We'd brought a collapsible stretcher, just in case he was hurt, and now I decided we would use it. We'd tie him down to it, gag him, and free him when we got back to base.

His captors must have been giving him hash to smoke. They must have passed the evenings smoking hash in front of a warm fire, getting friendly. Stupid bastard! No wonder he was pally with them.

We got his limp body out of the window we had come in through. He was tall, at least six three, but painfully thin. He wouldn't have weighed more than seventy kilos. Good, I thought, it made the stretcher-bearers' job that much easier. But the stretcher was too short. His feet stuck out at the end and we had to lash his ankles to the poles to keep them from moving around. Four men could carry the stretcher fast enough over the inhospitable ground in the dark—they would all wear NVGs, night vision glasses, to help them navigate—and they'd have a point man to lead the way. It was thirty kilometres, nearly twenty miles, to the point where we had arranged to cross over. The stretcher-bearers would try to make it in six hours and the others would take an hour less.

We rendezvoused with another team two kilometres away nearly half an hour later, and then split up into five teams. Hari insisted on leading the stretcher-bearers. 'You have to get back quickly,' he told me, and wouldn't listen to me when I argued against that. There are times when you give your juniors their head, so the stretcher-bearers went first, at a jog-trot, along a trail to the east. A group of two followed three minutes later. They would tail the stretcher-bearers, and in case someone found them, create a diversion and let them get away. I hoped it wouldn't come to that. The rest of us waited another ten minutes, and then took our own trails into the forest, all in two- or three-man teams.

The trail we took was faint, but my buddy had been up and down it a couple of times while surveying the land three days ago. He'd found little landmarks, odd-shaped rocks, old trees, even unusual patches of moss. In the moonlight he followed his marks smoothly and jogged up the slope at an even pace that was beginning to leave me breathless. We climbed higher. It was no longer possible to keep silent; our breathing was harsh and laboured enough to be heard thirty yards away by someone with keen ears. But then there was no need to stay so quiet: we could maintain this pace long enough to get clear of any pursuit on foot . . . Unless someone radioed the Rangers at the border.

Until we got to the crossover point, the stretcher-bearers were the most vulnerable. We couldn't afford to give up the American. We were all following more or less parallel trails, not more than a mile or so apart. If the stretcher-bearers came under attack, at least two teams besides the one following them would hear, and come to their assistance.

We took a ten-minute break two hours and nearly ten kilometres later. The going had been rougher than we'd expected, and I was holding up my buddy who seemed exhausted due to lack of sleep and the exertions of the earlier part of the night. Nature's deadline, dawn, drew inevitably closer. In this season, first light was a little after six, and my watch said half past one. Four hours to go. We'd be there before six at this rate, allowing for two more breaks. If nothing happened.

Something did. An hour later, jogging along a better-defined trail now, my buddy turned a curve and almost bumped into another group of two men dressed more or less like us, the lower halves of their faces covered by scarves. They were going the other way, carrying SLRs, not sub-machine guns. Not one of our teams. They had passwords, the men who wandered these mountains, passwords we didn't know. My buddy held up a hand in greeting. They responded by lowering the barrels of their SLRs. A rifle shot or a burst from a sub-machine gun would carry miles in this still air. Any noise and we'd be in a pitched battle that we couldn't afford.

From under my blanket I drew my silenced pistol and fired even before their rifles were trained, and my buddy leapt off the trail, taking cover behind a boulder, throwing a knife at the men as he went.

The man I'd hit went down silently, but the other was on his knees, making strange noises in the back of his throat, trying to scream words that wouldn't come. The knife had hit him below the breastbone, just below the diaphragm, so he couldn't breathe. As I reached him, a burbling scream did emerge from his open mouth, cut off almost immediately by a burst of blood as he died.

We took cover, in case someone had heard that scream. Fifteen minutes later, when no one else turned up, we continued, hitting a rocky stretch in the valley. The moon was full, and down at the bottom of the valley was a small pond gleaming silver. In peacetime this was a beautiful land. I'd been all over the border, the Line of Control, and nowhere was it as heartbreakingly beautiful as it was here. To the north-east, where the mountains rose higher, the border was a snow-covered moonscape, jagged edges blurred by snow. To the south, the forests were replaced by orchards, and human habitations were more common.

We made it at half past five to the 'hole' in the border, picking a gap in the frequent Pakistani patrols between border posts. The border in these parts wasn't fencing or walls, just a string of landmarks—boulders, big trees, water—stretching off in both directions, and we crossed over into safe territory at twenty to six, with the sky still dark ahead of us as we did.

The stretcher-bearers came an hour and fifteen minutes later, behind time but safe.

chapter two

The rescued hostage had slowed his rescuers down.

We discovered that his captors had hooked him on heroin. Morphine derivatives are easy to get in those parts, and the terrorists had figured correctly that the hostage would be easy to keep under control if they kept him hooked. He'd come awake desperate for a shot, and Hari had had to lay him out twice again. Even tied to the stretcher he'd squirmed and struggled, making it impossible to carry the stretcher steadily. When we untied him, he went wild. His forearms showed signs of injections, all recent, all beginning to blacken. No wonder he was so thin, I thought. Maybe his wife, who had haunted the Indian embassy in Washington, wouldn't be so happy to get him back.

At the border post, the fierce-looking scar-faced Major from 9 Para had transport organized. 'General Kelkar wants you back right away,' he said when we met. 'There's a plane waiting for you at Srinagar.'

'What's it all about?' I asked. I knew there'd been some trouble with the LTTE in Tamil Nadu, near Kanyakumari.

Days before I set off for Uri we'd discovered a safe house in Nagercoil where LTTE heavyweights gathered for meetings. We'd left it untouched because there was no immediate violence in the offing, and, besides, if we could bug the safe house we'd get top-grade information directly.

'I don't know, sir,' said the 9 Para man, 'but I heard there was a FLASH message.'

A FLASH is an emergency tag used only by the Chief of Army Staff (COAS). 'Funny,' I muttered, wondering what it was all about, while the signalman radioed Kelkar. Kelkar came on the line. 'How did it go?' he asked.

'No serious damage,' I replied. 'We got him out. Lucky.'

'Good,' he said. 'Get back to Delhi right away. Your driver will meet you at Safdarjung.'

'What about the debriefing?' I asked.

'Hari can do that, can't he?'

'Yes,' I replied, 'but . . .'

'I can't explain,' Kelkar said, his voice terribly, uncharacteristically tired, 'Raja, just move.'

Thirty minutes later I was in a Chetak—modified Alouette—helicopter headed for Srinagar. I got a field dressing for the scratch on my arm, changed into combat blacks but didn't get to wash. I still smelt strongly of sweat in the warmth, the three-week-old beard itching and uncomfortable. The changeover at Srinagar, to an Ilyushin transport, was smooth and quick, and I sat on a pallet cocooned in engine noise, feeling my ears pop as the craft took off. Some minutes later, the co-pilot, a Flying Officer who looked about fifteen years old—he hadn't outgrown his acne yet—emerged from the flight deck with coffee in a thermos and blankets on his arm. 'You might try to get some sleep, sir,' he advised. 'It'll take a couple of hours to get to Delhi. We should be there at eight. A little earlier if the tailwind keeps up.'

'Too noisy,' I replied, 'too bumpy. Too cold.'

'The bumps'll ease off in a few minutes,' he smiled. 'There's cotton here for your ears and a blanket for the cold. Sleep.'

I accepted the blanket and the cotton and shook my head. Sleep came hard and rarely lasted long. 'Some more coffee in an hour or so would be fine. I'm good at just sitting around. But thanks all the same.'

'My pleasure,' he grinned. 'We were all a little curious to see what kind of a person you are.'

'No need to be,' I said, 'I'm just the same as anyone else, worried mostly about middle age and my son. Mostly my son.'

He smiled disbelievingly before returning to the flight deck, closing the door behind him. I'd spoken the truth. I worried about my son—stepson, actually, my wife's son from an earlier marriage—and about middle age. At thirty-eight I was taking far too long to get over bruises and aches and pains and losing my wind far too quickly for comfort. The cut on my arm ached mercilessly under the dressing, a reminder of my vulnerability, of the ever increasing possibility that the next man would be a little too fast.

I could stop going on these operations, of course. As chief of 1st Battalion, Special Operations Force, I could sit behind a desk or in a safe command post. But we were woefully short of officers. Just a year ago, when I was second-in-command, we'd discovered that my predecessor as chief, Colonel Ismail Qureishi, had been turned decades ago by Pakistan's ISI. The Army were all for covering up, and much to the relief of the brass at Army Headquarters, Ismail had never made it to trial: I had killed him on a bleak winter's evening in Sandhya's flat.

The SOF had barely survived the silent purge that followed. Nearly a fifth of the officers were found to have faint political blots on their copybooks. Now I had to build up strength and morale once again. Today's job should help, I thought. Getting one hostage out of POK wasn't a spectacular mission, but doing it without losing any of our own would be seen by the men as a major victory.

The aircraft bumped, dropped some height, and I felt the vibration increase as the pilot turned on the power to pass the air pocket, climbing past the bad patch to the relative calm above. When the craft settled down at its new altitude the Flying Officer emerged again, with another cup of coffee and a bunch of newspapers. 'We're not supposed to know this,' he said, 'but we believe you've been out of contact for a while. You might like to have these.' He handed me the papers.

There was little in them barring the coming elections, scandals and stories of bribe-taking, some involving the Prime Minister himself. And there were the stories on the Mehta diaries, now in the custody of the CBI. News about these diaries had first broken only a few days before I'd left for Uri. It had seemed to me then that this was something huge, and what I read in the papers now confirmed that. Nemish Mehta had been a stockbroker until he was found to have forged certificates worth a hundred crore rupees at current stock market rates. He'd borrowed money on the strength of the forgeries, and used it to start several companies, all part of the fastest-growing industrial and financial group in the country. He'd been caught and arrested, and during the ensuing search of his house the CBI had come across a set of diaries in which he had kept records of money paid to politicians and bureaucrats.

Mehta had been killed in prison before his interrogation was complete. There were dates and names in the diaries, all in Mehta's own hand, all easily verifiable. Rumours were that most of the Cabinet were listed there, including the PM. The CBI, of course, was taking its own sweet time investigating.

I put the papers away, worrying vaguely about how much money could buy. If someone with a few crores to play around with targeted the Army . . . Ismail had turned because of his loyalties, he'd never been bought. But what of the others?

I dozed, fatigue catching up with me. The next thing I knew, the young Air Force man was waking me up. 'Coffee, sir,' he said. 'We'll be there in twenty minutes. Your transport will meet you at the airfield.'

The coffee warmed me up. The tablet the medics gave me at Srinagar had worn off long ago and my arm hurt incessantly, a throbbing, biting pain sharpened by the thin, cold air. There was something bad coming up, Kelkar wouldn't interrupt an operation—it was on until the end of the debriefing—for anything less than war. And there was the Chief's FLASH message.

My usual SOF driver, Venkat, was at Safdarjung airport to meet the plane. He brought the jeep out onto the runway, halting a few feet away from the end of the ladder that the Air Force crew put down for me. I waved my thanks at them and climbed down the ladder, leaving my injured arm hanging limp. 'Where are we going?' I asked as I climbed into the jeep.

'The Prime Minister's house,' Venkat replied briefly. 'What happened to your arm, sir?'

I was so stunned at his reply that I didn't register his question, so he had to repeat it. 'Somebody used a pistol on me,' I mumbled. 'It'll be fine.'

He looked pointedly through the windscreen. 'The Colonel shouldn't have been there at all,' he said. 'If I might speak . . .'

'Go ahead,' I told him. I rarely, if ever, muzzled him. Men like him were disciplined. With such men, censorship brought disaster in the long run.

'The Colonel would be better employed keeping the Generals and the politicians off us. We can take care of the enemy but sometimes the politicians are difficult . . .'

'Be more specific,' I told him. 'What's been happening?'

'Charlie Company has been on a two-hour alert since yesterday morning. There's no sense in it.'

I'd been away six weeks, and had no idea of this. 'Why?' I asked.

‘They were on alert yesterday morning. Delta went off on exercises. Something happened last night and now everyone’s running around like headless chickens. If the Colonel will excuse the language.’

The Colonel did. I didn’t have time to say any more to him as we were already drawing up outside the PM’s residence at 1 Safdarjung Road, a stone’s throw from the airport. The security cordon, the outermost layer of it consisting of squads of Delhi Police, stopped us at a steel barrier. They looked at the jeep, at the insignia, and my uniform, and were completely unimpressed, as was proper.

I heard a police officer, a sub-inspector or perhaps an Inspector, speaking into a walkie-talkie. He repeated the jeep’s registration number twice, checked something off on a list, and motioned to an underling who in turn motioned me out of the jeep. Another underling made me lean forward, hands on the jeep’s bonnet, and frisked me thoroughly. The results were alarming: he found the knife in my belt besides the .22, and reacted violently, hauling me off the jeep by the collar. Out of the corner of my eye I saw another SOF jeep drawing up just behind mine, and the battalion adjutant Ramu jogging up, his usual grin conspicuous by its absence.

Ramu arrived at my side just in time to see the policeman push me back onto my knees. The Inspector took two negligent steps forward to examine the booty. ‘Take him to the station,’ he said, ‘I’ll talk to him there.’

‘One moment,’ I said, ‘ask for Major General Kelkar on your walkie-talkie. He asked me here because of some emergency. Check with him.’

The policeman ignored me. He repeated his order to the constable holding me and Ramu went berserk. Before anyone knew what was happening, the Inspector was on his stomach on the ground and with a sub-machine gun in his ear. 'Do like he says,' Ramu hissed. 'Check on your radio. Now.'

For a moment I thought the other policemen were going to open fire but they just froze in position, rifles at the ready, all pointing uncompromisingly at us. The Inspector, his face red, reached down to his belt for the radio, asked for some high-up, then for Kelkar. I heard him pronounce my name, and seconds later he handed me the radio. 'What have you got into, Raja?' Kelkar asked over the crackle of the speaker.

'Some clown in police uniform frisked me and found a knife and a pistol,' I replied, keeping my voice steady. 'He was going to lock me up when Ramu arrived. Then Ramu—ummm . . . intervened and made him check with you.'

'You're not supposed to bring those things in here. Only the PM's guards are armed.'

'He could have asked for them,' I replied. 'After he found the stuff I asked him to call you. He didn't. Will you speak to him? He can keep my stuff if he likes but he's got to give it back when I leave.'

'Don't worry,' he said, 'I'll have someone sent out to fetch you in. Now give the radio back to the policeman.'

The Inspector's hard, flat face changed as he talked on the wireless. When he was through, Ramu moved away, allowing him to get up. He turned to me and behind his smile I could see the acid rancour building up. But all he said was, 'Please wait, sir. Someone will come to the gate and we will see what is to be done.'

The someone arrived two minutes later in a white Ambassador, a chubby, dark-skinned, fortyish man in a grey safari suit that is the summer uniform of the bureaucrat. Behind him came a trim, moustached man with short hair, watchful eyes, and no expression at all. I could see the ID card hung about his neck on a steel chain. One of the praetorian guard, a hard boy, a very different proposition from the roughneck policeman. The man in the grey safari stuck his hand out. 'Bhaskar,' he said, 'Bhaskar Reddy. Special Assistant to the Prime Minister's Private Secretary. I'm sorry about that little row you had, but the police were just doing their job, you know. And now, if you'll hand over your weapons to my friend here,' he waved at the bodyguard, 'we can proceed.'

Hard Face took the stuff impassively, inspected it, and put it in a plastic bag. 'I'll give it to you as you leave, sir,' he said, 'we can't let you keep it inside these gates.'

With the escort, getting in was a breeze. Two more ranks of security men—one ring of Indo-Tibetan Border Force (ITBF) men, and a further one of plainclothesmen, all clones of Hard Face sitting in the front passenger seat of the car—waved us through. 'I understand you were in the middle of an operation when you were called here,' said Bhaskar.

'We'd just finished,' I said. 'I can't talk about it. I was told the COAS sent a FLASH message for me. That can't be much short of war. Otherwise I'd have gone home to change before coming here.'

'Just as well you didn't,' he said, suddenly grim-faced. 'It's not a matter I'll discuss with you here, but I'll arrange for fresh clothes and a bath for you before you see the PM. General Kelkar will brief you first.'

Kelkar was in one of the anterooms with N. Somasekhara Rao, chief of the CBI. Kelkar introduced us, then got straight down to business, as was his wont. 'There's been a kidnap,' he said. 'Night before last, the PM's granddaughter attended a wedding in a village near Mysore and from there she went to a Karnataka state government lodge on the banks of the Kabini river. Last night she and two of her friends were kidnapped.'

I could see now why the police at the gate had been so tetchy. Having the PM's granddaughter kidnapped was itself a disaster. And with the elections coming up everyone was on edge: the PM was scheduled to travel all over the country leading the campaign, spending more time in the air than on the ground; they couldn't afford to lose time. The ruling party's election campaign would be thrown entirely out of gear.

Rao of the CBI took up the narrative. He put some photographs down on the coffee table, all of a girl of sixteen or seventeen. 'That's her,' he recited, 'Priya Reddy, seventeen years old, wheatish complexion, black hair, brown eyes, one-sixty-three centimetres tall, forty-eight kilos, last seen dressed in a yellow nightgown in the lodge.' I looked at the photos of the PM's granddaughter—large eyes stared back at me, smiling a vulnerable smile. Another set of photographs landed on the table as Rao went on. 'That's one of her friends, Urmila Shetty. Same age, one-sixty-five, fifty kilos. I don't yet have a description of how she was dressed when they took her. They studied together. Her father's a Bangalore-based businessman, has known the PM's family for years.' This one looked less vulnerable and much more photogenic. A third set. 'Mallika Deshpande. Same age. One-fifty-nine, fifty kilos, no description, same college, father's in Bombay.' This one looked the youngest, the baby fat still softening the outlines of her face.

'The wedding was at noon the day before yesterday. They drove there in a group the day before yesterday morning, driven by a man who works for the PM's son's company in Hyderabad. They arrived at eleven and went straight to the wedding hall, stayed until four, meeting people, then left for Kabini. They got there at half past five and were shown their rooms immediately. They did nothing the rest of that day.'

'What time did the snatch happen?' I asked.

'Two in the morning. It was all over in three minutes, but for the chase.'

'Who else was in the lodge?'

'This programme was fixed up five weeks ago. The staff were warned, and the management of the lodge didn't permit any other reservations. The girls and their entourage were the only occupants of the lodge that day.

'The lodge has rooms and cottages—independent suites.

Her security men thought it wiser for her to stay in one of the rooms rather than in a cottage. The rooms are all in a row, eight of them, each meant for two people. She stayed in one of the centre rooms, with a girl in the rooms on either side, and security men in all the rest. There was one bodyguard at the front door to her room.'

'Was there a back door, then?' I asked.

'Yes, there was. Attached to this room is a bathroom, and to the rear of the bathroom is a door that opens out onto the lawn behind. The whole residential area is set in a huge lawn dotted with buildings. There are the office buildings, staff quarters, a hall where they show video movies in the evenings, a store for cigarettes and liquor and souvenirs, all set in these lawns. Here's a map. As you can see, the complex is on a riverside, and one of the dining halls actually overlooks the river. That circular open-air dining room is there,' he pointed.

'What's the perimeter like?'

'The lodge itself is fenced in. The fence is not much of a deterrent to a determined man, but there are other deterrents. There are animals about, leopard and deer and so on. But the side of the lodge facing the river is not fenced in. In fact, the security men were afraid of an attack along the river. Anyone can float downstream and get into the premises along the bank. They can do whatever they want and continue downstream afterwards.'

'The way you say it these men didn't come along the water. How did they, then?'

'They came from above. From the air.'

'Parachute?'

'No.' His smile was laden with irony. 'They came in ultralight aircraft. Basically hang-gliders with small engines attached, all canvas and struts. The engines are noisy but you can switch them off for landing. They're slow, but fast enough. And they're expensive. They have to be imported. These came in from the US.'

'I've heard of them. They can land in twenty metres of flat space, or even less.'

'Yes. They landed on the lawns. There are lamps all over the lawn in front of the rooms but not behind, beyond about thirty feet from the rooms. There the lawn is like a little jungle, dark and overgrown in parts. They landed there, dressed in camouflage clothing, and came in quietly, taking cover behind small trees and shrubs. They shot the security men at the back with silenced weapons, blasted their way into the bathrooms and then into the rooms. They took the ladies, then a car, and drove off.'

'In one car?' I asked.

'Yes. From what I've heard there were only four men. Seven people in all. They'd fit in one large car.'

'Didn't you say the security men gave chase?'

'Yes . . . The kidnappers had a heavy weapon as well, an RPG-7, probably. It's old but effective. They fired a rocket in the direction of the village, and a second at the chase vehicle. Then they drove off. The police followed their tracks. About twenty kilometres away, in a clearing, there were tracks that indicate they had a helicopter waiting. Beyond that we have nothing—they just . . . disappeared.

Must have kept the chopper below five hundred feet because Bangalore radar stations say they did not see anything. It's risky, flying that low among all the trees there, the surrounding hills and tricky winds, but possible if they had NVGs and a good pilot. I've got men looking for reports of a helicopter in the area.'

'Anything on who did it? Demands, anything?'

'Nothing so far. I think they want us to sweat for a while. They know we're under tremendous pressure.'

'What else do you have?'

'The gliders . . . the ultralights. We got four of them. We don't know if any more men came by road. They could have had men waiting along the road whom they took on their way out. We don't know.'

'They didn't fumble at all, did they?'

'No. They knew exactly where to find what they wanted. But it's not hard to find out about the resort. It's open to the public, after all. Anyone can put down a few thousand rupees a night and look all over the place.'

'But they knew the rooms where the girls were. Someone must have told them.'

'Yes. We're interrogating the staff now. I still don't know what progress we've made there.'

'Any suspicious guests in the recent past, since the hostages' schedule was fixed?'

'That was five weeks ago. I've told my people to list all occupants other than family groups with small children, and known corporate figures—some companies entertain there—also foreigners who have left the country, and regulars. We'll look first for single men, or groups of men with no women.

'So far we've got more than fifty such groups or men. My people are checking their addresses, if we get a false name or address we'll treat that as a lead. We're going to question the whole lot of them anyway.'

'How long do you think this exercise will take?' I asked.

'The rest of the day, Colonel,' came the reply. The CBI chief had retired, and was on his first extension of service. His face was lined with exhaustion and he sat limply. 'I must go now,' he continued, 'one of our Deputy Directors, Chauhan—you know him, and I believe you get along well—he'll head the investigations into this case.'

'Where is he now?'

'On leave. We called him back last night, just like we called you. He should be in any time now.' He looked at his watch. 'Not more than an hour from now, in any case.'

'Who's headed it so far?'

'We got the news only hours ago,' he said, 'and I've been pushing everyone to their limits. Including myself.' He smiled in utter weariness and left.

Kelkar waited until the door had shut behind him, then turned to me. 'I asked you here because they might get in touch any time. I want you here when they do. You should be available for the negotiations.'

'I'd expect them to get in touch with someone near the site of the kidnap, not here,' I said. 'Mysore, or maybe Bangalore. They'll make us go there.'

'I know. Get someone from your unit to go down to

Bangalore immediately, with at least a platoon force first, then a company. Keep them there, on the ready. I've spoken to the Sub-Area Chief in Bangalore, Brigadier Kalra, you know him. He's got a Para unit down there near Jalahalli. They'll keep your men supplied.'

He seemed dispirited. I knew it wasn't because he'd been rousted out of bed in the wee hours; he could go without sleep for days without losing his energy. 'What's bugging you about this, sir?' I asked.

He looked up at me, surprised, then down at the coffee table. 'The bumsucking,' he said softly. 'The Chief came here and crawled. There are more people here just to hold the PM's hand than there are to run the search. They're all getting tough with visitors, just to prove how big they are. You saw some of it at the gate, the same thing is happening here as well. No one here seems to understand the logistics of a search . . . I don't know if anyone is looking for possible hideouts yet.'

'There's some pretty heavy cover in those parts,' I said, 'the Mudumalai and Bandipur sanctuaries. Veerappan's been operating out of there for years but they haven't been able to catch him yet.'

'I don't think they'd hide out in the jungle,' he said. 'Communication would be a problem, and logistics. Unless they have some pretty advanced communication equipment and a prepared hideout in the hills.'

'Don't rule all that out,' I said. 'Remember the ultralights? Who'd have thought of that?' I couldn't help a grin at the thought of the security men surprised from above.

For the first time that morning Kelkar's face lost its grimness, then hardened again. 'It seems the PM asked the Chief who would be the best person to send out to handle this. The Chief named you. It's a terrific opportunity, Raja, but if you mess this up you'll spend the rest of your career patrolling the Nagas.'

'Thanks,' I said. 'Anything more?'

'Yes,' he said. 'The principal hostage is a spoilt brat. Not that that should change the way you do your job. And don't expect to get much support from the local authorities. The opposition has a powerful presence in Karnataka, they won't like the Army coming in at all, except to take the blame if the operation fails.'

There was a knock on the door and Bhaskar walked in. Behind him was a uniformed bearer carrying a bag. 'Colonel, some fresh clothes for you, and basic toiletries. The PM will want you in half an hour. Please don't keep him waiting, he has a lot on his mind.'

Inside the bag I found a shaving kit, a toothbrush, fresh underwear, trousers, a shirt, a pair of socks, even a tie, all brand new. The bearer led me to a bathroom at the end of the corridor. Half an hour later, Bhaskar led me into another anteroom with a male secretary working furiously at a typewriter, on the table beside the machine was an intercom. We waited a few moments, then the intercom buzzed. The secretary lifted the handset, spoke his name, then said, 'Yes, sir.' He hung up and nodded at Bhaskar, indicating the door behind him with a thumb, and went back to his typing.

The PM usually looked remarkably chipper for a man

in his seventies, even when he was busy campaigning, but we found him looking ancient and worn out, as if the weight of all the troubles in the world rested on his shoulders. His eyes were red-rimmed and bleary and his thinning hair, normally combed carefully across his scalp to cover his bald patch, was tousled. He fidgeted with papers on the table in front of him, his fingers trembling and twitching, his hands refusing to stay still. Bhaskar stepped forward. 'Colonel Menon,' he said, leading me forward.

The PM didn't offer me his hand, or make any sign of greeting. 'Colonel,' he said, 'I asked the Chief of Army Staff to tell me which man under him has the best chance of getting my little girl back. He named you. Don't let me down.'

All my resentment, all the anger and the ill-feeling that had been building up on the way here, dissolved when I faced this tired old man overwrought with worry for his granddaughter. 'I'll do my best, sir,' I told him, 'but I need to talk to you alone.'

'Go ahead,' he said. 'Don't worry about Bhaskar.'

'I must insist, sir, one-to-one.'

'All right,' he said. He motioned Bhaskar to leave the room and then he turned to face me, all business. 'Why?'

'I need to know about your granddaughter, sir,' I explained. 'I need to know things that only the two of you know. That's essential if at any time I have to confirm that she's alive, and that she is who they say she is. If it comes to that.'

‘Why send Bhaskar away?’ he asked, ‘he’s my right hand.’

‘I’m assuming that they wouldn’t have been able to kidnap her without someone inside here,’ I said. ‘As far as I’m concerned, everyone in your inner circle is suspect. And anyone else who knew where she was going.’

‘You cast your net wide,’ he said, considering. He was silent for a moment, then continued, ‘I have no choice but to agree with you. I am in your hands.’

‘In that case I’d like you to tell me some of those things,’ I said. ‘I’ll make note of them. You don’t have to tell me a lot right away, but I need one for positive identification. Just in case.’

He paused, swallowed, and hid his eyes, which I suspected were beginning to water. When he spoke, his voice was hoarse with the effort he had to use to keep it from breaking. ‘She was born when I was in the wilderness, politically speaking,’ he whispered. ‘Two years after she was born I even resigned from my party posts and lived in retirement at home, near Mysore. I . . . I watched her grow up then. I have never had time to spend with my own children but by an accident of fate I had time to spend with her. She is the only child I have been able to watch at leisure, Colonel . . . She made those years bearable. Do you understand me?’ He looked up and this time he didn’t bother to hide the tears. I nodded, not knowing what to say. ‘I taught her to make paper boats, Colonel. We spent afternoons floating paper boats in a tank by my ancestral home near Mysore.

‘Eventually she learnt to make them herself. She tried

several times and failed, but eventually she made one. We named it together. We gave the boat her own name, and that was a secret between her and me. And now it is yours as well . . .' His voice trailed off, choking.

'We'd best have this over and done with, sir,' I said gently. 'It might hurt but you have to do it for her sake. We will need this kind of information to identify her. If . . .' I couldn't complete the sentence: If she lives . . .

The intercom buzzed, and he reached for it with a trembling hand, relieved to have this little break from my inquisition. 'Yes?' he said. 'All right. Put him on.' Pause. 'Good morning, Mr Prime Minister,' he spoke heavily. 'Thank you for calling, and for your concern. Yes, I'm aware your people are extremely good at hostage-rescue work. Thank you very much, and I'll certainly let you know as soon as possible. But for the time being I'll let my own boys go ahead . . . Yes, I've spoken to them personally. One of them is here with me right now . . . I appreciate it, Mr Prime Minister, thanks once again. I'll get back to you if need be.'

He hung up and turned to me. 'That was John Major,' he said, 'a personal call. He offered us their SAS or whatever. I told him I'll leave it to you for the time being. If you can't handle it, tell me immediately so I can call the British in. Or the Americans . . . their President called earlier.'

'I'll tell you straightaway, sir,' I promised.

'Where were we? Yes, my granddaughter. The paper boat. We named it Priya, after her. Isn't that enough?'

'For now, yes. But after the kidnappers get in touch I'll

need more. Each time they get in touch we'll have to reconfirm that she is alive and well. I'd like at least half a dozen such questions and answers.' The pain came flaring up in his eyes and I wanted suddenly to shield him from dwelling on her any more.

'You don't have to tell me now, sir,' I said, 'I'll spend time on this with you later, after they get in touch.'

'Do that,' he said, nodding, sitting up in relief. 'Can we have Bhaskar back now?'

I nodded, and the PM called Bhaskar on the intercom. He must have been waiting in the anteroom because he was back immediately. No sooner had he taken his seat next to me than he rattled off his strategy. 'The CBI says we should prepare a team of negotiators and hostage-rescue experts as soon as possible, preferably by the time the kidnappers get in touch. After that we follow everything the kidnappers tell us, look for a weakness, and move in if we think there's a good chance of getting the girls out without harming them. We can also use rescue teams if it looks as if they're going to kill the hostages anyway, but primarily we should do as they say and worry about chasing them after we get the girls back.'

'No,' I intervened, 'we can't do that. Two things. First, the only way to counter terrorism is to resist. It works, in the long run. Second, if we give in to them too easily they might get the idea they could have got away with more. Once they get that feeling, they might get frustrated and harm the hostages, or they might escalate their demands. I'd say we prepare for everything, like the CBI say, and after they get in touch, play it by ear. And if it's a political kidnapping we'll have to be extra careful.'

'Why the difference?' asked the PM.

'Professional kidnappers do it for the money. They want that, and the time in which to enjoy it. They won't kill or seriously injure a hostage because they're spending their capital doing that. But political ones, especially the fanatics—and I've come across enough of them—they don't think like that. Most prefer a glorious death to living in obscurity. They have very little consideration for their hostages. Dealing with them is like walking a minefield. If there's a psychopath or two among the kidnappers, you could agree to everything they say and still have your hostages blown up in front of your eyes . . . And they're likely to stretch out the drama. You see, terrorists, from what I've seen, are in it for the fun of killing, or the power they enjoy of having a whole country's population jump to their commands. They get high on the feeling.'

'What else?'

'We must make sure the hostages are all right. That's why I asked you all those questions earlier. We have to have a regular procedure to verify this from time to time. And we need to watch out for the exchange—ransom for hostages. That's when things are most likely to go wrong. So we've got to negotiate the exchange most carefully and make it foolproof.'

'So what do we do now?' he asked.

'First, we shift the base of operations to Bangalore,' I replied. 'The kidnappers took their hostages in Karnataka and I suspect they're holed up somewhere not far from Kabini. They're likely to have stayed in the state, it's not easy to transport three people clandestinely across a state border, and it takes time besides. Finally, you have an election campaign on. The campaign and us would just get in each other's way if we stay here.'

'How should we organize things in Bangalore?' asked Bhaskar.

'The kidnappers need to get in touch with us without fear, that's the first thing. The moment they get in touch we have to set up a communication system so they can keep in touch without any hassles, from anywhere. Set up a board for that, and when they contact us, give them a number that they can call from anywhere, any time. Set up equipment to trace all calls to the number. I know it'll take a little time so you could get started on it straightaway.'

'We'll do that, Colonel,' Bhaskar acknowledged. 'And what do you intend to do?'

'I'll move to Bangalore as soon as I can, set up things there. I can liaise either through you or through General Kelkar. I'll be more useful there than here.'

'Yes,' said the PM. His eyes were blanking out now and again, and it was clear he was having trouble concentrating.

'And if I might offer some advice . . .' I began.

'Go ahead,' said the PM.

'The worst part of it is the waiting. The kidnappers know this. While it is in their interest to collect their ransom and leave as soon as possible, they will let you stew as long as they think they can, to make the negotiations that much easier for them . . . Don't give in.'

'I won't,' he promised. He seemed to collect himself. Suddenly the politician was back. I could see it in those eyes, now unblinking, steely.

The intercom buzzed again. Bhaskar reached out and picked it up, and his face went still. He listened for a moment and said, 'Come right in,' and hung up. He looked from the PM to me. 'Something else has come up. Mr Somasekhara Rao will tell us about it. Colonel, you could listen to this as well. I don't have to tell you that it's confidential.'

Rao looked defeated when he walked in a minute later. He slumped into the chair to which the PM waved him, and dropped a sheaf of papers on the table. 'I just got a message from Madras. It seems there's been another kidnap. The son of the Chief Justice of the Supreme Court.'

'Is it related to the Kabini kidnap?' Bhaskar asked.

'We don't know yet. I would tend to think it is. I just spoke to a DG of the Tamil Nadu police. He says the CJ's son was taken by a group of professionals. Minimum violence, minimum force. They knew exactly where and how to take him. It happened at about three in the morning. The police were informed by the milkman who came to the house at half past five. He found the watchman dead, the front door broken and the wife of the CJ's son gagged and tied up in the bedroom on the first floor. That's all we have now.'

'We should assume the two kidnaps are linked,' I said.

'Why?' asked Bhaskar. 'There's no evidence to that effect.'

'I don't trust coincidence,' I replied, 'and both the kidnaps have been good jobs.'

'I've put my people in Madras on to it,' Rao said. 'Menon's right. Until we know for sure we'll assume that the kidnaps are related and that, therefore, whatever the kidnappers will demand is likely to require judicial intervention of some kind.'

'Terrorists to be released?' I asked. 'That's not enough. They've done it before . . . Why would they threaten the judiciary?'

'I don't know,' said Rao, 'and I'm not going to try to anticipate them. We'll know when they tell us.' He excused himself and left.

'We'll need all our resources to take care of this situation,' said Bhaskar, on his feet and pacing the room as soon as Rao had left. 'We will have two committees here, one a Cabinet-level ministerial committee, consisting of the ministers of home affairs, defence, telecom, finance, and perhaps civil aviation—' A play for power. Sit in Delhi and pull strings.

'You can't do that!' I protested, horrified, 'that'll blow our security out of the water!'

He gave me a cold look. 'I suggest you keep within the limits of your remit,' he said and continued as if he'd never been interrupted: 'We'll also have a Special Combined Task Force, on which we'll have representatives from all these ministries, Chiefs of all the Services, and the Director of Special Forces.'

'No,' I said. 'Look, these guys have sources all over the place. The committees will make minutes, they'll leave paper around, there'll be stenographers and other staff.

How do you think you'll keep anything confidential?'

'We'll have to have these people informed,' the PM said, 'we need their help. That's democracy for you.'

For a moment I was tempted to tell the PM to call the Brits in, or the Yanks, but I held back. Maybe Kelkar would be able to persuade them to drop it. I excused myself and left, and found Kelkar waiting in the anteroom where we'd talked. 'What happened?' he asked.

'Disaster,' I told him. 'They want two committees, one of ministers, the other of bureaucrats. Heavyweights from all over the place. My mistake—I asked the PM to send that man Bhaskar Reddy out of the room for a bit. This must be his revenge.'

'I'll try to sort it out in a while,' he promised. 'But I'm out of my depth as well. The Chief's involved, remember, and he's trying to be noticed around here.'

'All right,' I said. 'Another thing. I've told them I'm going to Bangalore, to set up communications and see to it that the unit is all right. I told them I'll liaise through you.'

'I'll do what I can,' he said, 'but I don't know if it'll work out. Chances are I'll end up with you in Bangalore.'

'The PM's thinking of bringing in Brits or Yanks to do our job for us,' I said.

He snorted. 'They'd be better off than us. None of these bloody committees to foul them up . . . When will you leave?'

'In a couple of hours. I thought I'd go home and see Sandhya on the way out.' We left together, escorted out by

Bhaskar, who with his point proven was altogether more confident than I liked. He led us as far as the outermost checkpoint—where Ramu had had his little dust-up—and waved us off. The policemen who'd stopped me stayed away as Kelkar's staff car rolled up, followed by my jeep.

chapter three

Home. A two-bedroom flat a kilometre or so away from SOF headquarters near Dhaula Kuan. Sandhya was standing on a stool fixing up new curtains on the drawing-room windows when I got there. Her mouth was full of clips, her forehead was damp with sweat and a curl of hair stuck to her cheek. But she looked all right to me. 'Hi, there,' she said rather indistinctly around the clips when she saw me. We aren't normally very demonstrative, but I could make out from her voice that she was glad to see me back. She took the clips out of her mouth. 'Your kit arrived twenty minutes ago. Aren't those clothes new?'

'Yes,' I answered. 'There's something cooking. They pulled me out of the last one before the debriefing and I didn't have time to get back here and change. I had to meet some of the brass, so they bought me new clothes.'

Her face went still when she got closer and felt the bandage on my arm. 'What's this?' she said, forcing a lightness she didn't feel. 'You've been up to mischief.'

'Take it easy,' I replied.

She looked away. We had an unspoken agreement not to interfere with each others' lives. She had a fair career now illustrating books and magazines, and generally kept busy enough not to mind my frequent absences. But of late I'd begun to notice a growing disapproval. 'I've got to go away again soon,' I continued. 'But this time I'll be safe. Behind a desk.'

'Where will you go?' she asked, turning around. 'And for how long? Or would it be a breach of national security to tell your wife where you're going and when you'll be back?'

'I can answer the first question but I really don't know how long I'll be away,' I told her, trying to keep my voice level. My life was richer for her presence, and I didn't want to do anything that would threaten our marriage. Besides, she'd know from the newspapers. 'The PM's granddaughter's been kidnapped.'

'Oh, no!' she said, her anger at me forgotten. 'Poor girl. Is she very young? I hope she's not a child!'

'She's seventeen,' I replied. 'They showed me photographs of her. Seemed a normal teenager, maybe a little spoilt. From what I hear, she's got a temper.'

'What will you do? Do you know where they're holding her?'

'They took two other girls with this one. Both friends, about the same age. I'm going to Bangalore because we think the kidnappers, when they do get in touch, will contact someone in Karnataka.'

'What do you mean, when they do get in touch?'

'They're keeping us waiting. Simmering. And there's another little twist.'

'What?'

'They took the son of the Supreme Court's Chief Justice as well. We don't know if it was the same group but it happened in Madras a few hours after the girls were taken.'

'Do you know why they were kidnapped?'

'No. The kidnappers seem to be professionals. Very well organized, high-tech. They're probably doing it for the money. Lots of it. If it had been political the chances are they'd have been broadcasting it all over the world by now.'

'Why are you going, then?' she asked. 'I thought the police would do that better.'

'They want me around to negotiate, that's all.'

The fight was over, nipped in the bud by her sympathy for the hostages. But I knew that the issue would come up again soon, probably the next time I had to leave in the middle of something, leave without telling her where I was going or why or for how long. This time I was lucky because she'd read all about it in tomorrow's newspapers, see it on TV . . . Take it one day at a time, I thought, and left it at that. 'Have you had breakfast?' she asked.

'No,' I said, 'I thought I'd have it here, with you. I went straight off to see the PM after I got back. I'm leaving after breakfast . . . You'd better explain to Kiran.' Kiran was her son, my stepson, who hadn't yet got over the damage inflicted on his mind by a group of terrorists who had taken him hostage—with some thirty-odd others—more than a year ago. He was past seven now, but had recurring nightmares from which he woke screaming, and he still wet his bed occasionally.

Living with a victim had given me a totally new and different perspective on kidnapping. Victims and their families bled for the rest of their lives. If the family had to pay a ransom—which was usually the limit of what they could raise—they had to learn to live on drastically lowered incomes, and the relief of getting the hostage back was soon overwhelmed by the discomfort of relative poverty. For the victim it was the greater burden of guilt for having caused such discomfort. The family themselves bore the guilt of not having protected the hostage better, or for just resenting the victim.

We'd been lucky. I could see the guilt in Sandhya sometimes but it receded as Kiran improved. He had been brought back with no ransom paid, and being young, he had got over the worst of it within weeks. He saw a therapist every other week now.

Forty minutes later, after a quick breakfast and a goodbye full of consciously repressed passion, I was at the office, reviewing with Ramu. I had taken Charlie company off the two-hour-alert before going home, and Beta had taken over. Delta company, just back from training, rested and fresh, was being readied to leave for Bangalore, with Alpha held in reserve.

There was still no news from the kidnappers. Kelkar rang up at the office minutes before I left. The CBI had found out that one of the servants at the Kabini lodge had talked to someone he shouldn't have. They were questioning him, but were getting nowhere. The man seemed terrified.

The ultralights, they'd established, were manufactured by a Minneapolis-based outfit the previous year, but nobody knew how they'd been brought into the country. The kidnappers, apparently, had taken off in their ultralights from a small plain in the hills about fifteen kilometres south-east of Mysore. Some villagers nearby had heard small-engine noises at about the right time. About fifteen minutes later, villagers to the east of Mysore had been woken by the clatter of a helicopter going by very low. But no one had seen anything.

All this added up to little. There was something sinister about these men. They'd planned it all to perfection, and spent so much on the equipment—they couldn't be doing it for just the money. I told Kelkar this and he asked me to take it one step at a time. He was in a tight spot himself. The committees were up and squabbling already. The only sane man he saw was V.M. Mankekar, a Congress Party stalwart, an old friend of the PM and also his unofficial adviser on home affairs. In his seventies now, Mankekar was due to retire after the coming elections. He'd never held a government post, but everyone knew him and respected him for his integrity. The PM, of course, knew him better than most: they went back a long way, to the time they were in jail together during the Quit India Movement. 'Lucky you,' I said to Kelkar. At least there was one good man on his side. I'd have my friend Chauhan of the CBI, he comforted me. He was already on his way to

Bangalore. And then there was Kalra, he would take good care of my men already there.

As it turned out, Kalra had done just that. He'd been waiting to go on leave for a week but when he heard of the kidnap he'd cancelled his leave. His men had been called on to cordon off the lodge after the kidnap and they were combing the areas around the lodge for traces of the helicopter. He came forward to meet me at the airport, a big man, red-faced, going grey at the temples, comfortably plump but still reassuringly strong, prickly at times. 'Let me know if you need anything,' he said, 'we've taken care of your boys.'

The men had been messed and housed well, their daily regimen provided for at the Para base, and in a couple of hours I was free to contact Chauhan to ask about the servant who had given the game away. The man had been detained in a hotel that the CBI had taken over in the old section of the city—Chauhan had anticipated that if the kidnappers had enough sources of information to enable them to kidnap the PM's granddaughter, they were quite capable of having the man killed in custody if he were kept in jail—and it was there that I went. The servant, an alcoholic called Basappa, had already been questioned several times by Chauhan's men, and was terrified and confused, for he didn't seem to know whom to fear more: the CBI or the kidnappers. He sat slumped in a straight-backed metal chair, eyes darting from side to side, mouth working all the time. The man was close to panic and, no doubt, thirsty for a drink.

From his record he was a petty criminal, always short of money to pay for his liquor, always in trouble with his employers, and a terrific cook. I pulled up a chair across the table from him, put his file on the table in front of me, opened it, and began to read the transcripts of his questioning, although I'd been through them twice already. He gave me my first faint break.

He'd been with the lodge two years now and he lived in a room inside the lodge complex on working days. On his days off he lived at his wife's house in the village nearby. His native tongue was Kannada, but he'd picked up English working in houses where only English was spoken. He'd been contacted first at night, in his wife's house, where someone had offered him a drink just after a quarrel with his wife in the course of which she had refused him money. The visitor had come at half past nine, and when Basappa had had a couple he'd threatened him with exposure. He'd told the cringing servant that unless he was very careful, information would be laid with the authorities to the effect that he had stolen a pair of earrings from a German tourist a month earlier. When Basappa tried to laugh that off, saying that no one had complained, the stranger told him that the jeweller to whom Basappa had sold the pair at a tenth of its price was willing to testify against him in court, and that the tourist, who had discovered her loss only in Bombay and had since left for home, would be willing to depose against him by mail.

The mention of the court had scared Basappa. His wife was expecting, he had explained, and there were many small expenses, and his salary was so small . . . A man had to take care of himself, after all. The visitor had then offered Basappa a deal. Money, in exchange for information.

Basappa, overjoyed at the discovery that instead of losing his job he was going to earn some money on the side, had jumped at the deal. Three days before the kidnap, he'd told the visitor about the sleeping arrangements which he had overheard the manager explain to the housekeeper.

'How many men came to meet you?' I asked him in English.

'Two men, sar,' he replied. 'I told the police so many times, now why are you asking me again?'

'Just shut up and answer,' I said.

He subsided in his chair. 'How many times did they come?' I asked.

'One man come three times, sar. He come first. On the second visit the other man also come. The first man tell me about earring, sar, he threaten me.'

'Did you see the man properly?' I asked. 'The first man?'

'No, sar. He always come at night, in the dark.'

'What did he look like?'

'Tall, sar, six feet tall. Moustache. Glasses. I never see his eyes. Thin face, big nose. Just like anyone else, sar. Ordinary.'

'And his dress?'

'He dress well, sar. Dark clothes. Both of them dress well. I think they are executives with big company. They using after-shave, sar, Old Spice, I know.'

'Who spoke to you?'

'Only the first man speak to me. The second man, he speak to the first man once or twice.'

'Did you hear what he said?'

'I hear, sar, but I don't understand. I don't know language.'

'Could you make out what language they spoke?'

'No, sar. Not Kannada, not English, not Tamil, not Hindi.' He ticked these off on his fingers. 'Not Malayalam, not Telugu. I don't know any other language.'

'What did the second man look like?'

'He is also well dressed, sar. Very good dress he is wearing. But sar, he is dangerous man. He get angry very quickly. His leg, sar, it is not all right. He is walking slowly.' He got up and imitated a stiff-legged walk, like a man with a knee that wouldn't bend. 'But he is walking very straight, sar, like Army man. Shoulders up. Like this.'

Something nibbled at the edges of my memory. I knew someone like that. Who? 'Was he a big man?'

'Yes, sar, very big. Bigger than the other man. Hefty, strong man. Moustache, sar, and short hair. Like Army haircut.'

The nibbles grew into bites. 'You said you heard him speak to the other man. What was his voice like?'

He smiled nervously, shrugged. 'His voice, sar? His voice is like any other voice only. Not like voice of big man.' Another lead.

'Did you see his hands?' I asked.

'Big hands, sar, very strong hands, very white and clean . . . Yes, sar, one finger gone. Small finger. I think small finger of his left hand missing.'

'All of it, or just part?'

'Only part, sar. This part.' He pointed at the first joint, just below the nail. 'From here it is gone.'

The minnow wriggled behind some rocks, then emerged. I knew someone who could be this man. He'd been with the Grenadiers, posted in Poonch. I'd first met him when I was a Captain with 9 Para Commando, on detached duty in the same area. The objective—of the Grenadiers, not the 9 Para team—was to encircle a nest of Pakistan-trained militants who had holed up in the forest some thirty kilometres from Poonch while fleeing from another Grenadier unit that had chased them. This man, I remembered, was a Major then, leading that unit.

The militants had had a local guide whose sympathies were with them but didn't run as far as supporting them in the field. In any case, they had forced him to lead them into the forest. When the militants reached the edge of the guide's territory, they dumped him and moved on. Some hours after that the Grenadiers arrived in the area and found the guide. The militants were long gone, and the sympathizer had no idea where they were, or which way they'd gone. The Major—his name popped into my mind out of the blue: Abhay Rawat—decided that the man did know, and would tell only under extreme pressure. In other words, torture.

The Major led the man off the trail into the woods that dark night to speak to him, taking with him a couple of soldiers who would cooperate. The guide was a tall, lean man, all trace of excess weight burnt off him by the hard life of the mountains. The Major was equally tall, a light-heavyweight boxer heavy with muscle and aggression, full of himself. Three hundred yards down the trail, the guide, his eyes accustomed to the dark, knowing every shadow around him, knowing what awaited him at the Major's hands, made his move. He jumped the Major, who was careless, and got his sidearm. He held the muzzle of the pistol at the Major's throat, and told the soldiers to withdraw. The soldiers withdrew, and the Major tried to get his pistol back. In the scuffle that followed, the Major was shot in the kneecap, which was why the big man now limped. He couldn't bend his left leg at the knee any more.

I'd been in the vicinity, heard voices and a shot, and moved in to investigate. I found the Major on the ground, swearing through his teeth gritted in pain, the two soldiers nonplussed, and their erstwhile captive holding the Major's own pistol to the Major's head. I jumped the guide, took him by surprise, and handed him to the soldiers, who knocked him out. The Major, meanwhile, had recovered sufficiently to shoot and kill the sympathizer as he lay unconscious.

The soldiers didn't care one way or another, but I complained, much to the Major's displeasure. The way he told the story, the sympathizer had taken his gun and shot him in the leg but the Major, taking advantage of my unexpected arrival on the scene, had heroically overcome the man and shot him back. But his testimony was ill-prepared, and there were contradictions in it that fairly leapt out at one.

And then he'd done this stupid thing. I'd testified against him at the court martial, where he'd been accused of using excessive force against a non-combatant. They'd found there that the Major had often interrogated prisoners on his own or in the company of one or two other ranks—never with another officer around—and the prisoners had always been shot trying to escape. The court martial had, to my disgust, exonerated him. But I found that the Army has wonderful ways of being obscure and the verdict had been cloaked in language that stripped him of any professional pride. After he'd limped out of the court, he called me up and swore to get his own back; he was extremely well connected. But in the following elections his connections had lost their power and nothing happened.

I remembered best his high voice, strange coming from so big and powerful a man, and I could remember it best on the telephone after the verdict, saying he'd get me yet. I couldn't remember his unit and his name had come only with effort, but the voice was still clear in my memory. The missing fingertip I had no recollection of. Maybe he'd lost if afterwards.

I must have been silent a long while, for Basappa, seeing some hope, began to plead to be let loose. I told him that that wasn't in my hands, that he'd committed a crime in any case and he'd have to spend time in prison for it. He began to cry then, and whine about his wife and children, and I left. From outside the room I called Chauhan and told him what I knew about the big man, his name, his rank, and his court martial. 'Try to trace him,' I said, 'pick him up for questioning. Get the servant to identify him. Get Army Headquarters to dig out the records of his court martial.'

'What about the servant?' he asked. 'Do you think he's reliable?'

'If you mean reliable as in truthful, no, but I think he's telling the truth about Rawat. I don't think he'd be able to make up a character like that.'

'All right. Do you want to hold him a little longer or shall I give him back to the police?'

'Give him back,' I said, committing my first major blunder, 'you can always pick him up afterwards to identify that officer.'

I called General Kelkar to tell him to contact the Grenadiers and find out if they had any idea where Major Abhay Rawat had gone after leaving the Army. Kelkar was in a meeting with the PM, the operator told me, but had left instructions that if I called he was to be dragged out of the meeting, so would I please hold. I did, and minutes later he was on the line. 'I'm glad you got me out of there,' he said, 'I was hoping you'd call. There was some kind of strategy meeting going on there and I didn't know what to do.'

'I've got a lead,' I told him. 'Remember that court martial where I testified against a Grenadier Major? I don't know what he did when he quit but he seems to be involved in this.' I explained about the servant, that I couldn't be a hundred per cent sure of the identification, not based on the kind of evidence that the servant had given, but it would be worth checking it out quickly.

'I'll follow up,' he said, 'I'll get the PM to talk to Army Headquarters. Or maybe the defence minister, that might be quicker. Anything further?'

'No,' I replied.

'I've got some bad news for you, then,' he said. 'There's nothing secure here. The committee's got about fifteen people on it and they're all too busy trying to impress the PM for any real work to be done. Old man Mankekar's been standing up for me, that's all.'

'Should we pull out?' I asked.

'I won't . . . Raja, take it easy. Don't put people's backs up, all right? You have a problem, you call me.' He disconnected.

Basappa was led away to a police jeep by two large constables, a woebegone figure now. He would be taken to a police station where he'd be kept in the lock-up until we needed him. I went back to my own temporary office near the TV tower to think things out. Rawat had been through the four-month commando course and learnt to be watchful and to live off the land. The Army would have given him some leadership skills. And for all his weaknesses, the man was very bright. If he'd organized this, he'd done a good job.

That commando course spelt trouble. With the knowledge he'd gained out of that, Rawat could well have the kidnappers hole up somewhere in the jungle for a couple of days, emerge anywhere at the fringes and take off to wherever they wanted. It wasn't so hard to hide out for a few weeks in the forests around Coorg and Nagarhole, to make friends with villagers and get them to supply him with what he needed. Veerappan, the sandalwood smuggler, had done just that. But he'd had political help as well, the odd legislator or parliamentarian offering him goodies by way of information on when the various Special Task Forces were going after him . . .

Maybe it was Rawat, after all. Even in the days I knew him he'd had political connections. One of his uncles had at one time been a Cabinet minister, and he'd had dozens of friends who were rich and influential.

The ultralights had me intrigued. They, too, pointed at connivance in some form. They couldn't have come into the country otherwise. You don't put an ultralight in your suitcase and walk out through customs with the thing in your hand. Four ultralights, and even the CBI had no idea where they'd come from, or how.

Reports came occasionally, on the telephone, or via messengers. The searchers—police, Army, and the Forest Service—had found nothing yet. Then came more news. As if by magic a local Task Force Committee had been formed. It included a Karnataka Police DIG, the Sub-Area Commander, the director of the Karnataka State Forest Department, the state's Home Secretary, Chauhan of the CBI, a representative of RAW, and myself. We were to meet twice a day to report our progress. Anything of note from Delhi would be presented at these meetings.

The first meeting that evening was the most useful. The helicopter had been found, about a hundred kilometres away from where it had last been seen, in a clearing less than a hundred metres from the road, but well hidden so that a casual passerby wouldn't spot it. The machine had been disabled thoroughly—someone had taken an axe to the console and the controls, and, for good measure, brought down a rotor as well. The Forest Service men who found the chopper found the pilot too, in a pit some thirty metres away. The police said he'd been shot in the back of the head, and the professor of forensic medicine, who had been called in to do the post-mortem, said that death could have occurred any time between three and twelve hours after the kidnap.

They must have forced him to fly them out. When they had no further need for him they'd dragged him out and shot him. That also told us something about the kidnappers: the pilot had known something about them. What?

And there was silence still from the kidnappers.

That night I couldn't sleep. Patience is the essence of soldiering and I'd told the PM that waiting would be hard, but now, even so far from Delhi, I myself found the tension building up. What if the searchers actually bumped into the kidnappers in their hideout? Or worse still, alerted them? The hostages were at risk. With such a large-scale but clumsy search anything could happen. They couldn't just comb the country, they'd have to ask around gently. I'd said as much to Chauhan and Kalra and the Karnataka Police DIG heading the search. Kalra called off his men—he was exceeding his brief anyway—but the others just smiled briefly and it kept on.

The lodge at which the girls had stayed was technically in control, I supposed. I wanted to see it, especially now that there was the possibility of an Army man being involved. Maybe I could work out something backwards from what I saw there. After the next morning's meeting I picked up the telephone and called the DIG.

The operator put me on hold for almost five minutes before DIG K. Subramanian's voice came on the line. 'Yes, Colonel, what can I do for you?' he asked coldly, discouragingly. 'Any more hints on how I should do my job?'

I ignored the barb and said, 'I'd like to see that jungle lodge where the girls were kidnapped. I thought I'd ask you if I can go there now. Your people must have finished with the place.'

'They finished long back. My lab staff gave it back to the CBI long ago.' I knew from his tone that he'd had some kind of territorial wrangle with Chauhan as well.

I was tempted to tell him to restrict his pissing contests to his own service and then thought the better of it. 'Your men sealed off the place until the CBI got there and took it over, didn't they?' I asked. 'Did they also go through the grounds and round up the locals?'

'All our papers are with the CBI, Colonel,' he said, 'we are just providing sentries to guard the place. If you want anything, talk to the CBI. And now, if you'll excuse me, I have my work to get back to. If you want anything further, call my secretary.' He hung up with a click.

I called Chauhan, who sounded too harassed to get into pissing contests. 'Go ahead,' he said when I told him what I wanted, 'but take a helicopter. Save you time. They might get in touch any time now and I'd like to have you around when they do.'

'Right, I'll come straight back if there's any movement.' Then I told him why I wanted to go to Kabini, to see if I could climb inside the head of whoever had planned this one, that people often showed preferences for tactics or equipment that might give us a lead on who the kidnappers were. He listened impatiently, with only passing interest, as if he had a pile of other things to do—which he had—so I kept it short. Less than half an hour after that I was at a helipad at Jalahalli, climbing into an Air Force Mi-8 helicopter.

Flying at eight hundred metres along the road to Mysore the pilot kept the machine going fairly fast, about eighty knots—a hundred and fifty kilometres an hour—but I had no impression of speed except for the wind in my face and the clatter of the engine biting through the ear-protectors we wore. The crewman tied a line about my waist and when I leaned out and looked down at the road below I could see that we were travelling much faster than the cars below, maybe thrice as fast. What took three hours by road took only an hour in the chopper and soon we were swinging south-west past Mysore, over the road to Kabini. Traffic on the road below slowed still more, to something under forty kilometres an hour, I estimated. The chase that night would have lasted only three or four minutes before the RPG-7 cut it off.

As we approached the forest, the ground appeared damp from the early rains. There was grass sprouting all over the place, still new and tender. Where there were trees, the forest, seen from above, was a solid layer of green. The Kabini river came into sight dead ahead. The pilot signalled to me that we would follow the course of the river from now, rather than the road, and we drifted serenely above the valleys through which the little river—at no point that I could see was it more than two hundred metres across—flowed sluggishly down towards the faraway coast.

On the intercom the pilot's voice was scratchy and almost drowned out by engine noise and static. 'There's a clearing nearby where they took off from,' he said, 'we can have a look.'

'All right,' I said into the mike in the helmet, and the helicopter slid southward to a dusty clearing.

Nothing there that I could use, not from the air. I'd have a look later on, perhaps. I told the pilot to go on.

Minutes later, I saw the lodge, set on the rising banks of the river, its lawns gleaming in the sunshine. The circular dining hall just up the banks from the river came into view, and then, up the slope from the hall, the office, the path between them flanked by servants' quarters, with a big tree to one side. In front of the office were the central lawns, watered and manicured, where we were going to land. At least fifty armed policemen guarded the area. Among them were senior officers, a few plainclothesmen, and a few quiet men in safari suits.

The pilot eased the helicopter to a stop over the spot, marked with white paint on the grass, where he would land, and drifted gently downwards. A wide circle of security men, all now with weapons ready and all looking upwards, gathered around the white mark.

The helicopter came down on the grass. Before I had the door open, one of the safari suits came running up, his hair blown about by the downdraft from the rotor, walkie-talkie in his left hand, his right hovering close to the sidearm concealed under his arm. 'Colonel Menon?' he asked as the rotors spun to a halt and the noise died down.

I waited a moment to get used to the silence before replying. 'Yes. Who might you be?'

'My name is Prakash, sir, and I'm with the Special Protection Group, now on duty with the PM's personal security detachment.' He looked young and hard and his eyes were restless, watchful even when he smiled. A more careful look revealed faint wrinkles. He wasn't as young as I'd thought. Mid-thirties, trim except for a roll of fat about the waist, a drooping moustache over a wide, thin-lipped mouth, a big, heavy jaw. Quick on his feet, he seemed used to taking charge. 'I was told you were on your way. We've been in radio contact with Bangalore control throughout. We were told there was a small deviation from the flight plan.'

The detour to the clearing had taken less than three minutes, and taken us less than a kilometre off our path, but these guys were already tetchy. 'I wanted to check out a clearing on the way,' I explained, 'where they took off on their ultralights.'

'You're welcome to do that,' he said. 'Look at what you like, when you like. But you must keep us informed.

Preferably in advance, so that we don't come to the wrong conclusions. It'll be much easier all around. The rules are tight, sir. I'm sure you understand. I have to keep my charges safe.'

I did understand. This man was smooth but inexorable. 'I'll remember that for the future,' I promised. 'And in the meanwhile, I want to go over whatever you've found here. Everything the hostages did after they got here.'

'Right, sir.' A colleague, this one in a fawn safari suit, slid up beside him. 'This is Ved, sir, my colleague, who debriefed the Princess's—sorry, that's our code name for the PM's granddaughter—Ved debriefed her security men after the kidnap. He can also put you on to the men themselves, some of whom are still confined here. As you know, two of the three dead men have been taken to Delhi and another four injured are in a Mysore hospital.'

'I thought only two men had been killed.'

'The third died just a couple of hours ago. A good friend. Everyone here, you'll understand, is in an ugly mood. You'll see when you speak to them.' I knew. I'd been through it myself. A dead colleague brought your own death close. I nodded and moved on to Ved, a younger, slimmer version of Prakash. More obvious, less polished, less mature, but all that would come with the years. He led me first to the room where the Princess—I liked that name—had slept that fateful night.

It was a square room, a bedroom some fourteen feet by fourteen, high-ceilinged, with an old white fan on a long rod still turning slowly. Opposite the double doors through which we'd come in was another, much smaller door, and to our left, a double bed with a bedside table on each side. The sheets on the bed were still rumpled, and the counterpane lay on a chair by the bathroom door. In the corner just by the doors was a mosquito repellent, a coil that had to be lit and would glow through the night. There was still a faint smell of smoke in the room. 'We haven't cleaned up yet,' Ved explained. 'We'll keep it like this until the lab boys say they have nothing more to do here.'

'What have they done so far?' I asked.

'Fingerprints. Blood. Photographs. But those were the local men. A team from Delhi is on the way. Everything will end up at the lab in Delhi. Flies are a problem.'

'You'll have to set up a table fan somewhere to blow them away,' I said. 'There're no signs of a struggle here. Did they knock the girls out, or were they conscious when they took her?'

'The security men I debriefed said that the men seemed to be half carrying the girls. They wouldn't have been totally unconscious, only half-way there, probably drugged. The kidnappers had shot the lights out, so our men can't be sure, but they're quite clear they didn't hear any signs of a struggle. No screams, no gasps, nothing. Just the thump of the door breaking and then the kidnappers were out in the veranda. Also, all our men complained of being very sleepy though no one was actually asleep. Maybe they had something that slowed them down slightly, just a few seconds. But you know how much those few seconds count . . . We've sent stomach contents to the lab. We'll know the results in a few hours.'

'Where did they land?' I asked.

He led me to the bathroom door, unlatched it. Inside the bathroom, to the left was a full-size bath, to the right a washbasin sink, above it a mirror, and beyond the sink a toilet seat. There was one light above the mirror, another over the head of the bath. Facing the door through which we had entered was another door. Double doors, actually, one of them hanging on a single hinge. The damaged door was burnt in parts, and the jamb side of it had been broken.

Ved pushed the undamaged door open, a kerchief covering his fingers, and there, beyond it, was more open space. The grass here wasn't as neatly trimmed as in the lawns in front but there was a reasonable amount of clear space, enough for the ultralights to land. Ved pointed at a spot some thirty metres away from the building. 'They came to land somewhere there, with the engines switched off. All the rooms here are similar, and they knew exactly which ones to attack. The other two rooms have the same kind of damage that this one has.

'There were two guards stationed here, they're both dead. They were the ones killed first. The kidnappers landed, moved in here, shot the guards, and broke the doors. They must have used some fancy explosives for that. The men in front heard the blast—they must have timed the explosions well, because the men heard only one blast—and then they charged in. They broke the doors between the bathroom and the bedroom in the other two rooms, but not here. The Princess must have left it unlocked.'

'One strange thing about the two guards, though,' he added and paused for effect.

'What?' I asked, irritated.

'One of the two guards at the back didn't die immediately, the doctor says. They slit his throat as they went. There was no need to do that but one of the men in the group slit his throat and killed him.' He pointed down at the bloodstains on the grass outside, brownish now and unidentifiable unless you knew what you were looking for. 'They needn't have killed him, and they knew it.'

'Leave that for the moment,' I said, 'we'll get back to it. Go ahead with what happened.'

'There were two men to the Princess's room, one each to the other two. They forced their way out of the rooms, one man coming out of the Princess's room ahead of the others. He ran into the guard in front, and shot him. By that time the other kidnappers had emerged with the hostages and our men had to hold their fire.'

'How did they get away?' I asked.

'Did you see the cars parked in front of the office block?' he asked, pointing. 'Well, they worked their way up there. All were dressed in black, masked, like you people on a raid. They didn't make noise or anything. The extra man was to carry the equipment. He went out and brought along a huge sack, also black. Then they gave a demonstration. They fired a rocket out of something they got out of the bag. Then they signalled some of our men to come close, and one of them tied up those he could see. Four of them. The rest they locked into a room.

'Then they went to the cars, picked a Mercedes 220 belonging to the father of one of the hostages, and took off into the dark. They left a cassette player outside the room where they'd locked the men, playing a cassette that had sounds on it of men walking around, some thumps and bumps.

'The security men ignored it and broke out but they lost some time doing that, and by then the kidnappers were almost out of sight. They chased the car, till somewhere past the gates the kidnappers fired one rocket at them. It hit the car but they got out in time . . . Lucky men. The car was burnt out. The round was old, it didn't go off as violently as it should have. Those rockets can pierce armour.'

'How did you find out about the helicopter and so on?'

'We found the Mercedes at a clearing. There were the tracks of a helicopter there, and the vegetation around had been blown flat. You know, the kind of signs a helicopter leaves.'

'What kind of a helicopter? It must have been an eight- or nine-seater. Pilot plus four kidnappers plus three hostages.'

'A Westland, sir. That's what it looked like. It's small but in reasonable weather and with a good pilot it can take that kind of load if the passengers are willing to be cramped.'

'Where did they get it from?'

'A charter firm. The doors were larger than standard, the owners did that. The people who hire these helicopters most are the big oil companies. They need helicopters to patrol the oil pipelines and to fly stuff in and out of rigs.

But the patrol machines are all smaller ones, two- or three-seaters.'

'The pilot? Any leads on him yet?'

'One of the firm's best, sir, very experienced. A stable family man. The craft took off from Bangalore. The flight plan said it was going to Mysore, to land in a private field. The passengers were supposed to be businessmen who wanted to survey a township off the highway between Mysore and Bangalore for a Japanese sponsored project. Bangalore lost the craft near Mysore. Then the charter firm got a strange call. The caller said that the helicopter had had a mechanical failure, a broken pin in the landing gear. The pilot could fix it, he said, but it would take a few hours. That was it . . . They must have taken the machine at gunpoint. One of them must have known about radio conventions, because otherwise the pilot would have slipped in a distress message somehow. He'd flown all over the world, in Africa, the Middle East, with all kinds of people. He'd have worked out some way to get the message across if he had a chance. They must have known the routine. They prepared well.'

'What about the other guests at the lodge before the day of the kidnap?' I asked. 'Have you prepared a guest list? Do you know if the follow-up has had any results yet?'

He shook his head. 'There are others looking at that,' he said. 'We might not know at all, officially. There are several agencies at work here. But like I said earlier, three of our men are dead, sir, we're not going to let it go so easily . . . I knew those men, played with their children, ate with them, took them home . . . We won't let it go.' I knew he wouldn't. The competitive fire in these men is fierce, as is the bonding.

'Do you know what my role here is?' I asked.

'Yes,' he replied. 'Negotiations. Hostage rescue if possible. Coordinating the exchange, consulting on logistics . . . We've heard about your unit, and some of your operations.'

'Good,' I said, 'since you know why I'm here, maybe you could tell me how these guys think. So far I've got little.'

He gave me a long, hard stare. I could see him revising—downwards—his opinion of me. 'Not really,' he said, 'I don't know much about that sort of thing. All I can tell you is that these people are well organized, they've got a much larger organization than the four men we saw. They have very good intelligence, and they can move very fast. They must have spent a week here digging up information on the Princess, on where she would stay, on who works here and how to handle them . . . what the weak points are. The trouble is, this place is open to the public. Anyone can pay their few thousand rupees a day and come and stay here as long as they like. If they give us false addresses we can find out that the addresses are false, but after that we hit a dead end. Unless there's some further identification possible.'

'Do you have the ultralights here?' I asked. 'I'd like to have a look.'

'We have one. The rest were taken away by the lab men and on to other specialists after they were checked for explosives and fingerprints and so on. The machines are

American, mostly tubular frame and canvas for the wings, a small seat without a cushion and a small Korean-made engine. Look like insects.'

'How do you think they brought them into the country?' I asked.

'Getting an ultralight shouldn't be a problem for people as resourceful as these. They got sub-machine guns, an RPG . . . You saw those bathroom doors, I think they blew them in with a kind of bomb you don't get in India. It's a credit-card-sized piece of plastic explosive with a fuse you can scratch and set off. You stick it between the door and the jamb, scratch, and take cover. Three seconds later it goes boom and the door's gone.'

I knew. We'd used bombs like that ourselves to get into houses. 'Did you get the RPG?' I asked.

'No. They took it with them. They fired it out of the car, like I told you. But we found the marks.' An RPG launcher—Rocket Propelled Grenade, a misnomer because it fires a rocket rather than a grenade—lets off a tongue of flame with each rocket. If fired low down, and if there's vegetation around, it sometimes leaves a scorch mark, like an arrow pointing in the direction of the rocket. The rockets are designed to go through the kind of armour used on light tanks and APCs. The 7 has been superseded in wealthier armies by later models, but it is still popular in the poorer countries. And, of course, among terrorist groups.

'Where are the scorch marks?' I asked.

He led me out of the front door of the bathroom to the bedroom, and then out onto the lawn towards the office building. The scorch marks were about thirty metres from the building, and very faint. The rocket had been fired in the direction of the river. Short marks, so it had been fired upwards. They'd have used it to demonstrate their firepower to keep the security men tied up: the ones who had gone chasing the kidnappers had been foolhardy, and were extremely fortunate to be alive.

RPGs are meant to be handled by two men, or one very powerful one. With three hostages keeping his three colleagues busy, the fourth man would have fired it all by himself.

'Did you find where the rocket landed?'

'Yes. On the far side of the river. Not much damage, except for a couple of trees. There's a small crater there, you must have seen it on the way in.' I had seen a small blackened spot but hadn't connected it with the RPG.

They must have known exactly where the rocket would land. If it had landed in the village nearby it would have killed villagers, caused a great uproar, even though in India a few dead villagers were insignificant beside the kidnaps. Preparation . . . I wished the police would hurry up with the guest list. And with Rawat.

'Lucky no one got killed by that rocket,' Ved commented.

'Do you really think they were lucky?'

He looked at me strangely all over again. 'Of course,' he replied eventually. 'No one would set off an RPG in the dark in a strange place and be sure of not hitting anything.'

'Ask yourself two little questions,' I said. 'Was it dark for them? Was this a strange place?'

His mouth hung open in surprise. 'But . . . They didn't have lights with them! They came and went in the dark!'

'Night vision glasses,' I told him. 'If they could get hold of an RPG launcher and fancy explosives and steal a helicopter, they could well get themselves NVGs.'

He kept quiet and looked away. I could make out that he didn't like the idea, because it meant that whoever had done it had extensive knowledge of weaponry and equipment, and could get hold of whatever he needed. Nothing was random. That meant, possibly, a foreign mercenary. Or a former services man with contacts, probably one who had served with counter-insurgency or anti-terrorist units, in Punjab or Kashmir or Nagaland or Assam. It could even be a former colleague of his. 'Do you have the ultralight here?' I asked.

'Yes,' he replied, 'I'll take you to it.' He led me to the office block along a wide gravelled pathway flanked with flowerpots. On either side stretched the lawns, dotted with shrubs. A pair of monkeys sat on a small ornamental tree some way off, unafraid of the human presence so close by. There were about four others in a larger tree some distance away. They'd definitely have chattered an alarm when they sensed the ultralights coming in. Strange smells at night worry monkeys, who fear tree-climbing leopards. The security men wouldn't have noticed their chattering that night because they weren't used to the normal pattern of noises in the lodge. This place had a fine alarm system laid on by nature: nesting birds, monkeys, lots of small animals—all useless that night because the security men hadn't been in place long enough to absorb the local atmosphere.

Whoever had come in here would have known about this—they struck on the first night the girls were there, when the lodge was completely new to the security men. Perfect timing. That argued special forces training. No ordinary hood would have been able to penetrate the security rings around the Princess and then find his way out safe.

Rawat?

There were too many ex-Army men around who could have worked this. But they'd need money. Lots of it. There would have to be someone much bigger behind them.

Who? And more to the point, why?

My first instinct was to think of the ISI, Pakistan's Inter Services Intelligence, run out of a large office in Islamabad by Major General Hamid Gul. During Zia's time he'd started Operation Topaz, which had cost us untold lives. He and his successors were behind most of the gun- and drug-running on India's western and northern frontiers, where separatists in Punjab and Kashmir offered fertile ground for the kind of mayhem he liked to cause. They were also behind much of the gun-running in the south, along the west coast, where his razakars found enough local support.

But there were limits even Gul's ISI wouldn't cross. For all their pointed ignorance of the conventions of intelligence-gathering and agit-prop, they wouldn't get into assassinations or kidnaps of leading figures. Unless . . . unless they could point with utter certainty at someone else. Did they have a scapegoat, then?

Another possibility, faint and receding every moment, was professional kidnappers. They operated more or less freely in parts of Bihar and UP for large amounts of money. They had their hideouts in the hills and many had links with Khalistani terrorists settled in the Terai who had the contacts, mostly in Pakistan, to get weapons and equipment.

But the ultralights were a different ball-game altogether. No Khalistani separatist would use an ultralight for something like this, if at all he thought of using one. More and more it pointed to the ISI, or one of the organizations it supported.

We would know only when the kidnappers surfaced with their demands. If they asked for money, that was fine. I would recommend in that case that the ransom be paid without too much fuss. But stepping on the shifting sands of political terrorism, especially the religious fundamentalist kind favoured by groups like Al Faran and Hamas, always left you with a sense of loss because you got to see human nature at its worst. Dealing with professionals was easier because both sides knew exactly what they were after and cutting your losses worked because the losses were measurable in money. The ultralight Ved led me to was behind the office block.

A spidery framework of tubular aluminium alloy, with wing surfaces of gaily patterned canvas. It had three wheels, two soup-plate-sized ones in front and a smaller one at the back, and a minimal seat, with just a couple of levers for control. A fragile craft. I wouldn't trust my life to one of these unless I had to.

From the office block we went down to the dining room by the river, where I had a hasty lunch out of a paper plate. The river, glinting grey-blue in the sunlight, now falling almost vertically down, flowed sluggishly past. There, were lots of birds around, yet not too much noise in the somnolence of a late summer morning, the buzzing of insects the loudest background noise.

The kidnappers had brought in some heavy equipment; the RPG, and God knows what else. The river would have been the logical way to bring it in. The RPG launcher was heavy and long, and if carried as dead weight on an ultralight would seriously reduce the craft's performance. Maybe some of them had got in along the river, hidden their stuff somewhere for the men who flew in to pick up. 'Has the river been checked?' I asked. 'They might have tossed something in. Or got something along it.'

'Yes,' Ved answered, 'we dragged the river immediately. Didn't find anything.'

I remembered something about the RPG-7. One model of the RPG-7 was called the Stroke D—RPG-7/D. Its barrel came unscrewed in the middle, thereby halving its length, which made the launcher a whole lot easier to manage. You could fire a rocket and have it folded down in something the size of a bag of golf clubs in under three minutes. They must have brought in a Stroke D and taken it back with them to avoid the possibility of their being traced via the serial number. But few people knew about Stroke Ds. Certainly not the average serviceman.

The sun went behind clouds coming in from the south and I looked at my watch. A quarter to two. Time to return to Bangalore, for the meeting at six, and to wait for the kidnappers to get in touch. More than thirty-six hours after the kidnap they were still silent, which said a lot for their poise. And nothing from Madras either, about the CJ's son. I hoped that the Madras kidnapping had nothing to do with this one.

Across the river was the small crater left by the RPG rocket.

They'd used it just to deter the security men, to let them know that they were well armed. Was there a message in there somewhere? I didn't get it.

Rain clouds gathered, bleak and threatening. It began to drizzle gently. I borrowed a raincoat and took a last look around, tracing my way around the bathrooms and the bedrooms and the corridors, and then out along the road to the gate where the burnt out hulk of the chase car stood.

The more I looked at it the surer I was that their actions were calculated and their violence measured. There must have been a soldier involved in this somewhere, a professional soldier who knew how to anticipate the kind of response a security man would come up with. He'd known about the natural alarms, the monkeys and the birds, and attacked too early for the security men to have got used to these alarms. And now he was making everyone sweat.

Only one piece didn't fit. The slit throat. There had been no need to kill that man. More than that, a seriously injured man, one near death, can in a desperate dying surge do considerable damage. Going close enough to slit his throat wasn't professional, unless there was a message there as well.

Either that, or the killer just liked killing.

chapter four

At the meetings the power play continued and the tension mounted to almost unbearable levels. The searchers reported blanks all over. The CJ's son too seemed to have vanished, like the PM's granddaughter and her friends.

By now the hostages' photographs were being flashed on every TV channel, and printed on the front page of every newspaper, with a notice of a generous reward and a promise of anonymity and protection, if required, to anyone offering information. A range of telephone numbers was provided, all manned by trained policemen or secretaries, but all they got were crank calls. The control room averaged a call every ten minutes, policemen rigorously taping and transcribing every call in the increasingly faint hope of getting something out of them, rigidly maintaining their calm through the calls no matter what was said.

The CBI, meanwhile, had been following up with addresses of guests registered at the lodge in the past six weeks. Three sets of addresses turned out to be false. The guests involved were all men, one of them American. All we had to go on was a description of the American from the forest rangers who took the guests out on the sightseeing trails. They remembered the Yank because he was almost always drunk and a big tipper. Interpol found him from his description twelve hours later. He was a drug-runner with a whole variety of passports and had been caught in Malaysia.

Nearly a kilometre from the lodge, up the river, a sharp-eyed policeman noticed a bit of black rubber floating on the surface of the water. He called for a diver who found under the water a black rubber inflatable dinghy weighted with a bit of chain and some stones. The lab, however, said that the dinghy had probably been in water more than a year.

Army Headquarters turned up Rawat's records. They were initially a little slow handing them over but a word from the top produced results. Rawat had been given the option of resigning from the Army after his court martial. Reading between the lines it was clear that he'd been shown this leniency only on the grounds of his injury. His photograph, too, was on TV screens all over the country now. This person, the accompanying notices said, might be able to help the law enforcement agencies in their search for the PM's kidnapped granddaughter.

To this notice there was a surprising level of response. Fifteen minutes after the first notices came out, the switchboards in Delhi, Bombay, Madras, Calcutta, and Bangalore were swamped with calls from people saying they knew the man. Most of them claimed business acquaintance, but there were also neighbours in Bombay, and colleagues in all the cities. Most of the callers were neutral, saying they knew who the man was and little else. His colleagues were uniformly indignant, saying he was a respectable man doing a respectable job in a respectable company, a pillar of financial society.

Former Major Abhay Rawat, it turned out, was now Chief Security Officer with West Coast Holdings Limited. West Coast, called Wesco, was a holding company, itself controlling a travel agency, a publisher, a struggling airline, an investment company, and two textile mills. It was growing fast, growing by purchasing existing outfits. Its Managing Director rang up himself to say that Rawat was a responsible senior executive with his company and could not have been involved in the kidnap because on the day of the kidnap he had been attending a series of meetings in Bombay, and had two hours before the kidnap been on his way home from a party, attended by other senior executives, at the MD's house. There were nine witnesses to testify to Rawat's presence throughout the party and his departure from it shortly after midnight. There were Rawat's own signatures in attendance registers maintained by the company to testify to his presence in Bombay on the days when the MD said he had been attending meetings.

How Rawat got the job with Wesco Holdings no one knew. A man who leaves the Army under a cloud has few options by way of civilian employment. If Wesco had been a small, shady operation I'd have understood, but it was one of the larger business groups in the south, and there were rumours that it would go public very soon. It was based in Hyderabad, promoted fourteen years earlier by a group of businessmen who'd made small fortunes in Europe and the Middle East. While it wasn't really a major player, its turnover of over Rs 1000 crores last year wasn't to be sneezed at. Why then would the company risk its reputation and pick a man with a dark past to head its security service?

Rawat had spent seven years with Wesco, always looking for ways to use technology to make the company's security tighter; they had been among the first to use burglar alarms and electronics extensively and their communication lines were among the most secure in the country. Rawat was a good man to work for; his security men, half of them from the Army or police forces, were by their standards very well paid. He avoided the prevalent practice of farming out security to security agencies. The MD said that Rawat had once told him that farming out security would keep out the average thief but not a determined one. An intelligent, observant man who figured out the security men's routines could always get through and out safe.

Rawat was clearly a smart man and the men at Wesco would have seen this. Maybe they needed him for industrial espionage. Or perhaps he ran a bunch of frighteners to help keep down the prices of the companies Wesco bought. All that was fine by me. But was he in on the kidnap? He certainly had the training to set it up, and the contacts to get those weapons. He had the organization, courtesy his employers, and via the travel agency could handle the transport as well . . .

'Can you check if there's a connection between Wesco and the ultralights?' I asked Chauhan at the meeting.

'I already did,' he said sourly. 'There's nothing. They must have been smuggled in. Not that it's a serious problem, smuggling in four relatively innocuous things like that. Not when you have Antonovs air dropping weapons and bombs all over the country, like they did at Purulia.'

'Check on what our friend Rawat did between his exit from the Army and joining Wesco. I'm still queasy about him,' I said.

'I'm doing that. I've got a few dozen photographs of the man out here, but that cook only said he might be the man . . . He wasn't sure. I even got a vidoetape of Rawat at somebody's wedding, but that didn't click either. His being in Bombay at the time of the snatch doesn't prevent him from being the one who planned it all, of course, but it seems he was in Bombay even at the time Basappa claims he saw him here. Must have been mistaken. I'll check again, just to make sure. I do know though that Rawat travels a lot. He's married but he likes to play the field, and has the money for it.'

I told him in detail of my own encounter with Rawat. He listened, then said, 'Look, there are twenty ordinary guys willing to testify that the man was with them when the snatch was on, and Basappa's testimony is shaky as it is. Besides, this man's got his signature on attendance records. You can't fake them, and I can't imagine someone taking the trouble to falsify stuff so far ahead . . . But I'll check anyway.' He looked grumpily down at his notes. 'You know what hurts? My men spend two days with this cook Basappa and get nothing out of him. You spend fifteen minutes with the man and come up with a possible lead just because you happen to be in the Army!'

'That's life,' I told him, my spirits rising under the influence of his good-natured wrangling despite the glowering looks from the others in the committee. 'You should perhaps spend some time in the Army. I'll try to get you in if you like . . . As a Second Lieutenant, perhaps?'

He muttered something unprintable under his breath and went back to his notes, and with that the meeting ended.

General Kelkar and the Chief, both holding the PM's hand in Delhi, managed to keep the politicians off my back. Then it got too hot for Kelkar and he managed to get out of Delhi. That night he called to say he would attend the following day's morning meeting at Bangalore.

The meeting never took place, for in between the kidnappers got in touch. They did it in a way we never expected them to. At six in the morning a distraught young woman, dressed in dirty clothes and with her hair in disarray, walked into a small police station near Srirangapatna, a few kilometres off the Bangalore–Mysore highway. Her face had been on TV several times, and was still on the front pages of some newspapers, but the head constable on duty had trouble connecting the dishevelled, weeping young woman in front of him with the pretty young girl in the photograph. He got his hands on a paper that had a photograph of her, looked at it closely, then at the girl, and decided that while it might be a hoax the girl looked sufficiently like the photograph to justify calling his superior, the sub-inspector in charge of the police station. He sat the girl down and passed the buck on to the officer.

The sub-inspector, in his fifties, nearing retirement and very much in favour of the quiet life, suspecting a hoax but not sure of himself, taken completely aback by this turn of events which pitchforked him into the hot seat, came running to the station. By the time he arrived, the girl had got her wits together sufficiently to convince him that she was who she claimed to be, and the sub-inspector called his boss, the Circle Inspector of Police.

The CI, rousted out of bed hours before his wake-up alarm went off, told the sub-inspector to bugger off and went back to sleep. The SI, now in a jam, called the local administrative services man, a young Revenue Development Officer fresh out of the IAS academy. The RDO, who had been praying for something to brighten up his term, responded instantly, calling the special switchboard in Bangalore for information to verify that the girl was who she said she was—Urmila Shetty—since she had no identification on her. He left his name and telephone number with the board.

Minutes later, Mr Shetty himself called the RDO from Bangalore. In a voice barely under control, he told the RDO that their Dalmatian bitch had littered earlier in the year, a litter of two. One pup they had decided to keep, and had given the other away to a friend of Urmila's. Which friend, could the RDO please ask the young woman?

When the young woman gave the right answer she was whisked off under guard—CBI men from Mysore had arrived on the scene by then—and in the company of a fat, matronly policewoman, to a nearby government guest house. The RDO, being a compassionate youngster, besides being sympathetic to a pretty young woman in trouble, decided to delay the interrogation until she met her parents, who were already on their way.

At this stage, the girl remembered the note that the kidnappers had given her to deliver to the police when they deposited her on the roadside some two kilometres away from the police station. The RDO opened the envelope, and found inside it a note on a single sheet of paper, and half a hundred-rupee currency note.

About this time, word got to me from Chauhan. 'Let's go to Mysore to talk to her,' I said.

'No,' Chauhan replied, 'she's on her way here. Her father insisted. It makes sense. Everything else is here.'

'What about the place where they left her?' I asked.

'She pointed it out to my men,' he replied, 'and they're searching around there for a place where she might have been hidden. She told the police that she'd been in a car for two or three hours before she was let loose. That helps.'

'What about the note?' I asked.

'I've got a copy here, on the fax. I'll fax it on to you.'

The fax arrived minutes after I put down the phone. The

note was short and to the point. It was addressed to the Prime Minister of India, and said, in anonymous block letters handwritten by someone with a steady hand, 'We have with us your granddaughter Priya and two of her friends. We are releasing one of those two friends with this message for you. We know you are searching for us. Call off your dogs. Wait for us to get in touch with you. We will contact you by mail. In the meanwhile, start raising money. You'll need all of it you can get your hands on. Our next message will contain the other half of the currency note in this envelope. This will eliminate verification problems.'

No signature, no other marks. The paper had been sent off to the labs, the accompanying note from Chauhan said, and the morning meeting would be held at two that afternoon, after the released hostage had been debriefed.

Urmila Shetty, when I met her a couple of hours later in a CBI safe house in Bangalore, was hardly more informative. She was still unsteady, on the brink of tears all the time, hanging on to her father's arm throughout the meeting. Her father, fiftyish, with greying hair and a strong jaw, seemed to fill the room, strangely imposing in his custom-made clothes. He was a successful industrialist with a work force of nearly five thousand working for him in a dozen plants all over the country. Also in the room were Chauhan, an official stenographer, and a uniformed Karnataka Police DIG heading the search for the hideout. He would now redefine the parameters of the search, he said, in the light of what the hostage said.

I led Chauhan and the DIG out of the room the moment I saw the girl's condition. 'She'll speak more confidently without all of us around,' I said. 'Last thing she needs now is bright lights, loud voices, hard questions and uniforms.'

'The idea of the joint interrogation is to avoid duplication, Menon,' said the DIG. 'If you want to waste your time with individual sessions that's up to you.'

Chauhan spoke up. 'Menon has a point. She doesn't want to speak to each of us separately, and she won't be comfortable with all of us in the room with her. One of us can talk to her. We'll write down our questions and the one who speaks to her asks all our questions. If her condition improves by tomorrow we'll talk to her again.'

'All right,' agreed the DIG, 'I'll speak to her. I need to know where she was.'

Chauhan spoke softly, kindly. 'Do you have much experience of dealing with kidnapped children?'

'No,' came the reply, stiff with indignation, 'but I don't need it.'

'You do,' Chauhan said. 'Let Menon talk to her. He'll know how. He's done it before. And he's the right kind of person to do it without scaring her.' I am average height, average weight, average everything. Even my hair, which I'd grown during the undercover stint in Uri, is medium long. In civvies I melt into the background.

The DIG swallowed hard, then agreed. He didn't want a jurisdictional dispute here. His face hardened as I opened the door to go back in but he didn't say anything.

Urmila was visibly more relaxed than she'd been with the others in the room. 'I can ask the steno to leave if you want,' I said.

'No, no,' she said, 'this is fine. Where are the others?'

'They've left me to speak to you. They won't be back unless you want them back.'

'No, this is fine,' she said.

'Give me a minute to go over what we have. Just to get the basics clear. Okay?' When she nodded, I continued, 'You were at the Kabini lodge the day before yesterday when a man broke into your room at about two in the morning. He and his men took you and your friends Priya and Mallika away. They kept you with them until early this morning, then released you not very far from the police station at five this morning. Is that right?'

She gulped, shook her head, and bit her lower lip, sudden tears shining in her eyes. 'I don't know what time they came. I was fast asleep. We'd had a tiring time, all that travel, and then we went all over the jungle trails in the evening.'

'Would you like to tell me what happened?'

'I was asleep in bed, in the room next to Priya's. There was a bang, I couldn't tell from which direction, that woke me up. Then there was a lot of smoke in the room and I thought the place was burning. I sat up and someone grabbed me from behind. He put his hand over my mouth and I felt him hold a knife to my throat. He was very strong . . . I was helpless. He told me to shut up and dragged me out of the room, opening the door as he went . . . I was disoriented. I didn't know what was happening, what happened to the security men. It was all so confusing.' Her composure wavered and broke. She sobbed into a kerchief while her father put his arm consolingly around her.

'I'm sorry we have to put you through this,' I told her as gently as I could when the sobs had begun to subside, 'but we have to get your friends back safe.'

She nodded through her tears. 'Daddy . . . Daddy told me all that. It's all right.'

Her father squeezed her arm briefly and turned to me with a grim smile. 'I know what we went through before she was released,' he said, 'that's why I was willing to let you people speak to her.' His face became bleak. 'I know what the others are going through. Otherwise you wouldn't have got within a mile of my daughter.' His voice was gravelly and authoritative, soft just now with concern for his daughter, but I suspected his normal tone would be harsh. His wife, well-dressed but giving an impression of being colourless and mousy, sat on the other side of her daughter. I didn't like Shetty's tone much, but there was an underlying solidity that commanded respect.

The daughter found her voice again. 'There was this hand across my mouth,' she said finally, 'and I was helpless. I tried to bite but I just couldn't. He was holding me with his other arm. I couldn't move.'

'She's claustrophobic,' her father explained. 'She can't take being restrained. There was a time when she wouldn't get into a lift. She's got over all that now, of course, but physical restraint throws her off balance.'

The daughter nodded, holding his hand tight. 'I . . . I don't know what happened, I just sort of passed out . . . It was ghastly. The next thing I knew we were in a car, all cramped, and there was someone on top of me and I began screaming and someone hit me.' She fingered a mark on her jaw. 'I kept quiet. Then there was the helicopter . . . That was equally crowded. There was a man in front with a pistol at the pilot's head . . . There was this man with a knife, he told us to keep quiet. They gagged us there, with a piece of cloth in the mouth . . . And the noise in that helicopter. My head was splitting.'

'How long did that ride last?'

'I don't know. It seemed to last years and years but it could have been anything . . . I'm sorry, I don't know.'

'Don't worry, just tell me what you know. We'll ask you questions to sort of jog your memory. That's what I'm here for . . . And after the helicopter, what?'

She burst into tears again, shaking her head. 'I don't remember anything,' she sobbed, 'I don't want to think about it.'

'Did they say anything to you about the other girls? Did they threaten you?'

'No, I just saw the other girls, like I said, before they let me go. And they never threatened me in the house . . . No, they didn't have to. I was terrified.'

'Do you have any idea where you were? How far from Srirangapatna? From Mysore?'

'No. I was panicked on the journey there . . . I told you how it was. And when they let me loose they drugged me, I think, so I went to sleep.'

'Take it easy,' I said. 'If you can't answer, just say so. Don't whip yourself for not remembering anything.'

She shut her eyes. 'You don't know anything about this. You just don't understand.'

'I do,' I told her. 'You're happy to be back but it's already disappointing. It's not as terrific as you thought it would be . . .' I paused, finding her staring at me. 'Think back once again,' I said, close to giving up. 'Did you notice any smells? Anything odd? Fresh paint? Animals? Anything?'

'I smell a lot of bullshit here,' her father interrupted. 'You don't know what to ask her and now you're just playing games.' There was authority in his rough voice and it was clear he was close to blowing his top. I held up my hand for him to stop but he was not impressed. 'Interrogation is all very well but this has gone too far.'

'Leave it, Daddy, I don't mind,' she said.

He ignored her. 'Look, Menon, you'd better leave.'

'We have to evaluate her answers,' I tried to explain, 'that's not easy. Why don't you just leave it at that?'

He didn't budge. 'I don't want my daughter harassed just because you people can't think and act fast enough. You've seen the condition she's in. Get out of here. Get out of here right now or I'll call the PM and tell him what you're doing. He'll listen to me, I guarantee you.'

I rose to leave. She'd given me nothing to go on. I signalled the stenographer to leave and went to the door myself. 'I'll be back,' I said, looking back at her father. 'I can get a court order if there's resistance. I suggest you accept this questioning without making it worse for everyone.'

Outside, Chauhan stopped me. The steno must have told him what happened. 'Keep your cool,' he said. 'That man contributed huge amounts to the PM's party in the last elections, and backed up the PM with staff and logistical help in the earlier ones. He's backing the party in the coming elections, too. And he doesn't give a damn about bribery scandals. He's relatively clean, as businessmen go. The PM might well listen to him.'

'It's the PM's granddaughter whose life is at stake,' I snapped. 'Will he listen to this man? Will he allow this guy to shut his daughter up?'

'Raja, this is the trouble with you Army types,' he said, 'you can't accept reality. We have every reason to think that these kidnappers are professionals. Out for money, huge amounts of it. The PM knows that as well as we do. He can raise any amount of money for the ransom. He'll get her back, regardless of whether you ask this girl any questions or not.'

I still didn't accept this, but just three-quarters of an hour later Chauhan was proved right. Minutes after I got back to my temporary office, Bhaskar called from Delhi. 'Menon,' he said, 'I heard you've been, er, over enthusiastic in your interrogation of the young lady whom the kidnappers sent back.'

'Look, do you want me to keep working on getting the other two back?' I said sharply. 'If you do, I'll keep at it my way, and if you don't, I'll get my men back in Delhi where they can do something useful.'

He backpedalled, but not much. 'Of course we need

you where you are,' he said, 'but you see, a little tact would be useful. There's a way of doing these things.' I began to see. Take no risks at all. Keep up the pretence of hunting for the kidnappers to keep the public from wondering. Do nothing substantial, and when the kidnappers get in touch, let them have any amount of money they want. The money wouldn't be a problem: party slush funds would take care of it, or enthusiastic supporters like Urmila's father. Before Urmila was released they were shaky, but now they are sure they would be able to buy the remaining hostages back.

'Right,' I said, 'tell me, Bhaskar, who'll handle the negotiations when they do get in touch?'

He hesitated. 'I don't know for sure. The PM has a list of five possibles. You're on it, Menon, don't worry. The others are from the CBI, the police . . . But it'll probably be a team, not a single person. A lone man might miss some angles.'

Do it by committee, I thought, and everyone's safe. The coming elections explained it all. The ruling party had been rocked by scandal, was facing questions in Parliament and from the media on where its funds had come from, and how much had come in. There were possibilities of senior ministers being linked, in incredibly shady ways, to leaders of communal and separatist groups. The party didn't stand much chance of getting a majority in Parliament in these elections. Naturally, then, the kidnap would help. It was already being put to use: Look at the sacrifices this man has made for his country, the posters said of the PM, with a photo of him, dark glasses covering grieving eyes.

'Okay,' I said, 'I'll probably want to talk to her again but it can wait until she's better. Tomorrow?'

'Of course,' came the reply, 'speak to her tomorrow. An hour or so, would that be all right? I'll have it fixed. Someone will get back to you about the time. And Menon—' his voice was no longer conciliatory, 'before you talk to her, clear it with me, okay?'

He cleared nothing. For the next two days, each time I spoke to him he said she was sedated, or indisposed, or whatever. I kept my men at peak, knowing that it couldn't go on much longer. These men were like a fine-tuned football team. You had to build up to a peak and there was a limit to how long you could maintain them there before they began to wind down. They couldn't stay at peak much longer.

The review meetings went on. Chauhan's men discovered several more false addresses among those given by guests at the Kabini lodge. The net had widened, putting a strain on the GDI's men. Now there were more than two thousand people working on the kidnap, excluding the Army. The helicopter hire firm produced records to show that their ace pilot had been on duty on an offshore rig for three weeks out of the four preceding the kidnap, and had spent the remaining week on leave in his village in UP, by the side of his ailing mother.

The search had become desultory. And there was nothing else. It was as if we had run into a stone wall.

Such things happened, but the ministerial committee in

Delhi got into the habit of ringing up every now and then for reports. General Kelkar handled them but some of the pressure inevitably came down on us.

Slowly the mood changed. I could see the stress in the eyes of the others at the reviews, except for Chauhan, who just looked tired. Nerves tightened perceptibly, and tempers shortened. Junior staff walked softly around their seniors. When the PM worried, the whole country worried with him. In the run up to the election the ruling party's strategy seemed to falter, their alliances with local parties seemed to weaken. They were unable to find anyone to fill the slot that the PM seemed to have left open. The search picked up momentum on the second day of silence from the kidnappers, but with much less hope.

And on the third day, with still no further news from the kidnappers, they began to talk of a rescue operation.

Bhaskar called me up after the meeting to say I could speak to Urmila whenever I needed to. I went immediately, in the company of Chauhan and a stenographer. Urmila's parents continued to hover about her, the mother as quiet as before, the father sullen and aggressive. 'Don't push her around like you did last time,' he said when I entered the room.

'We'll try not to,' I replied, then turned to her. 'How do you feel now?'

'Better,' she answered, though she looked worse, if anything. Her brown eyes were lifeless, her hands twitched, and her clothes had been selected hastily. No, it wasn't her clothes that were sloppy, it was her posture. The last time we met there'd been the joy of her release and of her reunion with her parents. That had worn off, leaving fatigue. But there was more to it than that. She was too scared. Had they threatened her? Threatened to rape or kill the others if she talked?

Her mother spoke for the first time, in halting English. 'She is not better. She is sick. She does not want a doctor. She does not eat. She cries without any reason.'

'You have to be patient,' I told her. 'Your daughter is full of guilt that she is free and her friends aren't. And I suspect she feels bad that she has some kind feelings for one of the kidnappers. She feels invaded . . . That she will never be safe again, because they can come in anywhere and take her again. The damage is there, and it's more than you can see. But it'll pass in due course.'

Urmila's eyes widened as I spoke. 'How did you know?' she asked. 'I've been trying to explain to them but they don't understand . . . And sometimes words seem sort of empty. As if talking won't make a difference . . . You know, don't you? You said something like this last time.'

'I've seen others in your position,' I explained. 'For many there's no return to a normal life. For others it's slow, agonizing, and in the end pointless because "normal" by then has no meaning to them. You're lucky. You were out there only a couple of days. You weren't threatened, though you must have been terrified when they broke into your room . . .' I changed my tone suddenly, to get her off guard: 'Or were you?'

'They didn't threaten me . . . They did threaten to do horrible things to the others if I spoke about them to the police.

'They said they would find out and they would get back to me, but I told you all the same . . .' She was crying again. 'I don't know what to do, it's so confusing.'

'What did they threaten?' I asked.

She shook her head. 'They said they'd . . . they'd gang-rape the others, and get the money just the same . . .'

'Is that the only time they threatened you?' She shook her head. 'Leave that be,' I said, 'they're putting on an act. There's little you've seen that can really help us pinpoint them. They threatened you with violence to soften the families of the other hostages so they'll pay up easily. It's just their way of negotiating.'

'But they sounded genuine!'

'Any effective threat must.'

'All right,' she said, her dullness lifting a little, 'I'll tell you what else they said. They said the others wouldn't ever get back unless I kept shut. That I'd never see them again if I stepped out of line.'

'Fine. Can we get back to the kidnap? After the helicopter?'

'There was a van. They bundled us into it. There were two of them in the back, and I don't know how many in front. We were all terrified . . . Those men wore masks, and they sounded horrible. You know, I kept thinking about those fairy tales with evil giants and stuff like that. Their voices . . . Ugh!'

'And where did the van take you?'

'They blindfolded us before taking us out of that van. I think I walked four or five steps, and then there was a single step to climb.' She shut her eyes, trying to remember. 'There was a single step, then a doorway. I tripped over something there . . . Then about a dozen steps. They gave me a chair to sit on. I heard other chairs being moved around so I thought the others also sat down. They took off our blindfolds then. They tied us up to the chairs . . . and then I couldn't take it any more and started struggling. The chair fell down . . .' She wept again, hiding her face in her father's shoulder, her free hand gripping her mother's.

A minute later she was back under control, 'I got hurt,' she continued, pointing at a bruise on her forehead. 'One of them sort of understood I couldn't take being tied up. He picked up the chair with me in it, and he told me not to worry. My face just goes red . . . He must have understood. He took off the gag they'd put on in the helicopter and asked what the matter was. I told him, and he said I wasn't to make a noise, or get up, and he would cut me free. He did it, too, with a knife. He said they were fixing a room for me and as soon as it was ready I would be alone there.'

'This man who cut you free, did you see his face?'

She shook her head. 'They all wore masks, the same black masks, with holes for eyes and mouths. He was big. Not very tall, but broad, with huge hands, very strong. He picked me up just like that. His voice . . . was soft, almost gentle. He was dressed in black, they all were. I remember his hands. They were very hairy. I saw him later on as well, without the mask, but he had a bandanna round the lower half of his face and a scarf over his head. I saw his ears. There were tufts of hair growing out of them . . . And his eyebrows were thick, too. I saw them even when he had his mask on. That's all I saw of him.'

'How did he move?' I asked.

'He moved lightly. Now that you ask, he was pretty athletic. Very strong, very smooth.'

'Did they blindfold you again?'

She shook her head, her hair bobbing. 'There was nothing to see. The windows were all closed, and so were the doors. The room was empty except for us, in three chairs against a wall, and there were two doors.'

'Did the other girls scream or anything?'

'No . . . I didn't hear them do anything. They looked wound up but I saw only their eyes. They were desperate . . . They must have seen the man in the car hit me.'

'Where was the room to which you were taken separately?'

'It was up a flight of stairs, I remember. One of them led me up to it. There was a sort of corridor with three or four doors leading off it, and the man opened one of them and pushed me into it.'

'What was the room like?'

'Small. It must have been twice as long as the bed . . . It was square.'

'Twelve by twelve?'

'Maybe. I can't be sure. There were two windows, both were sealed and boarded up. It was dark and the man switched on a light. There was a peephole in the door, about an inch big. There was a cover, too, on the other side. They could look in whenever they liked but I couldn't look out. There was a bathroom attached, an old-style bathroom, no tiles on the floor, you know how they are.'

'Were there ventilators?'

'Yes. One in the bedroom and another in the bathroom. I climbed onto the toilet seat to try to look out but it was too high. Then I managed to hold on to the cupboard door or something and stand on the cistern and the door just came off in my hands before I got a good look outside.' Brave girl.

'What did you see?' I asked.

'Nothing . . . I think I saw a broken minaret. Like mosques have at the corners. You know, with a crescent at the top. I saw two and one was broken.'

'Broken in what way?'

'The top seemed to have fallen off. The crescent.'

'And what did they have to say when they saw the broken door?'

She smiled suddenly, a sunny, mischievous smile. 'I told them I blacked out and grabbed the door and it just came off in my hands.'

I smiled back at this first sign of returning normality. 'Did they come in immediately when they heard the crash?'

Her face became serious. 'Yes. They just broke in . . . It was horrible. We had no privacy for anything. They could come in whenever they liked . . .' She shook her head again.

'Do you want a little break now?' I asked. 'I have more to ask you but you might want to think for a while.'

'Come back tomorrow,' her father said, 'she'll be better.'

'I doubt it,' I said. 'She'll take a few days to get over it. She's been through something harrowing, but her friends are still going through it and once she's past the relief of getting out, the guilt will catch up. The sooner we're through with it the fresher the details will be and the faster she'll be able to make her own peace afterwards.'

'And what do you know about these things?' he flared at me, the voice rougher, the eyes rimmed with red.

'I've seen this before. I've done some hostage-rescue work. I've dealt with some of the problems of hostages.'

A memory stirred in his head. 'They said you were in the Army, Menon. You were involved in that Madras thing, and the poison gas scare in Delhi, right?' The anger began to recede, but not much. 'I'm sure you know what you're doing, Menon, but you can see she needs to be left alone.'

'That's the last thing she needs right now,' I said. 'Don't leave her alone for some time.'

The anger receded some more. 'I won't. And what are you planning to do? Get the girls back?'

'Figuring out how to get them back safe,' I replied, 'how to handle the exchange—ransom for hostages, and so on. And if possible how to get the kids out.'

'But what will my daughter be able to tell you?'

'She's already told me something useful. Old-style house, at least two floors, compound large enough to accommodate a van, a driveway. We know the general locality.

Now it's a matter of elimination. There's more. The man who she said was gentle, he's got some experience at this. He knows how to soothe and sting. The hostages tend to believe him. You might have noticed, she has to make an effort to tell us anything that might get him caught.'

The anger returned, mixed with incredulity, as he rasped, 'Are you trying to tell me my daughter doesn't want her kidnapper caught? You must be nuts!'

'Perhaps not consciously, but in the back of her mind, yes. Look at it from her point of view. When things were at their worst he intervened and helped. There's a name for this kind of thing—the Stockholm Syndrome. It takes a long time to take hold properly, but the seeds have been sown . . . Her claustrophobia helped things along.'

I broke off when I saw her eyes fixed unblinkingly at me.

'How did you know?' she asked in a whisper. 'How did you find out?'

'It happens all the time,' I explained. 'It's perfectly natural. Don't feel guilty about it, just tell us everything.'

Instead of saying anything she sobbed loudly, eyes wide in a terrified face. 'I feel so bad . . . They've got Priya and Mallika and god knows what'll happen to them,' she managed eventually. 'I don't know what to do about it . . . I feel so helpless . . . It's like being tied down again.'

There was visible distress now in her parents' faces too. For a few moments they both sat in mute grief at the loss of her innocence. Feeling it had gone on long enough, I brought them back to earth. 'Tell me more about the room you were in. The furnishings. There must have been a bed.'

'It was just a room with a bed . . . Okay, a wooden bed, flat. No table. There was a white sheet, a single pillow, a blanket . . . a ceiling fan. The switches were next to the door. Just a room.'

'What colour walls?'

'Off-white. The doors were wooden. Solid doors.'

'The ceiling?'

'Yes, the ceiling was funny, sloping to one side. It was made of planks. Now that you ask, yes, it was an old house. It must have been built at least thirty or forty years ago.'

'Yes. Tiled roof and so on . . . The questions help, don't they?' She smiled and nodded and I continued, 'Did you smell anything while you were there? Cooking smells, animal smells, factory smells, farm smells, anything?'

'The toilet stank.' She wrinkled her nose and shook her head. 'No, nothing like that . . . Yes, I got a whiff of the kitchen once. I don't remember exactly what. And . . . and the hairy man—he used some after-shave. I think it was one of those foreign ones . . . And I forgot to tell you, the flush handle was gone. There was a bucket and a tap. There was just that empty tank there, with the lid stuck on. I couldn't take it off . . .'

'That's because bits of the flush mechanism can become weapons. There's a brass rod inside, with a float valve. You could get that off, sharpen the end, and stick it between someone's ribs.'

Her eyes widened. 'I didn't think of that.'

'You would have, given enough time. What did you eat?'

'They brought us food. I don't know how it was with

the others . . . I suppose it was the same. The food came in paper plates, and we had to eat with our fingers. They gave us water to drink. There was a plastic bottle of it in the room, and a glass, the disposable kind.'

'What kind of food?'

She made a face. 'Bread and jam and cheese and stuff like that. No cooked food. As if they didn't want to waste time cooking. Not that I was hungry, anyway. I . . . I ate very little.'

'And the rest of the time? What did you do?'

'I just lay around, half asleep. That's not usually what I do . . . But in there I just lay around and it was comfortable. Every now and then there was the prayer call from a mosque, that was it. The room got very hot but they didn't give us towels or anything. I didn't change my clothes once.'

'And how about when they released you? Do you remember?'

'Not very well . . . They gave me coffee and I was sleepy. They gave me that letter. They took me to another room with a peephole. When I looked through it I saw Priya and Mallika, both asleep . . . It was a bigger room than mine. I wish they hadn't left me alone. After that they took me out to the van. I went to sleep in the back, and the next thing I knew someone was shaking me, telling me to get out. They gave me some money, a hundred rupees, and told me the way to the nearest police station . . . And I made my way there . . . in the dark . . . I was terrified.'

'Did you see anyone on the way?'

'Yes. I saw a milkman, and asked him the time. He just looked at me like I was crazy and kept going. I saw someone else, he looked like a labourer going to work, and I asked him the way to the police station and he just looked away. Then I understood . . . I was still in my nightdress . . . They would have been surprised to see a girl dressed like that roaming around at that time of the day.'

'Anyone else?'

'Yes, a couple of others. I didn't try to speak to them. Then I saw an autorickshaw and asked him to take me to the police station . . . He did and he took the whole hundred rupees. He said he didn't have time to wait and I wasn't thinking straight . . . And when I got into the police station the policeman didn't believe me . . .' She was crying again, the sobs shaking her body. Soon she straightened up and wiped her eyes angrily.

Good, I thought, she's mad at them now. 'How many men did you see during the time you were there?'

'I don't know. There were never more than three of them together at any time. Then there was the fellow with the hairy ears. At least four, maybe one or two more. Only the hairy one spoke to us. The others were silent. They seemed to have rehearsed . . . They communicated with signals, and they all knew exactly what to do.' Pros. Or well-trained fanatics. And this wasn't the first time they were working together.

'Why didn't you tell us all this earlier?' her father asked in some bewilderment. 'You knew we wouldn't tell anyone if you didn't want us to!' He saw now the distance between him and his daughter, and there was the beginning of panic and distrust in him as he tried to close it up.

'I tried,' she answered, without looking at him, 'I didn't know . . . I tried to explain but you didn't understand.'

'Don't worry about it,' I said, 'you're back, your friends will probably be back soon, and you'll feel better. And the kidnappers will screw all the money they can out of the families . . . Look at it this way. That nice guy with the hair must be one of the best-paid actors in the country. He's no different from the rest. He puts on an act for a few hours a day for a few weeks and gets paid more than Amitabh Bachchan ever got.'

She gave me a watery grin that fitted well with the grey outside. It was a beginning, anyway. 'To get back to the kidnappers, did they wear a uniform?'

'Not really. All wore dark clothes with those masks I told you about. They wore black shoes, and gloves some of the time. They didn't wear their masks all the time but when they didn't, their faces were always covered. Handkerchiefs or scarves. And all of them had beards.'

'All of them?'

'All of them that I saw.' Disguise, perhaps, or an attempt to make them all look the same, to avoid her getting any idea how many men there were. 'And they all seemed ruffianly. Except Hairy Ears.'

'More actors, perhaps. Leading you to false conclusions.'

She looked away. 'There's deceit . . . in everything,' she said quietly, 'everywhere. We're full of it.'

She had grown up fast these last few days. Her father

looked at her with deepening disquiet, her mother with open-mouthed astonishment.

'Yes,' I replied, 'we are. But you've got to learn to live with it, and come to terms with the deceit in yourself, first.'

She shook her head at me. All that was yet to be thought of, and there were more pressing concerns in her mind. 'Do you think . . . Do you think they'll have kept Priya and Mallika drugged like they kept me?'

'In all probability, yes,' I replied. 'Drugging hostages makes their lives easier. They're less liable to scream or struggle or try to escape. If the police turn up they can be hidden. They'll prefer sedatives to tranquillizers. A sleepy hostage is a good hostage.'

'Then . . . those threats, what the man said about . . . about rape and so on . . . That wasn't true, was it?'

She was beginning to understand. Good girl. Now she'd be able to shed a fraction of that heavy load of guilt. 'Yes,' I said, and smiled at her.

Instead of smiling back she burst into tears. Of relief, apparently, for in a few moments she straightened up and sniffed and blew her nose. 'I thought I'd never be all right again,' she said, 'but I will, won't I?'

For a seventeen-year-old that was par for the course. 'Sure you will,' I said, 'you're on your way already.'

'I want to talk to you alone,' she said suddenly.

'About what?' her father asked gratingly, anger giving his voice an extra edge, 'what can you tell this man that you can't tell your own parents?'

The mother answered, taking the rest of us off balance. 'Let her do what she wants. Mr Menon will not harm her. You can see that he understands her better than us.'

He turned on her and raged at her for a full, fluent minute in a language I didn't understand at all, perhaps Telugu. The lady, instead of crumpling under the barrage as I'd thought she would, gave back as good as she got. They sat back after that, glaring at each other in a distinctly hostile silence, and I began to see what Urmila meant by deceit everywhere. She must have seen it at home, been a pawn in husband–wife squabbles. She must have seen her mother put down in a hundred different ways by her successful husband. Not something she'd want to talk about in their presence. 'If you'd give me a minute to speak,' I began, and they looked set to transfer their anger at me, but said nothing. 'Listen, Urmila,' I said, 'I'm on an Army base, with my hands full, hoping to get the others back. There's nothing else on my mind. If what you want to tell me has anything to do with that I'd be glad to hear you out. Otherwise it'll have to be some other time, when all this is over.'

'Okay,' she said. 'Promise?'

'Promise,' I smiled, 'I'll even invite you to spend a few days with my wife. You see, she and my stepson were held hostage for a while year before last. In a railway coach, you might have heard about it.'

'Oh, yes!' she said. 'I remember. Of course I remember. But I didn't connect you with that . . . I'd expected someone more . . .' she broke off in confusion, 'someone different.'

'Someone a great deal more impressive?' I grinned. 'So do the opposition, and when they get me instead it takes them aback. Gives me an edge.'

It was time to go. I couldn't sit here listening to her pour out her heart. But where would she go if I turned away? On impulse, I offered her my Delhi telephone number, and told her Sandhya's name. 'She'll listen to you with understanding,' I said. 'Try her if you like. And if you can visit her she'll be glad to see you.' She took the contact gratefully, with her parents watching in mounting resentment. I stopped at the door. 'One last thing. You've made some progress today, but chances are you'll feel worse again. You'll go up and down and up again and down again. Don't worry about those swings.'

chapter five

Back in the temporary office at the Para base the pressure was beginning to show. I had many routine things to do, mostly about keeping the men up, but it was getting tougher. They were bored, ill-equipped, on strange territory, and the edge was coming off their alertness. Without that work to do I wouldn't have been able to take the pressure. Work was a great cure for many ills. Chauhan was equally busy, monitoring the teams, now several hundreds of people, searching for contact with the kidnappers. He'd got a good machine set up now, working smoothly despite the constant sniping from local police chiefs.

The PM was increasingly wound up these days, I'd heard, needing sedatives to get through the nights and tranquillizers through the day. His wife, on tranquillizers even before the kidnap, was now bedridden. The election campaign was losing steam before it even began. But photos of the young hostage were everywhere, reminders of what the man had lost.

I called Chauhan to give him a summary of my talk with the girl. He'd get the details anyway but typing up the transcripts would take time and I had a couple of clear clues, about the mosque with the broken minaret and the sounds of the muezzin's call. He digested the news in quiet, then thanked me. 'What news from Delhi?' I asked.

'Nothing. The usual election stuff.'

'How's it going?'

'Good for the government. They're using it to get votes. This time there are no real issues other than corruption. If they can get a few hundred thousand votes on the strength of the kidnap, so much the better for them.'

'What about the scandals?' I asked. 'The slush funds?'

He chuckled. 'Who cares about them? The special court asks for reports, and gets them, but how long do they stay in the public's mind? And at times like this anyone would sympathize with the PM. Even you did.'

'Yes,' I agreed, 'but that sympathy disappeared the moment you explained things to me, and turned into something else when I saw the posters. I'm not a political animal but I'm beginning to pick up the nuances.'

'Listen to your own lectures sometimes,' he said, 'I heard you go on about how the kidnappers are play-acting.'

'What do you mean?' I asked.

'There's no difference between the kidnappers and the government. They're both acting. Posturing. The money doesn't count. The ransom doesn't count. If they ask for fifty terrorists to be released, the fifty terrorists will be released, even if they're all psychopaths and confirmed murderers.'

'Then where do I come in?'

'Ah!' he said. 'First, they can't appear to give up just like that. Second, when the kidnappers don't get in touch for so long, the men at the top get queasy. It's a flip-flop they're doing up there, you know. Now they're beginning to doubt if they'll get the girls back so easily, so they want you around and they're nice to you. The moment it's clear there'll be no need for a rescue operation they'll send you back, just you watch. And if you do run a rescue and it fails, my lad, you're finished. You've no idea how vindictive these guys can be.'

I hung up, a great deal more thoughtful than I'd been before calling Chauhan. His deeply ingrained cynicism was catching. And I could see he was right. Suddenly I was sure that I wouldn't ever reach the top of the ladder. The infighting, though necessary, was too much. I didn't want any more money than I had, or power, or anything . . . Maybe Sandhya was right, after all. Maybe this whole thing wasn't worth it.

Evening brought evidence that Chauhan had been right. After the meeting Bhaskar called to find out what progress I'd made. I could almost see him purse his lips in disapproval when I told him what I'd got out of Urmila, and that we'd lost two days because he hadn't allowed me to see her earlier. 'Look,' he said, beginning to get aggressive, 'there's pressure on all of us. Yes, we changed our minds, that's why you lost two days. You don't know what it is like out here.'

'I don't,' I said, 'and I don't want to. Ever.'

He must have caught the tiny note of contempt because

he froze immediately. 'Don't talk to me like that, Menon.'

'Don't give me that garbage,' I said. 'Remember, the higher up a tree a monkey goes the better you see his bottom.'

He blew up, in a civilized kind of way. 'Colonel,' he said, his voice edged with ice, 'I suggest you keep to the subject at hand. I did arrange for you to meet her today, after all.'

'And I've passed the results on to the appropriate quarters,' I told him. 'Call them if you're antsy about what I found out. And remember that I take my orders from General Kelkar. Don't jerk me around, okay?'

There was silence. Then, 'Given the situation I'll ignore what you just said, Menon. But do it again and you're in trouble. I can see why you're not very popular.'

I hung up. It was no use talking to the man. And I wasn't here to win popularity contests . . . But his life, and the PM's, were perpetual popularity contests. That was what kept governments alive, winning those contests. No wonder he had a different view of life.

One more night without progress and I was beginning to think of swapping my force here for another company when at the morning meeting relief arrived, in the form of another note from the kidnappers. It came in the mail, posted from Mysore, which meant we'd got the general area right—we were within a hundred kilometres of it, for whatever good that did us—and it was addressed, like its predecessor, to the PM. Identification was easy: the envelope contained, besides a brief note, the second half of the hundred-rupee note they'd sent us with the first.

Also included in the letter was half a ten-rupee note, to verify the source of their next letter. 'Mr Prime Minister,' the note said peremptorily, 'Please find enclosed the rest of the currency note we had sent you with Urmila Shetty. Also enclosed is part of another currency note. Following are our requirements for the release of the two remaining hostages, Priya Reddy and Mallika Deshpande: first, the sum of ten million dollars is to be deposited in our account in the Liechtenstein Bank. The account number is at the end of this letter. Second, you are to arrange for the delivery of Rs 2,00,00,000 in hundred-rupee notes—used notes, not in serial order—to a spot to be designated later. Third, gold worth an equal amount is to be readied for delivery along with the rupees. Finally, to dampen the enthusiasm with which your law-enforcement agencies will search for us after we depart, we want the Mehta diaries, all four volumes, to be delivered along with the money and the gold.

'In return for this you will get back your granddaughter, Priya, and her friend, Ms Deshpande. Also Mr Jagdish Mishra, son of the Chief Justice of the Supreme Court.

'Please acknowledge receipt of this letter through an advertisement in the classified advertisements of the *Deccan Herald*. In case of any hitch in arranging for these resources, please advise us through an advertisement in the same place and we will get in touch with you again.'

There was no signature, no marks: in that it was identical to the first note we'd got. The letter had been faxed to

Chauhan and to the local police under the TOP SECRET label, because the reference to the Mehta diaries was embarrassing. But it soon became clear that the confidentiality was useless. Whoever had sent the letter to us had also sent copies to the Bangalore offices of all the major dailies. They had, of course, left out the currency notes for identification, but they had instead included Polaroid photographs of the remaining hostages, all three of them holding copies of a daily newspaper dated two days after the kidnap.

The newspapers had a field day with the letters. The telephones at police headquarters were besieged with callers from the media, and at a hastily convened press conference at noon the DIG said that the kidnappers had at last announced their terms for the release of the hostages. When angry pressmen asked what the government intended to do about it, the DIG said that the matter was in the hands of the Cabinet Committee. All papers printed the text of the letter, and a few the photographs. Most also speculated that the kidnap was arranged by some of the guiltier parties named in the diaries, recipients of huge amounts of elbow grease for facilitating industrial licences and permits and for permitting public issues without enough supervision. Others, unwilling to sling mud, said it was a definite threat to the PM because it effectively crippled his election campaign and would clearly make a large dent in party funds; the PM would certainly not pay the ransom out of his own pocket—though it was possible he could afford it. A few saw 'a foreign hand' behind the kidnapping, perhaps Pakistani or American, especially in the light of the high-tech approach of the kidnappers.

All of it was pie-in-the-sky. The money at this stage was the least of the PM's worries. He could well persuade the Cabinet to sanction the money out of government funds. The real problem was the diaries. They were now in the CBFs custody, not yet admitted as evidence to the special court, run by a Justice of the Supreme Court, that had been set up to try the case. If the diaries were handed over to the kidnappers the country would go through a constitutional crisis; kidnapping would become an easy way to destroy evidence. Coming as it did so soon after the Vora Commission's report, which spoke of shady dealings among politicians and bureaucrats and criminals, it would destroy political careers, blow the country apart. But there, too, the PM seemed relatively safe: he had not been directly implicated by the diaries, while political leaders of every persuasion, including his own, had. There was the possibility, therefore, that the PM would be back, and with a fair bit of the opposition both in his own party and in Parliament taken out. With the emotional content of the kidnap, he could make a powerful campaign of it. If he were politician enough.

The arrival of the second letter sparked off a flurry of activity. The mood changed from uncertainty to even greater uncertainty. No one dared predict whether the diaries would be handed over. Towards evening, the Chief Justice of the Supreme Court issued a dignified and sorrowing statement to the effect that he would not involve himself in the decision of whether or not to hand over the diaries because of a possible conflict of interest. He also announced his retirement with immediate effect. The ruling party rallied around with a statement calling for donations to raise the ransom money. The Cabinet Committee, who were to decide whether they would apply to the Supreme Court to order the diaries released to the kidnappers, stayed purposefully silent.

After the evening's review meeting Chauhan called. 'The PM wants you to go for these guys,' he said. 'I've got orders saying we should go all out to find them, and you should now look at building up for a raid to get the hostages out. You have a time frame: three days, or whatever's in the note.'

'Do you know what's in the diaries?' I asked.

'Roughly yes. They're records of payments to politicians and bureaucrats. This guy did a smart thing. He put down the names of the bagmen and the people they represented. So if the politicians named in the diaries try to wriggle out saying they were elsewhere at the time, we can pick up the bagmen. Mehta's was a gigantic scam, he used false share certificates to raise capital, bribed people to ignore the fact that the certificates had been forged, paid off politicians left and right, and used his money to start up massive industrial projects, which went public. From these projects he could siphon off as much as he wanted. You'll not believe the kind of money the man talked about.'

'Like how much?' I asked.

'Like we did some translation and found that there's no mention of a payment under a crore of rupees. Most are tens of crores, and a few hundreds of crores. One, I think, was eight hundred crores. Each time the man came close to being caught, he sprayed his money around . . . Someone must have got fed up with him.'

'You think he was killed?'

'There are rumours . . . I wasn't involved in the case but I get to know. They say someone paid to have Mehta killed. Someone whom the diaries implicated fair and square. That Mehta was behind bars was no problem at all.'

'Are the diaries much use with Mehta dead? He can't testify to the contents.'

'They're explosive. They're explicit, unlike the others. You see, the man kept four books, and maintained them rigorously. He kept them with him wherever he went. No computer records, no nothing. Just four volumes of diaries.'

'How did the CBI get those diaries, then? He died before you got them, didn't he?'

'The killer ransacked Mehta's house and office but didn't get them. We got them out of his in-laws' place. Look, I have other stuff to do. Catch up later.'

The phone rang as soon as I put it down. 'Menon,' I said, picking it up.

'Raja, this is Kelkar,' said the General at the other end. 'They stopped waffling once they heard about the diaries. They want you to go in and get the hostages out. You're expected in Delhi tonight. With me.'

I raced to the airport to find a transport waiting. This one was a little more comfortable than the bare Ilyushins and Antonovs I'd got used to—courtesy General Kelkar—

and the jet made good time to Delhi, getting there a little after ten. By eleven we were at the PM's residence, waiting in an anteroom for Bhaskar to brief us before we met the Committee.

Bhaskar's briefing was short. The objective had changed, he told us pompously, and we were to suggest an approach to any planning that had to be done. Only constructive criticism would be acceptable. Kelkar stood it as long as he could, then told Bhaskar in poetic but unprintable language to talk sense or shut up. He shut up.

The Cabinet Committee met in the large conference room at the PM's residence. A communications cell was set up whenever it met, and when we were called in there were people streaming out, carrying files under their arms and looking worried or important. Inside, the members of the Committee sat at a polished teakwood table at least thirty feet long. The Chief was there, sweating in his full-dress uniform, with the two other service chiefs.

The Committee consisted of the PM himself—still in dark glasses—who was the chairman; the home minister, Siddharth Varshneya; the defence minister, Pravin Kumar; the telecommunications minister, Keval Ram; the law minister, Shankar Pai; and their respective junior ministers. The defence minister, plump, jovial, and almost totally ignorant of defence issues, sat next to the PM. Lower down sat the home minister, lean, articulate, once a highly successful lawyer and reportedly a terrific backroom manipulator. The telecom minister, here because of his large vote bank rather than any functional skill, sat hunched beyond the home minister, looking as if he had swallowed a rat. The law minister, also a lawyer but nowhere near as successful as the home minister, sat next. Right next to him was the minister of state for defence, Subhash Varma, a bull-necked, powerful man, a former airline pilot with a taste for the better things of life. The surprise member of the Committee was old man Mankekar. He held no official post, of course, but had been called in, as a former lawyer, to consult.

Besides the politicians were the bureaucrats, Secretaries of all the ministries, and a couple of Joint Secretaries who would for the time being be devoted to supporting the Committee, leaving their routine work in other hands. Some of them I knew, but most were strangers; the Telecom Secretary, for instance, a thin, constipated-looking man who was supposed to have his minister in his pocket, was a stranger.

'We have come to a decision, all of us together,' said the PM when we were in and seated at the foot of the table, 'that the kidnappers cannot be allowed to get away with this. We cannot allow them to interfere with the judicial process.' The Chief and some of the secretaries nodded like good schoolboys, while the ex-pilot glowered. 'Since these people have given us no way to negotiate with them quickly, we will have to locate and rescue the hostages. I am told that the search for them has so far been unsuccessful; we will have to make our search more effective.'

General Kelkar grimaced, then asked, 'Sir, how long do we have to find them?'

The PM fiddled with a pen before answering. 'I have just met people from the CBI, RAW and the police. They say that they will have a better idea of the location of the hostages by tomorrow, thanks to the information we got from the released hostage. Perhaps they will confirm the location by early the day after tomorrow. In the meanwhile I have called on the Americans for help . . . . They have satellites capable of identifying individual people in any area. We have the satellites but not the cameras. They have offered to divert one of their satellites over the Mysore area and photograph it thoroughly. When I spoke to their State Department some hours ago they said, if it can be seen from above we'll see it. If the kidnappers look up while the satellite is overflying them we'll be able to count their eyelashes on the picture.'

The man's political persona seemed dominant then, the enfeebled grandfather receding easily into the background under the threat to his own position. He took off his glasses and I noticed that while his eyes were red-rimmed he seemed under control. For a moment he looked directly at me. Those black eyes lost their dullness and seemed almost to burn through me, and then he smiled grimly. 'There are times, Colonel,' he said as if reading my thoughts, 'when one has to put away considerations of friends and family. Can you imagine the damage that would inevitably occur if those diaries fell into the wrong hands?'

I could well imagine it. Given a choice between a cover-up and the damage, I found myself choosing the cover-up without even thinking about it. 'Yes, sir,' I replied.

'I'm glad you understand,' he said, continuing to look squarely at me. 'Your superiors—General Kelkar here in particular—have said many good things about your contributions to our anti-terrorist forces. Colonel, you will personally plan and lead the mission. You will ask your Chief, who is also here, for whatever resources you might need. If you need assistance from any of the other services—armed or intelligence—you can speak to Bhaskar here, he will arrange it.'

He paused and was silent for a moment, looking down at his dark glasses on the table. Then, without looking up, he said, 'And you *will* get those hostages back, Colonel.'

'If we can, we will,' Kelkar replied on my behalf. 'We can't guarantee success, sir. After we know where they are, Menon will be able to give you a clearer picture, but still no guarantee.'

The PM gave me a hard look, and the junior minister for defence glowered directly at me. Then the PM turned to the Chief. 'General,' he said, 'you will ensure that General Kelkar and his people get whatever they need from the Army. Kelkar will coordinate that and you will supervise it, ensuring that nothing is held up for want of permissions. All intelligence from foreign agencies and Interpol—yes, we have asked for Interpol's help as well, to identify the one kidnapper about whom we seem to have got some physical details—all intelligence will be made available to you by the CBI. You will pass it on to Kelkar and his group. And you will assemble a group of qualified Army officers here to critique Kelkar's and Menon's plan when it is ready.'

I held up a hand, feeling like a schoolboy in class. 'If I may interrupt . . .' I began. The PM looked at me with the beginnings of anger smouldering in his eyes, then nodded to indicate I was to continue. 'Two points. One, there might not be time for a critique. Two, having a review by a group here will loosen security. Both would hamper us considerably. If you're setting up a group like that I'm afraid you must excuse me . . .' My voice trailed off under the concentrated glares of all the heavyweights in the room.

Support, not surprisingly, came from Kelkar, who cleared his throat nervously. When the PM turned to look at him, he said evenly, 'Sir, I have to agree with Menon.'

'Why?' glared the PM. 'You elite don't want to mix with the common soldiery, is it, General? Or do you think your people are above criticism?'

Kelkar cleared his throat again to cover his confusion but didn't flinch. 'Sir, in the first place it'll slow things down. Second, this is not the kind of objective a normal infantryman thinks about; he's trained to go in and get rid of the enemy and take his place. Third, the fewer the people who know about this plan the better—and safer. There are enormous inducements to give it away. Finally, getting enough qualified people together will itself be difficult and time-consuming. I believe most such are already with us. I have to agree completely with Menon.'

'All right,' said the PM, 'no reviews here. You have permission. I haven't the time to arrange for alternatives.' He turned to the COAS. 'Do your best, and keep me personally informed every twelve hours, at nine. As well as this Committee, of course.' The meeting was over. Kelkar and I were the closest to the door and the first out of it into the corridor beyond. As we emerged into the corridor the COAS, who had maintained a carefully impassive demeanour throughout the meeting, signalled Kelkar to wait for him.

In the anteroom where the Chief took us, I saw from a glance at his purpling face that Kelkar would never make Lieutenant General, not while this man was around. 'How could you drop me in the shit like that,' he ground out in a menacing whisper, 'after what I told the PM about you chaps?'

The COAS was one of the PM's blue-eyed boys, a former Signals man with a solid technological background. But he'd never been in combat except as commander of a Signals unit in the eastern sector in the 1971 war. And now he was running a standing army of a million plus.

'Sir,' said Kelkar, unaffected, 'I'd be happy to hand over charge the moment you choose to, to anyone else who can give you guarantees. After, during, or before this operation. I'm not used to evaluating without the benefit of basic information.'

The COAS's face resumed its normal ruddy hue. This man liked the good life and it showed in his complexion, in his jowls and in his softness. He had two years of his three-year term left, and wanted after that a gubernatorial appointment in a peaceful state. If he lost the hostages he could kiss that governorship goodbye. No wonder he was angry, I thought. But now he collected himself, perhaps with the recollection that if at all anyone could get the hostages out it was Kelkar and us. 'All right,' he said, 'what's past is over and done with. You people come up with your plan and position and equip your teams properly and let me know if you run into any problems. I'll have the Quartermaster General supply you. But keep me informed on logistical problems as early as possible.'

He turned then, and walked away, absurdly self-important. Kelkar shook his head and sighed. 'You go back to Bangalore, Raja,' he said, 'I'll stay here to handle the Chief and that man Bhaskar. You keep away from them. I suggest you liaise through me. You're not political enough to handle them.'

'Yessir,' I said. 'But with due respect, you're no better at it than I am.'

I could almost imagine the old man grinning at this. 'Relax, Raja,' he said, 'I've come as high as I ever will. I won't get that second star on my shoulder flaps, not with this Chief in place. There are half a dozen companies waiting to hire my services as a consultant the moment I retire. And I have a farm waiting for me back in Ratnagiri. What the hell do I stand to lose? And look, go back to that wife of yours for a minute.'

'I will, thanks,' I said. 'But she's learnt to get along without me.'

'Advice from an old soldier. These little visits make up for a lot of absences. Go.'

'Advice accepted. I will . . . I'll call you from Bangalore tomorrow morning.'

Sandhya was asleep when I opened the door with the latchkey, curled up in bed with Kiran. I switched on the bedside lamp, lay down beside her, put a hand on her shoulder and pulled her gently towards me. She turned over in her sleep, then woke up with a little gasp. 'Raja, you bum, you scared me!' she whispered when she got her breath back. 'You had a lousy day. It shows.'

'Yes,' I said, 'those meetings. The PM and the Chief. Also various heavyweights. I rubbed a lot of them the wrong way, so my career's up the creek. I'm glad I have a rich wife to support me in my declining years.'

'Trust you to put your foot in it.' Under the banter I could sense her wound up state. 'If you do it often enough maybe I'll walk out on you as well.'

'Did Urmila Shetty call?' I asked, to get her to ease up.

'Yes . . . I didn't know what to say to her. She cried a little and promised to call again. What do you want me to tell her?'

'Nothing. Just listen. Get her not to whip herself.'

'And shall I tell her you're away playing hero, trying to get those others out? Doing it for people you despise?'

'What was that again?' I asked uncomprehending.

'You're a dinosaur, Raja, that's what. You're openly contemptuous of the people whose orders you take. The general populace, who put those leaders there, couldn't care less about what you do except that it gives them an evening's entertainment. And yet there are fools like you who risk their lives to serve a country like this.'

'Hey, take it easy,' I said, 'you're worked up about this.'

She was crying, something I hadn't seen for a long time, mainly because she hated to seem vulnerable even in my presence. 'Raja,' she sniffed when the tears began to subside, 'I wouldn't feel so bad if you were putting your life on the line for something you thought worthwhile. I wouldn't question it. But when you do it for a bunch of thieves, it hurts. They're taking you for a ride and you're going along unquestioningly, like a lamb to the slaughter.' She blew her nose into my kerchief. 'And you don't even see it!'

'Yes, I do,' I protested. 'I don't like it, but that's my job. Let's just leave it at that, okay?'

She got out of bed abruptly and went to the bathroom. I lay back and edged closer to Kiran, who had slept through all this. Strange how kids are.

When she emerged from the bathroom some minutes later, her face bore the traces of a crying fit but she was back under control. 'I'm sorry about this,' she said, sitting beside me, 'letting you have it so suddenly when you've come for a few minutes. But the basic point is this, Raja, that you're a moral person and you're doing a whole lot of very hard things for a bunch of completely amoral people. Is it worth it?'

'It's a good thought,' I said, 'but it's come up at the wrong time.'

'I'd rather you were a mercenary,' she said. 'You soldier for someone and you take your money and that's the end of it.'

'That's a rather romantic picture you've got of a mercenary,' I said, almost mocking her, and though I regretted it immediately, I couldn't change the tone of my voice. 'Mostly they're in it because soldiering is all they can or care to do. And they do it well, selling their skills to the highest bidder, whoever that may be. They'll kill anybody and any number.'

She shook her head. 'I don't know what to say,' she said, 'I don't know how to explain. But it's because of people like you who are willing to do their dirty work for them that the clowns in power stay where they are.'

'You've read too much Ayn Rand,' I said. I was mocking her again, but I was too far gone to make amends. 'In any case, it's no use telling me anything now because I'm in the middle of something and I'm not going to walk out of it halfway through for anyone. But when this is over I'll take a break and we can talk. Maybe we'll settle something that you and I can live with. All right?'

I stayed another half-hour but the distance that had come up between us refused to close. I felt strangely out of place in that house, which seemed cheerful and bright even in the dark of the night. The cheer refused to touch me. Sandhya came to the door to see me off when it was time to leave and at the door she held my hand for a long time and said, 'Remember to come back, okay?' I bowed and grinned at her, but the good humour was false and we both knew it. I turned and ran to the jeep waiting below to take me to the airfield. I felt her eyes on my back but didn't turn to look at her as the jeep rolled down the driveway towards the gate.

chapter six

Kelkar stayed back in Delhi to liaise and steer us past the shoals of the bureaucracy in the defence ministry. When I got to Bangalore I called the men and told them that we had permission to go in, that we'd know in twenty-four hours where the hostages were, and that this would be the most difficult job we'd faced so far because we knew nothing about the terrain. They straightened up and went back to their exercises with renewed vigour, glad to know they were required, and I went back to the dreary rounds of meetings after the morning's run along the streets of the city.

Over the next twelve hours I got supplies of chutes and armaments that we would need for precision jumping if we were to go in from above, and a detachment of eighteen men from the IMSF—Marine commandos, trained by American SEALs—just in case we needed to go under water, and another team of frogmen to investigate the Kabini river to check if the kidnappers had indeed left any clues behind.

We also got enough space at the base to put the men through a rigorous routine for the remaining days. Reporters hung around the gates of the base, but the guard had been doubled and they didn't venture past. The meetings were more urgent now, with more specific reports of progress. Chauhan or one of his men called every hour on the hour, and the radius of the search shrank visibly, but it also became grindingly slow. 'We have to do it subtly lest the opposition get wind of the search,' Chauhan explained, 'but we also have to move fast, which means we use lots of light-footed men . . . And I have very few of those left.'

'What about the satellite photographs the Yanks promised us?' I asked.

'They're not much use. I had a look at some but they're not very clear. It's not much use unless you have the ground equipment they have over there.'

'And the stuff the girl told us?'

'That's the most useful stuff so far. I've checked out mosques with a cracked minaret . . . There are a few there. That's our best lead so far.'

'What are they looking for?'

'A largish house, at least two storeys, within sight of a mosque with a broken minaret.'

'Can't you just get a list of mosques? There must be some kind of an organization that lists them.'

'Asking for a list like that will surely alert those guys. Besides, there are enough private mosques. All these guys who come back with some savings from the Middle East decide to pool their money for a mosque. We have to operate a little more skilfully than that. But take it easy. It's only hours away now.'

'But still, they must be easy to trace.'

'There's nothing difficult about it,' he said, beginning to show traces of irritation. 'It's the volume of it that's slowing us down. It's overwhelming. And there just isn't time. Now get off my case, please.'

He was right. There wasn't time. The broadcasts to the kidnappers had begun the day we arrived, offering them safe telephone numbers to call, but had had no effect. The morning's *Deccan Herald*—and indeed all newspapers—carried an advertisement in the classified columns to the effect that the money was ready but that judicial permission was required for the diaries to be taken out of CBI custody, which would take a few days extra. Perhaps three. This was only partly true. Judicial permission could be issued in hours, not days. But this was the sole red herring we could produce that had any likelihood of convincing the kidnappers.

I'd said at the morning meeting that the ads were overdone, that they sent a clear message of panic in government ranks, but everyone else just ignored me so I shut up. Chauhan caught me afterwards and advised me gruffly to keep such thoughts to myself, that several others had said as much and been told to shut up by none less than the PM himself. 'It'll get them alert,' I protested, 'it'll tell them we're panicking and they know that panic will almost certainly drive us to attack. You might not care but I do because I'm the guy most likely to be shot first when we go in, and I would greatly like to keep my skin intact. I hate to think of what my wife will do to me if I don't.'

He laughed at this, and said that if I wanted I was welcome to try and persuade them to be a little more restrained. I called General Kelkar. 'I know,' he said. 'They wanted to advertise in papers all over the country, and on all the TV channels, government and private. They'd even got companies to pay for the ads on prime time, but I held them back. You know policy around here: never say in one word what you can say in four thousand. I managed to keep it down to about five hundred instead, but I can't go further without running a serious risk of getting kicked out.'

When I told him what I'd told Chauhan, he said he'd said exactly the same to Bhaskar. 'Why not the PM himself?' I asked. 'Nothing doing,' he said, 'I tried but couldn't get through. He's too busy with the campaign.'

'What kind of a campaign does the man run?'

'He doesn't,' came the sarcastic reply, 'his presence is enough. People come up to him and offer him their sympathy and slip his bagman some money and he just sits there wearing dark glasses and lapping it up. The campaign's running itself, and they've got some ad agency types telling them what sort of image to project. Anyway, I'll try to interrupt. I'll call you in an hour or so.'

He was as good as his word. An hour and five minutes later the phone rang again and there he was. 'Raja,' he said, 'the PM would like to speak to you. Hold on.' There were a couple of clicks and a burst of static and the PM's highish voice came on the line. 'What's your problem, Menon?' he asked. 'General Kelkar says you want the ads reduced. Don't you want to get my girl back?'

'I do, sir,' I replied, 'that's why I'm asking for the ads to be withdrawn. When the other side see such a frantic, overwhelming reply to their demand that we advertise in the *Deccan Herald*, they'll understand that we're cracking under the pressure. This advertising blitz is necessary only if they don't respond to our ad, which we won't know today because they seem to be intent on communicating through the mails alone.'

'So what do you think we should do?' he asked.

'Continue the ads in the *Deccan Herald*, as they said. Stop the rest. Tell the networks to go back to normal.'

'Do you realize, Colonel, that the ads might be doing us some good? It might make them think we're panicking when we're not? Won't it make them think we've got nowhere in our investigations?'

The man was sharp, but the purpose of the ads was now clear. They'd blend into the election campaign. No one in the country would be permitted to forget the hostage crisis. 'I see that,' I told him, 'but I don't think it'll work. Unless I'm mistaken, they have sources of information among the law enforcement people and maybe even the Army. I've already told you that. So we should cut off the noise now, before it establishes itself. If we cut if off later, they'll be inclined to think that the noise has died down because of some sudden progress with the investigation.'

'I can't cut it off now,' he said, 'too many things are

already scheduled, too much material already in print, for me to backtrack now.'

'All right, sir,' I said, anger now giving my own voice a rare edge, 'I leave it to you. Do as you wish, sir. She's your granddaughter, after all, not mine.'

There was a silence and then he said, quietly, deliberately, 'I'm not used to people talking to me this way. Don't ever do it again.' He hung up.

Now it was falling into place. The PM had initially been shaken by the kidnap, and scared. Then his political sense had taken over and told him that it was material for his campaign. Then his party PR men had moved in and packaged it for him and now he was stuck with it. And the package would get his party votes on the strength of sympathy for himself alone, thereby strengthening his position within the party as well. God, what a manipulator.

The noise went on. At the next morning's meeting even the police were complaining, but it went right on. And there was an answer from the kidnappers. It contained the usual pieces of currency notes for verification, more photographs of the hostages, and a note which said, in effect, that three days was far too much for judicial permission, that they would extend the deadline for the preparation of the money by one day and no more. Two days hence. The mode of delivery and the place where the gold and the cash were to be delivered would be supplied later. The brevity of the note, the rigidity it conveyed, and the absence of any attempts at lightness seemed to indicate that the kidnappers were getting tense as well. Whoever was leading them on the spot—Hairy Face, I thought—was under pressure. I couldn't make out how far they were from breaking, though.

Besides the letter were more Polaroid photographs. In one there were the two girls, sitting in chairs with their backs against a smooth, white wall. What we could see of the floor was shiny black. In a corner of the photograph was the back of a young man clad in jeans and a yellow t-shirt, a thin young man with curly hair. In the next photograph the same young man was shown alone, full face, only his face didn't look so young, with bags and dark shadows under the eyes. It was the CJ's son, head and shoulders, against a white wall. All three hostages were dull of eye, as if they'd been fed some kind of tranquillizer. All drooped, slouching low in their chairs. And there was something wrong about them.

'Something fishy here,' Chauhan said, echoing my thoughts. 'This doesn't fit.'

I looked once again at the set in my hand. 'You're right,' I said finally. 'The young man in the photographs is actually two different young men. They've kept these people at different places and they're trying to get us to think they're all at the same place.'

'Yes,' Chauhan said carefully. 'This complicates things, especially if they have an alarm system . . . if the men at the site we attack can signal the ones at the other site, we lose hostages anyway. How are you placed for simultaneous attacks, Menon?'

'Simultaneous' in my book is a four-letter word. Two

simultaneous related operations reduced our chances of success by a factor of ten or more. It complicated logistics enormously. If the other side were alert, it doubled their chances of spotting us as we positioned ourselves, or on the way in. 'Simultaneous' is a marvellous word for a presentation but for nothing else. 'Terribly,' I said, shaking my head. 'If you ask me, we should do something to neutralize at least one site ahead of time.'

'People as sophisticated as this are bound to have some system of communication between the sites.' True. A simple radio system would do, one that sets off an alarm when a button is pressed. And it can be made small enough for an alarm to be carried around by everyone in a small team. 'Having second thoughts now, are you?' Chauhan continued.

'I'm willing to go in if we have a clear set of priorities,' I said. 'Who's more important? And how much more important? I need to be clear once we get there about who is expendable and who is not. Otherwise we could lose the lot. Do you see?'

'Yes, I do,' he said. He signalled the steno to the effect that what he was going to say next was not to be minuted. 'The most important hostage is the PM's granddaughter. Next in importance is the CJ's son. Third is the other girl. Look at it from the point of view of not yourself but of a kidnapper or an extortionist.'

'And election propaganda,' I said sourly.

'That's not to be spoken,' he said, 'but yes, that too.'

'What about the diaries?' I asked.

'Since we haven't handed them over yet, that question

doesn't arise. And if you're going in, it won't arise.'

'It might . . . What if we go in after the delivery? While they're verifying the diaries and counting their chickens, we move in. They'll have most things to watch out for at that stage.'

'Later. We haven't found even the first site yet.'

And then, in the middle of the meeting came the first big break. A telephone rang and one of the junior police officers picked it up. We could see from his face that it was something big, and he handed the instrument to the DGP immediately. The DGP said 'Hello' and listened for a minute arid then flicked a switch so we could all hear both ends of the conversation on speakers set in the wall. 'Tell us who you are,' said the DGP.

'I am an SP of the Crime Branch now on special duty searching for the site where the PM's granddaughter and her companion are held hostage. We found a possible site ten minutes ago. The location is perfect, and it matches in every way with what we have been told to look for. A two-storey house, old construction, two hundred metres from a mosque with a crescent broken. I have arranged for photographs of the mosque and will fax them on to you immediately. Can the witness substantiate?'

My heart leapt. Good man. I nodded at the DGP, who was looking at me. 'Yes,' he said into the telephone. 'Don't give up the search but let me have those photographs right away. And make sure they're from the proper angles.'

'Yes, sir. Can you tell me from where the witness saw the mosque?'

The DGP said, 'I'm passing the phone on to Colonel Menon, who spoke to the witness.' He passed it to me across the table.

'The witness saw it from a bathroom ventilator on the first floor,' I told him. 'If you look at the building from the mosque side I don't think you'll see more than two or three ventilators. Some will be close by. At three hundred yards, a few feet won't make much difference, but cover all of them. And get the height right. As best I know, there were no trees in the view.'

'I have photographs of the building with me. There are four ventilators on the mosque side but two are covered by trees. That leaves two. I will send you photographs, black and white ones on the fax, colour photos by courier. You should have them in three hours.'

I disconnected and rang Urmila to ask if she could come over to the office and confirm that we'd found the right mosque.

Twenty minutes later she came into the conference room, her dress a bright splash of primary colours in a room full of dull men. My mood brightened just looking at her. The grainy black and whites had been sent on the fax, and the colour photographs had arrived, with a little loss of resolution, on a computer. Someone had scanned the photographs into a computer, then sent the results across the Internet. We'd got them printed out on a colour ink-jet printer. The results were nowhere near as clear as photographs, but they were usable.

Urmila took one look at them and said, 'Yes, this is it.'

She pointed at one of the jagged ends of the break in the crescent. 'You see this place, where there's that little bit sticking up? Like the nose of a man lying down? I remember that.'

'Would you be willing to go there and identify it?' I asked. 'That would be the quickest way for us to verify it. I'll come with you. We'll take a helicopter to Mysore and drive from there. You'll be safe, I promise.'

A set look came over her face. She didn't want to go. 'Think of your friends,' I said.

'Yes,' she nodded, her hair bouncing, 'I'll come.'

An hour and a half later we were getting off the helicopter at Mysore to transfer to an unmarked police car. 'Is this how you usually dress?' I asked.

'Yes,' she replied, 'but for some time I didn't really care about how I looked. I was sure I looked terrible, and dirty . . . Strange.'

'And now you look like a bird of paradise,' I grinned. 'I'm glad you're getting better.'

She looked down at herself self-consciously, then threw her head back and laughed, teeth gleaming, fresh skin glowing.

'You were right, you know, about relationships never being the same again, about growing up quickly. I wanted to speak to you about that . . . About being caught between my parents. Then I understood that they were doing it on purpose, creating that conflict to force me to choose a side. I was the prize, sort of . . . That's come to a stop now. I don't take sides and I don't judge them for what they do.

And now they fight less, now that they can see it doesn't work any more.'

I could have guessed. I also knew that having parents and being a pawn—a prize, to use her words—was better than not having any parents at all, but this wasn't the time to say such things. I let it go, smiled, and settled back in the seat.

As we approached the mosque, her face tightened. I reached out and held her hand. She looked at me in surprise, then her fingers closed around mine. Then she saw it. From a different angle, perhaps, but that nose pointing at the sky was unmistakable. 'That's it,' she said hurriedly, 'I know.'

The car slowed down and I pointed at a house nearby—from the descriptions of the SP, the house in which she must have been held. 'Do you recognize that place?' I asked.

'N-no,' she said, holding my fingers tighter, 'Not really. It might be vaguely familiar but I can't say I remember it. Please . . . Let's go.'

We took the long way around and in Bangalore I was able to confirm to the committee that we had found the house where the girls were kept. I started the men shifting to Mysore immediately and with the SP who had accompanied me back to Bangalore, went over the location of the house and the surrounding terrain once again.

It was twenty kilometres out of Mysore, on the way to Hassan, in quiet farm country. Around it was a two-acre coconut plantation and behind it a large pond from which I assumed they drew water for the plantation. The SP couldn't give me anything about the house itself, for he hadn't been able to trace the owners yet, and I left it at that and returned to the business of moving a whole company of SOF to Mysore in two dozen lorries borrowed from Brigadier Kalra. The men would be housed in three government-run guest houses, and I was to be billeted in a PWD rest house. It seemed a mess but since the men couldn't move into the neighbourhood of the target house without alerting the opposition, I had to leave it at that.

I borrowed an unmarked government car at four the next morning and drove out to have a look at the house with NVGs. In the limited contrast offered by the glasses, I couldn't make out much except that the pond was large, and offered shelter to birds who were already beginning to make a racket as they prepared for the day. The coconut palms were widely spaced, yet gave some cover. The ground itself was irregular, offering more cover, and there were weeds growing thickly all around the house.

By the time I got back, the SP had got in touch with the people in the house behind the one that was our target. They hadn't been able to tell him much, but were willing to help in any way. Tentatively they offered us their house for use as a base of operations, and I jumped at the offer, although with some reservations.

I went back there later in the morning, at about eleven, in a borrowed government car, wearing a chauffeur's uniform. In the day the house looked completely different. It baked in the sun, the clouds having receded beyond the horizon for the moment. It had an unplastered four-foot brick wall running right around it, a frontage of a hundred feet facing the road, with a gate in the middle. It enclosed an area of perhaps a hectare—two and a half acres—and the house was set forward of the centre. The coconut plantation covered almost half the area around the house, some of the rest being devoted to an overgrown kitchen garden, and a patch of lawn in front. By the side of the house was a shed that could also be used as a garage to house three cars . . . Or the van.

The driveway was muddy and uneven and led to the garage, passing by a porch. The front of the house was relatively new, painted a dirty off-white, but its rear side was older. The rear half was roofed with tiles, the front with concrete. The front door was in the centre, painted a dull grey, flanked by windows, all shut. There wasn't a single window open anywhere in that house as far as I could see.

There was no TV dish visible, but there was a cable operator near the mosque and we could see the cable snaking into the house. It looked neglected and run down—no one would want to live in a house like this for any length of time.

Parthenium and touch-me-not grew in profusion along the driveway. There was a mango tree somewhere to the rear of the house, and another smaller tree I couldn't identify. The room in which Urmila had been kept must have been to the rear, then, because the SP had said that the view from two of the ventilators was blocked by trees. The mosque wasn't visible from the gate of the house, but from the sides and the rear it loomed large. At the tops of the minarets were loudspeakers for the prayers.

Cover was patchy. The coconut plantation was the best bet, but inside the walls there was no vegetation more than six inches off the ground, except for the clumps of parthenium. The ground was irregular, with many dips and rises that offered more cover than the vegetation. There were weeds all over, except in the area around the house, which was clear, showing signs of having been trimmed recently. The kidnappers would have done it; weeds would have sprouted with the first rains and after that they would be hard to clear.

A lookout posted at the top of the house, on the roof of the new section, would be able to keep an eye on anyone coming in from the road, or over the front wall. The rear was a different matter because there was the pond there, and beyond that another house, the one that had been offered to us to base ourselves in for the duration. We'd be able to check out the rear after dark without being noticed, unless they had NVGs in constant use.

We had no idea what the inside of the target house was like. The owner and his entire family were abroad. They had left the house in the care of a distant cousin who had in turn rented the house out for six months. The rent had been paid in advance, and a deposit left behind, so the cousin had asked no questions of the tenant. And since he saw no point in paying tax on the rent, the transaction had been conducted in cash, the tenant being willing to accept his word that the deposit would be returned when the house was vacated.

The cousin, whom the police traced, was an engineer in Belgaum and knew nothing about what was going on in the farmhouse, which he had seen only in childhood and hardly remembered. What he did remember was that it had been built seventy years ago, with rooms or wings added on whenever the number of residents increased sufficiently. There was no plan, no architect. One of the members of the family himself knew enough about construction to do the needful, but he was away in the Middle East and couldn't be contacted.

The police were doing their best to trace people who might know the interior of the house—servants, neighbours, anyone—but had yet to turn up anything useful. They did come across one maid who had worked there until five years previously, but the front had been built since and she knew nothing about it.

I like to take my time over planning these operations. In the process I go over the ground several times, experiment with little details here and there, waiting for a glimmer of weakness to show. Once you have that glimmer it gets easier; all you have to do is work it into a shape that your strengths accommodate, fit in details like timing and staff and equipment and logistics. Generally there's a longish period of low-risk preparation, as much training and rehearsal as can be crammed into the time available, and then a brief hit, rarely lasting more than a few seconds, when the exposure and risk are substantial.

The idea is to keep that substantial risk low without increasing the time. The key to it is time. Since the hit lasts only a few seconds, anything that can save a stumble during those seconds becomes important. Anything that can shave a fraction of a second off our time, or delay the opposition, is worth looking at. The placement of furniture in a room, the smoothness of a floor, the height of a ceiling, the thickness of a wall, the strength of a hinge, all these make a difference. And therein lay the problem: on this, perhaps the most important of all my raids so far, there was little available by way of useful information.

I stalled the car at a corner of the compound between the house and the mosque and stepped out to open the bonnet. I hoped the chauffeur's uniform, white and spotted with grease stains, a dirty cap that I pushed to the back of my head, cheap shoes, trousers frayed at the ends, would lull the opposition. I stuck my hand into the engine well, found everything in order. I unscrewed the distributor cap, examined it, put it back in, and wished for a puncture. And all the while, Hari, who had joined us two days earlier, hunkered down in the back with an improvised periscope, examining the house. After less than a minute and a half, I lowered the bonnet and climbed back in. Under the cover of my cap I asked, 'Done?'

'Yes,' he replied, 'more after dark.' If he'd said no I'd have pretended to have trouble starting the car and opened the bonnet again.

Not a movement from the house. No sign at all of life, except fresh tyre marks outside the garage—at least one car and a larger vehicle, probably the van. The walls of the garage were filthy . . . All the windows boarded up, opaque.

I wondered how they lived in that airless house.

The area around the house was clear for a distance of at least ten metres throughout. The nearest coconut palms in the plantation were fifteen metres away. A well in a corner, with a pump next to it, provided water to the house. The large windows on either side of the front door had wooden shutters and were probably barred. There were half a dozen windows in front, and as many more at the sides. The tiles on the rear part of the roof were old and cracked and there were skylights set in them. For a moment I wondered if that were the way in, through the roof, but gave up the thought almost immediately; if it rained, which was a very real possibility this time of the year, the sloping roof would be deadly.

With the palms and the fruit trees and the bumps there was enough cover, but not if they had NVGs, or sharp-eyed watchers . . . If they had people outside who'd told them about the Kabini lodge and the PM's granddaughter's schedule, they were probably informed of our progress as well. If they had any idea when we were coming, we wouldn't make it.

Getting to the door was no problem. Neither was getting to the windows at the side. There was a kitchen door at the back, the police had said, which looked considerably weaker than the front door. Getting there, too, was possible . . . but from where? They'd expect us to go in from the coconut palms. That was the logical thing to do. The pond in the rear would be a deterrent, and there was much less cover in the other directions. If the house had been newer I'd have considered going through the walls, but sometimes old houses have surprisingly strong walls that stand up to much stronger blasts than one would expect them to.

A thought flickered through my mind. Use the pond. Take the bastards by surprise.

I turned in the car and drove back to the house behind. A command post had come up quickly enough there. The owners were two brothers—whom I privately named Salt and Pepper; one was white-haired and the other black—who lived there with their parents. They were both bachelors despite their age—both were in their forties—and, according to the police, impatient to get away from their village, preferably to some place in the Middle East, to make some tax-free money. They had no idea who had moved into the house behind theirs, they'd seen only one man enter or exit from there and they couldn't describe him since they saw him only after dusk. The police had told them that the occupants were drug smugglers using the house as a depot to cache heroin and cocaine. Not a story that would stand up to serious examination, but the two men accepted it.

They were twins, I discovered when I met them that afternoon, who had spent most of their lives right there, and had got used to the laid-back pace of life. Even their ambition to leave, I discovered, was more fantasy than ambition. Surprisingly enough, Salt, the white-haired one, was friendly with a girl who lived nearby, a Christian girl half his age of whom he was sure his parents would not approve. He had got into the habit of slipping out of the house surreptitiously after dark to meet her somewhere near her place, and had once seen a truck drawn up outside the garage of the house behind. He thought he'd got a glimpse of a man with a rifle, but couldn't be sure. What he'd seen was of little use to us, but enough to substantiate the drug smuggler story in his mind, and he was glad we were there to take care of the smugglers.

The brothers weren't comfortable speaking English and my Kannada was less than rudimentary. The answers came much faster after I arranged for a police Inspector to act as interpreter. The brothers were nervous, faced with so many uniforms all of a sudden, and probably awed by the fact that the District SP had come to their house. 'You know that house fairly well, don't you?' I asked them together.

They understood, for both nodded. They spoke in rapid-fire Kannada, the narrative switching smoothly between the two and to the policemen, then sat back smiling. The translation came immediately. 'They say their grandfather once owned that land. His father put up the first building there in the twenties. The family who own it now bought it about forty years ago. When they were children they used to play there. There were children there, too. The high wall between the two properties came up only about ten years back. Before that the edge of the pond was the border.'

'And whose is the pond?' I asked.

'Public property,' came the answer via the interpreters. 'There is, as you can see, an access road to it. We used it to water our land but for some reason the water is not good. Hardly anyone uses it. But it is public property.'

'Do people visit it often?'

'Yes. People bathe there in summer when there is a water shortage, and they wash clothes there. Many years ago someone used to shoot fish there, with a rifle. But now many houses have water piped up to them so the pond is no longer as heavily used as it was twenty years ago.'

The answers tended to be long rather than short and I had to be patient. 'I'd like to look over your property. Can you show me over it tomorrow? Can you act as if I'm a prospective buyer, and on that pretext introduce me to your neighbours?'

They nodded in unison, gesticulating and grinning, and spoke to the interpreters again in their fast Kannada. 'They'd be pleased to, any time you like,' said the policeman, also grinning. 'They haven't had so much fun ever in their lives.' They looked like young boys planning a prank as they sat there, rail-thin and bright-eyed and alert. Nice guys.

'How about right now?' I asked. 'I can't be the buyer because I don't know the language and I can't imagine an outsider buying land here. We'll find one of my men who speaks Kannada and I'll be his servant. His driver, who comes from Delhi and speaks only Hindi.' They agreed, and less than ten minutes later, Salt (we didn't want a crowd, so Pepper stayed back), a plainclothesman, Subedar Raghunath Poojary and I were walking across to the other house.

The twins owned six acres of land, most of it under coconuts. 'It's relatively new here,' Salt explained to Subedar Poojary, who was gleefully playing the role of my boss, while I followed, cap in hand. 'We thought coconuts grew only by the sea but now we've got them growing here and it's very popular because everyone drinks coconut water.' Some of their land—about an eighth of an acre—was set aside for vegetables, mostly in the area skirting the pond. The coconuts and the vegetable patch wouldn't provide much cover—the vegetables were too low for comfort and the coconut palms too far apart. As we got to the pond I caught a glimpse of a brown-and-white bird flying to the bank. So did the plainclothesman accompanying us, for he asked, 'What was that? That bird on the bank?'

Salt shrugged and replied, 'It's some kind of a duck. It lives by the pond and makes noise at dawn and at dusk. It quacks loudly.' They'd effectively got an alarm system laid on by nature. Anyone getting into that pond at night would set the birds making noises and an alert lookout would spot the disturbance quickly. Doses of weed-killer in the water would kill the ducks, but since it was public property used by people we couldn't take the risk. I couldn't help thinking of the young man in Uri who had noticed when the crickets went silent that night. These guys were likely to be as good.

They had picked their spot well . . . Like the Krait. But it couldn't be him again. Ismail was dead. And this wasn't a political group, at least not overtly.

The penny dropped. If Ismail's control got hold of the diaries, he wouldn't need to worry about a political front, or an organization like the Free Kashmir Front: the ISI would be able to entrench itself in the government on the strength of the contents of those diaries alone. I felt my pulse speeding up at the thought.

Other considerations arose. The PM didn't want to hand over the diaries. He was willing to risk his granddaughter's life for them, and while the politician in him scored over his private persona, I was sure he cared for her enormously . . . Perhaps more than he could afford to admit. He was therefore in the clear; otherwise he'd have been for handing the diaries over, assuming that the diaries in the hands of the kidnappers would probably be less dangerous than in the hands of the judiciary. Anyone who suggested handing the diaries over was automatically suspect.

No one had suggested that yet. Not one politician, bureaucrat, or cop.

There was much more at stake in this dusty farmhouse than the lives of the hostages. I looked around at the terrain with new, frightened eyes. It wasn't a farm any more. It was a battleground and the odds were heavily against us. And there was worse to come; we hadn't even found the second battleground yet.

chapter seven

The reconnaissance wasn't particularly useful. Salt, the prospective 'buyer' and the chauffeur—myself—walked up the drive to the house. Salt looked for a bell-push and not finding one, knocked firmly on the door. The hostages, the two girls at least, could not have been more than fifty feet away, and for one delicious mad moment I considered blasting my way in right there and fetching them out.

The madness disappeared very quickly. The front door opened six inches and part of a head showed. Dark glasses on a beak of a nose, stubble on a firm chin, baseball cap on a squarish head.

And a tuft of hair on a single shadowy ear.

The dangerous one, the leader, the one who spoke gently but acted viciously. Medium height, good thick shoulders as far as I could see. The fingers that showed on the door were also thick and strong and hairy. The overall impression was one of strength. 'Good day,' said Salt in Kannada. 'My name is Vishwanath and I live in the house behind yours, past the pond.' He waved a hand in the direction of the Subedar. 'And this is Dr Ramnarayan Rao, who wants to buy a house and some land in this area . . . He is thinking of buying our house. We were showing him around. Then we thought we would show him your house as well . . . Can you show us around?'

'I don't understand Kannada,' said Hairy Face, slowly, unsmilingly, in English. The plainclothesman, a Kannadiga, quickly came in as the interpreter.

'This is a rented house,' said Hairy Face after the plainclothesman had finished, 'it is not for sale. The owner is in Belgaum. Talk to him and then come here.' His voice was strong but on the high side. It didn't quite fit with his hairiness.

'Can we show the doctor around the compound, then?' asked Salt. 'This plot used to belong to my grandfather. I want to go around myself. Sentiment.'

'There is nothing in the compound,' said Hairy Face. 'I am alone in the house right now and I have a terrible headache, so can we keep this short?'

'Oh!' said Salt, 'it must be terrible for you, standing here in this bright sunlight. Shall we talk inside, then? You'll be better there.'

'No,' came the brusque reply, even before the plainclothesman had finished translating. 'I have conjunctivitis. That is why I have these glasses on. If you come in here you might get it as well. Come after a week or two, when this is better, and I will show you around.' His other hand appeared on the edge of the door, his right hand. On the middle finger was a red coral in a gold ring.

Along his knuckles was a scar, black and ugly and spreading, probably a burn. The door opened another inch and I saw clearly the beak of his nose, thin lips, gaunt cheeks, big cheekbones. A toecap showed, then the rest of a small foot. Dancer's feet, light and strong. Powerful shoulders, slim waist. Not an ounce of fat on this man.

On his hands were the little telltale scars that anyone who works with his hands has. This man used weapons and bombs, and if he himself had cut the throat of the bodyguard at Kabini, a knife as well.

His English was fluent, with an accent I couldn't place. Certainly not any of the common Indian accents . . . Perhaps Arabic?

We'd have his description sent out to Interpol, and to police headquarters in all states. Get people hunting for his background. If he had a record we'd pin him down within hours.

Salt, conceding that there was no chance of getting into the house now, acquiesced gracefully. He smiled. 'I'll see you next week. If you're better then you can show me around, otherwise it can wait . . . If you need anything, drop in.' Hairy Face disappeared with a silent, perfunctory nod, and a moment later we were looking at the blank front of a closed door.

We retreated in good order, with me still a couple of paces behind, still looking around, still eager for cover. There was some, which we could use best if we went in on a moonless night. Maybe we could make it across the garden, through the plantation . . . But that clear area just beside the house would be hard to get through. At this time of the year, hot spells were usually followed by clouds and rain . . . A good spell of rain would be useful, and if it came at the right time, would be wonderful: we'd go right through the water without being seen, the sounds of our approach disguised by the patter of falling rain.

Maybe . . . If . . . Suddenly a mood of dull despair came up out of nowhere, despair and defeat. There was no progress anywhere.

At the evening's meeting were raised the questions of how we were to hit the house where we knew the girls were, and how to find out where the CJ's son was, assuming that the kidnappers had indeed tried to trick us into thinking they were all in one place. I had no answers to the first, and no one had answers to the second.

That night we moved a team of twenty of my men into Salt and Pepper's house. We had figured a route for the lorries to take by which they could get to the area without being seen from the site. It involved some tricky cross-country driving, but two SOF drivers who came along to check it out handled the drive with ease. Salt and Pepper's parents, both in their seventies and both unexpectedly spirited in their willingness to help the police, were shifted to a government hotel by the riverside on the Bangalore–Mysore highway. Salt and Pepper themselves refused firmly to leave, preferring to take their chances, but were gently ordered away by the SP, who overawed them with his magnificent moustache and Ray-Ban.

All the Army lorries went away before daybreak. From

the viewpoint that the kidnappers had onto our command post, there were no traces that nearly a platoon of men had moved in, or that there was a compact but effective command post set up in the house behind. More equipment arrived, ferried in by the soldiers from nearly a kilometre away.

A ring of unobtrusive Crime Branch watchers went up around the kidnappers. They stood in the dark, unassuming men hidden behind trees and in some of the houses nearby, armed only with binoculars and sharp ears, waiting patiently.

And at long last, the kidnappers moved.

At four that morning, Hairy Face emerged from the house and unlocked the garage. He backed a white Maruti 1000 out of the garage and drove off. A relay of CBI men—four teams, two in cars and two on motorcycles—followed him discreetly to a two-storey house some eleven kilometres away, in a suburb of Mysore. There was a power failure when Hairy Face drew up outside the house and in the dark the plainclothesmen following on a motorcycle managed to get close without being seen. They noticed lights showing in some rooms: it was the only house with electrical power in that street. And strangely enough, although it was occupied, all the windows were shut.

The detail about the power, while small, offered some secondary evidence. We saw, through cracks in the shutters, lights in the other house as well, though there was a power cut in that area too. In the absence of generator noises, we assumed that they were using inverters and car batteries to keep the supply going. They had reason for it: in the first place, the hostages were more likely to try to escape in the dark, and second, if they had any means of communication with each other they needed power for that.

The plainclothesmen behind Hairy Face passed by his parked car after signalling another team to take over the chase. They radioed us the car's registration number, KA-04-J-904. The SP had this radioed on to the Regional Transport Officer in Bangalore. The grumbling RTO staff who followed up on it told us there was no such number in the state and went back to sleep while the police began looking through reports of stolen Maruti 1000s. There was only one that hadn't been traced, a metallic grey car stolen three weeks earlier from the parking lot outside St Patrick's arcade on Brigade Road in Bangalore.

The second hideaway, we discovered, was owned by a computer engineer who had been transferred out of Mysore. When the police traced him in Bangalore at seven in the morning, he told them that he hadn't planned to rent out the house, but someone had come to him six weeks earlier with an offer of a deposit and a rent that were both twice the going rate, and in cash if he preferred it that way. When he agreed they had paid up immediately, settling the estate agent's fee of one month's rent on the spot as well. No complaints from anyone.

And he remembered Hairy Face. The man was civilized and pleasant, he said, relaxed and well dressed. Clearly wealthy. He had paid without negotiating, offering a pile of cash which he was carrying in his briefcase. When the landlord murmured something about income tax he had smiled and nodded and agreed fully. The whole process had taken less than two hours.

This had happened the same day the hostages had reserved their rooms at the guest house.

The police had decided the young owner had something to do with the kidnappers and were keeping him in custody while they investigated. It seemed unlikely to me that he was involved—not because he seemed innocent but because those men were too smart to include in their plan someone so easily traceable. But I kept my mouth shut and went to the police station to talk to him.

Set as it was in a residential area of Mysore, the second hideaway wasn't as well-chosen as Salt and Pepper's house. At the police station the young engineer gave me a description of his house. There were four bedrooms, one on the ground floor and three above. On the ground floor, besides the bedroom were a living room, a dining room, a study, a kitchen and two bathrooms. The staircase rose from a side of the living room to a landing above from which four doors opened, three to the bedrooms and one to a bathroom. One bedroom had a bathroom attached while the other two shared the second bathroom. The tenant had wanted a furnished house, and since he had been willing to pay for it, the owner had left some minimal furniture in the house.

'What did you leave behind?' I asked him.

'A double bed in the large bedroom upstairs and singles in all other bedrooms,' he said and paused briefly to remember before continuing. 'A sofa set—one three-seater and two one-seaters—and an occasional table in the living room, a dining table and six chairs for the dining room. A fridge in the kitchen, and a toaster, and the gas stove . . . He offered me an extra deposit for all this. He didn't want to waste his time looking for the basics because he'd be here only six months anyway. He said he intended to have a couple of computers in the house, and needed steady power for them. When I told him there were long power failures here, he told me to get a UPS—uninterruptible power supply—to take care of two personal computers and an inverter for two fans and five lights. He was willing to pay for it so I got it done.'

'What's the master bedroom upstairs like?' I asked.

'There's a cupboard, a built-in cupboard, and one walk-in closet. There's the double bed there, and a dresser with a mirror, and a stool. He told me that was enough. When he came to see the house there were heavy, dark curtains all over. He looked at them and said they were fine, and could I leave them there. I agreed. You know, good tenants are so rare and this one looked excellent. He was exceptionally nice. He told me then that he was with a computer company who were thinking of starting a branch here, that he would often come back late at night. I told him that this was a quiet neighbourhood, that the next door neighbour was a policeman, and that what time he got back at was his business, but he shouldn't make noise coming in. He smiled and said of course not.'

A simple man, this engineer I thought and smiled at him. It seemed to put him at ease; he was confused by all the extraordinary drama that had resulted from what to him was a routine affair—renting out his house to a nice, accommodating tenant. I asked him a few more questions and for the address of the architect who had designed his house, and when I was through, two constables led him away.

One of the sub-inspectors at the station turned out to be a neighbour of the engineer. He came to me and rather shamefacedly confessed that he'd been foolish. Apparently he'd run into the tenant—Hairy Face—when he arrived at the gate of the engineer's house in the wee hours of the morning after the kidnap of the CJ's son, holding up a young man he said was a cousin. The 'cousin' had been unsteady of foot and glazed of eye, and the policeman had accepted Hairy Face's explanation that the young man was drunk. His head had been shaved, and he sported a small toothbrush moustache, enough to stop the police or anyone else who saw him from connecting the drunk youngster with the judge's son, whose face with its neat beard, topped with thick, curly hair, had been flashed on all the TV channels.

Anybody would have been fooled, I told the policeman. But he could still help. He could go to that house on the pretext of having a message from the landlord, and on the way look for clues on how many men were in there, where exactly the hostage was, and possible points of entry. With luck he might even get a look at what kind of armaments the kidnappers had.

The architect who had designed the engineer's house

was summoned. He arrived an hour later, bewildered at being dragged out of a meeting at his office, protesting that he wasn't involved. The policemen who fetched him hadn't told him why they wanted him, and he in fact thought that a house he had built had collapsed, and spent the first two or three minutes with me trying to convince me that though he used some—very few—substandard materials, everyone did much the same, and in any case he didn't break any safety regulations, that it wasn't his fault, that he knew the minister, and so on. 'Enough,' I told him when he paused to take a deep breath. 'All that is none of my business. I just want you to explain these plans to me.' I pushed towards him the plans of the house that the engineer had given the police.

'Why do you want to know?' he asked craftily, looking for a way to profit.

'There might be someone hiding there whom I want to blow out,' I replied, sure that if he knew what the purpose was he'd be able to pinpoint weak spots for us, 'but keep all this to yourself, please.'

His demeanour changed as the meaning of the words sank in. He could see now that there was nothing in it for him. He shook his head. 'The owner,' he explained, 'is an old friend of mine. I did the foundation well, and the walls are solid. Not easy to break into. The window and door frames are fixed solidly into the walls. They will be difficult to remove. It is not like some other houses here that you can break through easily.'

'I don't want to destroy the house,' I told him, 'I just

want to get in without being seen or heard. Just tell me how to do that.'

'There are people inside who will be waiting for you?' he asked.

'Yes,' I replied, 'several.'

'After you get in, then what will you do?'

'I'll check all the rooms first, in a few seconds. For those few seconds I need surprise, quiet. After that I don't care if the roof falls in.'

'Where do you want to go? Ground floor or first floor?'

'Both together. But the first floor is more important.' It was a pretty sure bet that the hostage was in one of the first-floor bedrooms, most probably the one with the attached bathroom.

He shook his head. 'It will be very difficult to do it silently,' he said after some consideration, 'but for what you need, the best place to enter is here.' He pointed to a spot on the plan, at the edge of the landing in the middle of the stairs. 'There are vertical windows here, very high windows that are only twelve inches wide. The owner wanted a lot of light there, natural light, and some breeze if possible. They are in two sections, and the lower section can be opened. A thin man can get through the window sideways, but a fat one would get stuck. But then you are not fat.'

'I won't be alone,' I smiled, 'but there won't be any fat men in this.'

'Good,' he said, 'I will show you how. You see, my friend wanted this house in a hurry. He told me that he wanted the window barred, and I ordered a frame with horizontal bars, set six inches apart. The carpenter didn't make that frame in time, so I got him to make one with a single vertical bar, with a support in the middle. The owner didn't want people looking in so we put in panes of ground glass. If you can break the glass without being heard, and then get past that one bar, you're through.' He pointed at the landing. 'You'll be here, eight steps from the upper floor, seven steps above the ground floor. From here you can move on to the living room and the dining room downstairs, and into the passage on the first floor . . .

'There is also a balcony on the first floor, with a door opening to the master bedroom, but if you get in that way you will have to break through some doors to get to the ground floor.'

If the hostage was in the master bedroom upstairs then the chances were that someone would be on the balcony. Going in from below, with grapnels on the balcony's railing, would be tricky. Going in from above would be impossible; there was no way to get onto the roof from anywhere nearby, according to what the policeman neighbour had told us . . . The landing, that was the best bet. We'd blow the frame right off.

'The doors inside the house,' I asked, 'are they as solid as the outer ones?'

'No, not really,' came the reply. 'You see, it's expensive fitting good doors . . . The internal doors I didn't pay much attention to.'

Good. That confirmed it. We'd go in through the landing. 'All right,' I said, 'you'll have to be with the police for some time, until all this is over, but let me assure you you're not in trouble, and you have my apologies for taking up your time.'

'Yes,' he said, relieved that we weren't going to lock him up. 'No problem. You want anything, you call me.'

At that evening's meeting I confirmed that we'd found the house where the CJ's son was held and that we had found a way into the house with a reasonable chance of getting him out intact, but there was no progress on the other house. The storm of protest that followed died down a little when I asked for details of the house, without which I couldn't promise anything. But there were still murmurs of incompetence that I didn't like. After the meeting, Kelkar called from Delhi at the command post in Salt and Pepper's house. 'Have you found a way in yet?' he asked.

'No,' I told him, 'we don't know what it's like inside. The second place, where the CJ's son is, should be an easier job but this one is the pits. We don't know what's inside, how many men there are, which rooms the kids are kept in. About the only good thing is that these guys seem to be professionals, so they won't slaughter the hostages as we go in.'

'That man Bhaskar's been getting after me, Raja,' he said unhappily. 'I can keep him occupied for a while but by and by he'll call in his heavy artillery and then I won't be able to stall him.' His voice was leaden, lifeless.

'What about the Chief?' I asked. 'What the hell is he doing there?'

'Nothing,' came the angry reply. 'Raja, the man's a paper soldier. He's got a sharp mind and he seems to understand technology and geopolitics and that's why he's got where he is, but he's got no heart at all. There's next to nothing he can contribute to a situation like yours. Do you have a plan? Even a half-baked one I can present to these guys? Give them some paper to chew on?'

'No,' I replied, 'nothing at all. But I do have an idea.'

'Spit it out,' he said impatiently, 'we'll see what we can do to dress it up.'

'You won't be able to dress it up,' I said. 'Don't say I didn't warn you.'

'Go on, tell me!' he snapped.

'We give in. We give them the money and the diaries. We give it to them in a form that's hard to count so they'll take some time to verify it all. We appear to fold up completely, to be on our knees. And while they're busy verifying it, we hit them . . . The chances are they'll be off guard at the time.'

'You're cutting down your own chances too much, I'd say,' he growled. 'What if they do the count and disappear in a couple of hours, before you even get a chance to move in?'

'I doubt if they can do that,' I countered. 'They've asked for a mixture of things, some cash, some gold, the diaries, whatever. In the first place, you can deliver these things slowly. Then they'll need time to count the money, unless they have a machine to do it, or someone among them who can count fast. And they have to make sure the money's not marked, not traceable. They'll take a few hours for that. I think we can stretch it out to maybe twelve hours between the time we deliver and the time they take off.'

'They'll have the hostages with them all the time, and the ransom, and they know they'll be vulnerable . . . They might not agree. They might accept the money without counting all of it . . . You don't know. I don't think the Committee's going to like this.' By Committee he meant the PM.

'Of course they won't like it,' I said. 'That's why I said you'll not be able to dress it up. But do we have an alternative? If we go in now, we risk losing the hostages. If we go in while they're counting and verifying we risk losing the hostages and the ransom, but that's when they'll be most vulnerable. Look, let me put it this way. That Committee doesn't really want to retrieve the diaries. They'd like them destroyed. The money doesn't matter, either. So what we do is go in and try to get the hostages out and to hell with the diaries as long as no one gets out of the place. We can retrieve the diaries later.'

'I get it, Raja,' he said, 'but what if they tell us to deliver the money someplace and the rest someplace else?'

'Gut feeling is that they won't. They've tried to keep their strength down to the minimum so far and I don't think they have enough people to split our attention so much. They're using technology to keep their numbers down, which is good thinking. My guess is that they'll have everything delivered to that farmhouse . . . they might even move the CJ's son there. That'll certainly free up some people while they count the money. I still think we should go in when they're counting.'

I knew he was now thinking along the same lines, but playing adversary so that we got our thinking straightened out. 'And what if they don't all move into one place?'

'We still have the advantage. They'll spend time preparing for their move, resting, whatever, before splitting, and they'll be under strength while counting. They'll be relaxed because they'll think they've won . . .'

'All right,' he said slowly, 'I'll pass this on. But work on it some more. Get the details worked out. And be prepared to come out here to meet the Committee and tell them about it.'

I spent that night in the command post looking at the plans and reviewing whatever we knew about the farmhouse, and turned up nothing at all. Anything I could think up was suicidally complicated, they'd catch us on the way in or very shortly after. By morning, on my tenth cup of black coffee in the past twelve hours, I was reaching the end of my tether. And at dawn, Kelkar called again, to say he had persuaded the Committee to look at my plan. 'Come on up, Raja,' he said, 'the deadline is tomorrow. Get here today, tell them about it. The Chief is against it, he thinks the risk is too high, and he wants to be in a position where no blame falls on him if this thing bombs. But the PM says we should listen. Thanks to old man Mankekar. I got him to push the PM into it. Any progress?'

'None at all,' I replied, 'except for a glimmer of an idea. We're still where we were last night except that now I know the terrain like the back of my hand and I know we can get into the farmhouse from a direction they won't anticipate.'

'Get to Bangalore, then, and I'll have a transport waiting for you. Anything you want me to do for you out here?'

'Yes. Find out how long they can delay things. Buy us as much time as you can. The more we delay the better it is for us.'

'I'll do that but they're shitting bricks out here already. No guarantees. Do you want to work out a timetable beforehand?'

'Yes. You'll have to get someone there who knows his bullion and his currency, and someone to tell us how they could test the notes, someone who can tell us how long it'll take, given the number of people doing it. He should also be able to tell us the clumsiest way to pack the stuff without getting them worked up. And I've been wondering . . . That stuff is going to be heavy. How do they plan to get it all out of there?'

'Staggered departure?' he said.

'That's the only way,' I agreed. They'd leave the house one by one at regular intervals, each carrying a part of the booty, reporting their escape over a wireless when they got to a sanctuary. The last to go would take the diaries with him, leaving the hostages behind. Our watchers, not knowing how many men were leaving, would not know when to move in. We'd be forced to wait until we saw that no more men left in a long while.

'See you in a few hours, then. You'll be taken straight to

the PM's residence, the conference room there. I'll be waiting for you. We should have an hour together before you meet the Committee.'

Something had happened. Instead of the no-frills transport that I usually got was a luxurious Gulfstream executive jet normally used by senior brass. Inside I was pampered by courteous Air Force staff, who aside from their uniforms, behaved like crew on a commercial flight.

All said and done, I preferred the transports.

Four hours later I was closeted once again with Kelkar in one of the anterooms. 'I spoke to the people you said I should,' he said. 'They all say you have a maximum of six hours, not the twelve that you'd been hoping for, for them to verify the delivery . . . That cuts your window by half. They've assumed there are three men doing the counting. They think that's optimal. More would get in each others' way and slow it down, and less would slow it down anyway.

'What the others here are worried about is the lack of stress on their side. It seems unusual. They've given us a fairly relaxed deadline, and when we asked for an extension they gave us one—a smaller one than we'd asked for, but they had a reason for it—and they handled it all coolly.'

'I think they're relaxed because they've got a source in here,' I told him.

'You do understand what you're saying, don't you?' he asked. 'So far, only the service Chiefs, the PM, Bhaskar and the rest of the Committee—all of whom have got the highest clearances—know anything about your plans. Even the CBI doesn't know.'

'I know what I'm saying,' I said, 'but can you think of another explanation? The other thing is that my involvement is known, and I've been here more than once. Ditto you. That means a raid is likely. And there must be people here who can put two and two together and come to the conclusion that a raid is likely in the near future. I'm sure any reasonably important politician would be able to get the police around here to tell him anything they can put together, from all those bits and pieces and dribbles. They might not have the complete picture but they will have a large part of it. I'd tend to think that they are in contact, and our problem is going to be to pinpoint the leaks.'

He nodded. 'I saw that,' he said. 'We can do three things. We can tell them all that we're going to do, or we can tell them just the principle of it and fine-tune the details ourselves. Or, if you think we must, we'll tell them a story to keep them shut and do what we think appropriate. I'd say we tell them the basic issues but not the details because they have control over the other things—deliveries and so on—which are critical to our timing.'

'Can't we get away without it?' I asked. Security where politicians were concerned was next to non-existent except when it came to ballot boxes.

'No. I have to tell the others when to deliver, and why. No getting away from that.'

'So be it, then,' I said, 'but can we make two plans?'

'If you think you can, yes.'

We drew up the two plans then. At the end of it I asked him the crucial question. 'We'll hit both places. If something misfires, what do we go for? Which do we try to save?'

'They'll say go for the hostages and blow the place as you get out. From their point of view the best thing that can happen is the destruction of the diaries, not their retrieval.'

The Chief joined us in the same anteroom just minutes after I wrapped up with Kelkar. He glared at the two of us, visibly the adversary. Then he concentrated his glare on me. 'What's all this Kelkar's been saying about our giving them what they want and you going in and fetching them out?' he asked when he had seated himself, pen and pad in hand.

'The basic idea is to divide their attention, sir,' I said, 'like they've been doing to us. We go in when their attention is divided between the booty and the hostages.'

He cut me off with a wave of the hand. 'I know all that,' he said testily. 'Have you forgotten the basics? Don't you know that the exchange is when they'll be most alert? When they'll be most tense?'

'I'm banking on two things,' I explained. 'First, we look like we've collapsed. Second, since they know the book as well as we do, they won't expect us there at the time.'

'Too far-fetched,' he said, 'but tell me more about your plan anyway.'

I took a deep breath and Kelkar gave me a warning glance. I brought out the doodles I'd made while working out the dummy plan with Kelkar. 'The hostages are in two houses. One is a house in a residential area in Mysore, where they've got the CJ's son. Getting into it is not going to be a problem, sir, we have two alternatives already.' I told him about my chat with the architect and what I'd decided after that. He nodded sceptically and told me to go on. 'The trickier place by far is that farmhouse. I really expect them to take delivery of the ransom there.' I described the layout of the place, then the dummy plan, which involved going in over the walls and sneaking in through the coconut plantation, ignoring the pond completely. 'The last few metres we'll be in the open,' I concluded, 'but if we move fast enough we should still be able to take them by surprise.'

'Are you sure you have cover to get that far?' he asked.

'No,' I said, 'we could be spotted any time. But we have a fighting chance of getting through without being seen, and if we make it that far, those last few yards we should be able to do in a short while. If we can figure out a pattern to their sentry duty we'd be able to make sure, sneak in while they're not watching. But there are no visible sentries. I'm sure there are people watching from cover, and if they have NVGs we run a high risk.'

'No way to make sure, is there?' he asked.

'Not unless we can set up the exchange so that whoever's doing the delivery gets close up enough to take a look inside. And these guys are too smart.'

'And where do you enter from?'

'Two points, maybe three. There's a ground floor and a first floor and we'll get in from the front and the back. It's only if the attack gets this far that we'll tell the other guys to go in and get the CJ's son. I'd like to investigate the possibility of someone getting up on the roof, but if it's raining that won't be possible. An airdrop is eliminated by the sloping roof.'

'And inside the house?'

'We know the rough position of the staircase, that the hostages are likely to be upstairs . . . We'll have to, play it by ear once we're inside.'

'No plans?' he asked acidly. 'I thought you'd made a plan. This is just speculation.'

'Yes, sir,' I replied, 'that's all I have at the moment.'

'That's not very encouraging,' he said, 'I don't think I can go along with this.'

'We don't have an alternative, sir,' I said. 'There's no other time at which we can take them safely. Their defences are just too strong: we have to have that element of surprise.'

'And what do you think is an acceptable risk?' he asked.

'Basically, sir, none of the scenarios is very good. The highest risk is during the delivery itself. That's the time they'll think some gung-ho idiot will decide to take them out with snipers or bombs or something. The second-highest risk of losing the hostages is before we deliver. After we deliver, they might think in terms of saving the booty rather than getting rid of the hostages and I want to exploit that. As far as I'm concerned, the diaries don't matter, the hostages do.'

'But won't they be focussed after the delivery?'

'Not as well as during. They'll be exhilarated that they have the booty, past the period of maximum stress. They might even be gloating. None of that makes for maximum alertness.'

'But their attention will be divided during the handover, too, won't it?' he asked.

'Yes,' I replied, 'but they'll be on edge then. They'll have more than one lookout and if one of them signals something funny, or if we make a misstep, they'll start working on the hostages. The chances are they'll have a hostage in front of them when they come to deal with us, and they'll cut her up right then. And they'll tell us to back off and come back with tighter controls and a bigger stake.'

He looked down at his impeccably manicured fingernails and grunted, clearly confused. I didn't really blame him. He liked things cut and dried, more or less in the orthodox military tradition, with the numbers and casualty estimates all worked out for him to calculate the percentages with. Here he had nothing. A few scribbles on a bit of paper and my words.

I was relieved when Bhaskar came in to tell us that the Committee was ready for us, and the four of us—Bhaskar, the Chief, Kelkar, and I—went down the long, hushed, white-painted corridor to meet the inquisition.

All said and done it went better than I'd thought. The apprehension in the faces around, or their laboured blankness, said loud and clear that they were near the end of their tether. The PM sat as usual at the head of the table, Mankekar to his left, and the rest in more or less random order along the sides of the long conference table. We seated ourselves close to the foot of the table.

The PM's face was drawn from sleeplessness, despite the medication he was under. He coughed a few times as we entered, an unhealthy, hacking cough that in a man past seventy could mean serious illness. Mankekar, sitting next to him, put out a hand as if to steady his old friend.

There was something touching about these two friends. I tried to imagine the two in jail together over fifty years ago, fiery young freedom fighters forging a bond that would last a lifetime. The PM had come a long way, of course, and so in his quiet way had Mankekar. A committed ideologue still, he commanded almost everybody's respect; in his ordinary cottons he looked like any man on the street, but in his eyes the fire that must have flamed in his youth still burned.

'The Chief of Army Staff has told us that you have worked out a plan of attack,' the PM began. 'He says you think you can carry it off if we all maintain the appearance of defeat.'

'Yes,' I said.

'Do you realize what this will do to the public?' he asked.

The voting public, you mean, I thought. 'Yes,' I said, 'but you can retrieve that if we succeed.'

'And if you fail? We will have been beaten comprehensively by a gang of criminals. How will I show my face to the public after that?' I kept shut. 'I hope you realize, Colonel,' he continued, 'that if we lose this battle we could tear the country apart. I know what you think. That we are fighting for votes. That I am fighting for votes to keep my place here. Yes, I am. I see nothing wrong in that. If that were all there were to it I would not speak to you in this fashion. But do you understand that what we are talking about is more than a simple vote-getting exercise? Do you realize that if those diaries fall into the wrong hands it could create an atmosphere of suspicion so pervasive that no one will be entirely free of it? We could stand to lose what little there is left here of the true democratic process. Do you understand?'

'Yes,' I said baldly.

He turned to Kelkar. 'And what do you think of the plan?' Kelkar cleared his throat before answering. 'Given that we can't let them get away with this,' he said carefully, 'and that we have to go in, it's the best we can do.'

'Aren't you confident it'll work?'

'Menon and I have both told you: no guarantees. We don't know enough about it to be utterly sure.'

'How sure are you?'

'I'm not sure it'll work, but I'm about as sure as Menon that it's the best thing to do.'

'And how sure *is* Menon?'

'Sure enough to be the first man in. In his place I'd do the same.'

He considered quietly for a while. The Committee awaited his pleasure. I became restless and found the junior minister for defence glaring at me as if to tell me to keep still. I ignored him. Then at last the PM spoke, to Kelkar. 'Let's have your plan, then.'

Mankekar held up a hand. 'Let the young man tell us. It's his plan, after all.'

I looked at him gratefully and waded right in with the

same dummy plan I'd told the Chief. They listened, the PM with faraway eyes, Mankekar sitting straight-backed in his chair, the others in postures that suggested extreme ennui in some and nervous attention in others. The PM seemed every now and again to have to jerk his attention back to what I was saying. The loss of his granddaughter had aged him beyond his seventy-three years that had sat so lightly on him until weeks ago. When I stopped, it was Subhash Varma, the junior minister for defence, who first voiced his opinion. 'I don't like this,' he said. 'It won't work. They'll see you coming if they're half as alert as you think they are.'

'I don't like it much either,' said the Chief, 'but we don't have much choice. I asked if we could go in while the transfer is on but both Kelkar and Menon say no.'

Varma spoke up once again, his voice compelling. 'How do we know there's no choice? Menon should have told us earlier. We could have called in the SAS from the UK or even the Americans.'

'I don't think they'd be able to come up with anything better,' Kelkar interrupted.

Varma glared at him. I could see that Kelkar had rubbed almost everyone around the wrong way. And then Mankekar spoke again, in that gentle voice of his that no one ever questioned. 'These men have done this kind of thing before,' he said, 'let's not forget that. They have experience, these two . . . they know what they're saying. Let them go ahead . . . That's what I'd say. But the last word is with my friend here. It's his granddaughter out there. All I can say is, give them a fair hearing.' Then he turned to us and added, 'And I would suggest you gentlemen tell us the whole plan. Not the bits you think we should know.'

The Chief's face flushed red, and his eyes seemed to bulge a little. The old man had seen through what Kelkar and I were trying—give the basics and withhold the entire plan. No one else had been sharp enough, certainly not the Chief. Kelkar looked at me and nodded. The hell with security, I thought. I took a deep breath and told them the crucial bit. 'There is a way we can get in with a much smaller risk of being seen. Behind the house is a pond that seems to be a natural barrier. We intend to use it. We will move into it at nightfall and stay there until it is time to attack. We will then be striking from a direction they don't expect anything from. There will be more cover as well. That's all.'

The PM looked at Mankekar. 'All right,' he whispered, 'let them go ahead. My granddaughter . . . she is in your hands now.' He buried his face in his hands for a moment, seeming almost to break down. Mankekar put his hand protectively on his shoulder and he straightened up. He looked at me with haggard eyes. 'You were right, Menon. The waiting is too hard. I thought I could do it but it's too much.'

Bhaskar ushered us out of the room, fussing like a mother hen, seeming busier now, and proud to be able to drive people away from the boss. The Chief, Kelkar and I went back to the anteroom where we had gone over the plan before the meeting. 'All right, gentlemen,' the Chief said, 'you have your permission. We'll set up the exchange for tomorrow evening, for dusk. We go in after the delivery, at two, in simultaneous attacks on the two sites. I'll call you if there are any developments here. Is there anything else you need?' When we shook our heads, he stuck out his hand to each of us in turn. 'All right, gentlemen,' he said, exuding distaste despite the polite words, 'all the best.'

On the way out Kelkar said, 'You haven't said anything about where they'll go to.'

'Not my job to speculate on that,' I said, 'but there are a few pointers. They plan to slip away one by one, at intervals. I suspect the ones who go first will take their payoffs with them: that's why they asked for the money and the gold in the first place. As each one that gets away reports that he's reached sanctuary, the next one will leave. My guess is it'll be an hour or more between departures. The last one to go will have the hardest job of all . . . And we won't know when the last one has gone. After the man who we think is the last one goes, we'll keep waiting, and when no one else emerges for a long time, we'll go in and find the hostages there.'

'So?'

'If they plan to pay off some of the men as they go, it means they've collected people together for this particular job. We should go looking for sources of such men. In other countries I'd look for mercenaries . . . But we've got none of those except in Kashmir, all those fellows from Afghanistan or wherever.'

'And where do they plan to take the diaries?'

'Not the faintest idea,' I said. 'They can put them in a bank vault somewhere and send people photocopies or whatever and threaten them to their hearts' content.'

'And won't the CBI men be able to take photocopies before they deliver the diaries? They'll begin their investigations based on the photocopies. The kidnappers will have to use the diaries before the CBI gets anywhere with its investigations.'

'Yes. But if the diaries contain what I've heard they do, the kidnappers won't need to worry about the CBI investigations. There are some heavy names in there, heavy enough to keep the CBI bogged down for years. The kidnappers will have all the time to use those diaries.'

'And how will they do that?'

'The chances are there's some information in those diaries that can be verified easily. They can just threaten to give it to a newspaper . . . I haven't thought about that yet.'

Bhaskar came running up. 'Two things,' he panted. 'We have news from the kidnappers. They accept the time for the delivery. Tomorrow evening is fine by them. And Mr Mankekar would like to speak to both of you.'

We went back to the anteroom where Mankekar was waiting, pale and tired but still spirited. 'Sit down, sit down,' he said when we entered. 'I find it hard to move around these days. Old bones, you know. I asked the favour of your time to speak to you about things my friend the Prime Minister cannot. You were asking him to decide on something that will affect the life of his granddaughter, and that he cannot do. I helped him out . . . You see, I have nothing more to do with politics, and she is more or less like my own granddaughter.

'You will do what is best for her, and if you need anything, you will let me know. I will be available at all times at this number.' He wrote the number for me, saying that it was unlisted and was used only by him. 'I will be available almost all the time, unlike my friend. And while I am not the PM, the ministers will all do as I tell them to in this matter. So do what you think best, and do it as best you can.'

'Yes,' Kelkar said, 'one of us will be in touch with you if we need anything. We might need your contacts for some equipment.'

'At this late stage . . . I'll do my best to get you what you need, if the need arises. Actually a better man for this is Varma, the junior man for defence He has contacts, but he will ask questions that I will not. So, keep in touch. And one last thing . . . I noticed there that you hesitated from time to time, Menon. Somehow I get the feeling you didn't tell us the whole plan. You're too much of an academic as a soldier to do anything so . . . so underprepared. I don't know your reasons for not telling us the whole plan but I would like to have them afterwards, when this is over.' Remarkably perceptive, the old man, and he'd done his groundwork well.

Bhaskar came in, carrying a fax of the kidnappers' latest note. The note had come in at the Bangalore office by mail, as before, enclosing a fraction of a currency note for identification. There were also photographs of the hostages—all alone, this time, heads and shoulders against a dull white background—holding recent newspapers, and answers to trick questions about the hostages' families.

'Bring in the ransom by late afternoon to the farmhouse,' the note said, 'in an open three-tonne truck to be parked at the gate, its rear facing the farmhouse.' Only one man was to be in the truck, the driver. He was to park the truck, come to the rear, and await further instructions. There was to be no one else around, and the driver had to be unarmed. The truck wasn't to be brought past the gate under any circumstances.

They mentioned, for the first time, how they planned to get away. After the counting and the verification, the members of their gang would begin to leave, in ones and twos. They would each report their getaway two to six hours after leaving, and then the next person or pair would move. All departing kidnappers were to be left strictly alone. If any of them spotted a tail they would be in touch immediately, with drastic results as far as the hostages were concerned.

Now they were telling us where they were, and how they'd get away. They were sure of getting away. Why?

Out in the corridor Kelkar said, 'It's like we thought it would be, the getaway. Where do you think they'll go?'

'God knows. If they time it right they might make it to Bangalore, to the international airport, and then to . . . Singapore, say? Or they might just disappear.'

'And what about the last bunch?'

'I wouldn't like to hazard a guess. They might have

something sneaky up their sleeves, or they might take one of the hostages as they go, and ditch her when they're sure they've made it. Or, like I said earlier, they might just leave without us knowing they're the last pair. They'll have planned on three hours in which to get away.'

He grunted his assent. 'We can't let them get away,' he said. 'Once they spread out we'll have too much on our hands. Anyway, leave that be. You have nearly three hours before your flight back . . . Will you go home now?' I nodded and he continued, 'I'll be there tomorrow for the exchange. If you're not available to supervise the exchange, I'd better be there.'

Kiran was playing some form of cricket in the lawns outside the block of flats when my jeep drew up by the fence. I told the driver to pull up to the side, hopped out of the jeep, and stood watching with some pleasure. It was once a rare sight, him playing, but now he went out to play just like any other kid. When you're recovering from a disaster the commonplace is reassuring. He was batting, with a bat almost as tall as himself, trying to swing as hard as he could at a tennis ball bowled to him by the eight-year-old from next door. One of the kids, the wicket-keeper, noticed me and waved, then said something to Kiran, pointing in my direction. Kiran looked around, saw me, and came running, the game forgotten. 'Hi!' he said from the other side of the fence, panting. 'Mummy never said you were coming!'

I reached over the fence and picked him up, hoisting him across it. 'Mummy doesn't know either,' I told him, putting him down on my side of the fence. 'You can finish your game and join us when you're through.'

'How long will you be here?' he demanded. The questions he asked were changing. Earlier he used to ask me when I'd be back.

'An hour or so, not more,' I told him.

'Wait for me, then,' he commanded, 'just a minute.' He ran to the fence and screamed something at one of the other kids—the gang-leader, I supposed—and bounded back, reaching for my hand. 'Let's go,' he said, 'Mummy said we'll have fried chicken for lunch.'

Sandhya was in the kitchen when we got to the flat. She opened the door and Kiran went in without wiping his shoes on the doormat. When she turned to yell at him, I sneaked in and grabbed her from behind. She gasped, shrieked, and whirled, and when she saw me her eyes opened wide in surprise. 'What are you doing here?' she asked, 'I thought you were in Bangalore or Kabini or whatever, playing St George to the kidnappers' dragon.'

'Came back for a meeting,' I replied. 'The brass, and the politicians. The PM's going out of his mind. Old man Mankekar's taken over from him for the time being. Fatherly presence and all that crap.'

'I don't like that old man,' she said. 'His halo's too shiny. Too good to be true, if you get what I mean.'

'Sure, but how did you know about him?'

'It's in all the papers,' she said. 'I get your secrets out of them, don't you know?'

'I don't get to read the papers,' I told her. 'Maybe the brass want us to stay in the dark.'

'Such shits they are!'

'Yes,' I said, 'and I thought about what you said the other day, about whether it's worthwhile, what I'm doing. Whether it's worthwhile doing it for this bunch of clowns. The answer is perhaps no. You were probably right. But then, that's all I know how to do . . . that's all I like to do sometimes. I don't know if I can get back to a more normal life now. So unless I'm told to do something I can't stomach, like murder and mayhem in an orphanage, I'll just keep going.'

Her smile congealed as I reached the end of my little speech. 'At least you agree it's not worthwhile doing it for them,' she said at last, 'but do you understand what you just said?'

'Obviously not if it's something as serious as you think it is,' I said. 'So tell me.'

'The thrills of the job, that's what it comes down to. They seem to count more than I do to you, more than family. The only thing is that I still believe it's not for the thrills that you do this, otherwise I'd have walked out on you by now. I guess we'll just have to learn to live with it, me with the worry each time you go out and you with the strife each time you come back. If you come back . . .' There were tears glinting in her eyes.

Enough of this, I thought, there wasn't time. It wasn't too bad, a few hours of strife every now and again was a small price to pay for a family. I grinned suddenly, taking her off balance. 'What are you so pleased about?' she asked angrily. 'It's not funny.'

'Nothing,' I said, 'I just thought an occasional scrap isn't so much set-off against the pleasure of having you around.'

She softened a little, not much but just enough. When I left half an hour later, I was exhausted from playing with Kiran, wondering where he got the energy from.

chapter eight

Kelkar got to the aerodrome minutes behind me, grinning with pleasure at having got away from the PM's house. 'I feel a lot better now,' I told him. 'Your friend Mankekar seems committed. And powerful.'

'Yes,' he replied happily, 'he is. That's why I came away. He'll get us whatever we need. We can just ignore the Committee from now on.'

Back in Mysore, at the command post at Salt and Pepper's farm, I sat with a two-man team that had just come off observation duty. 'Any movement?' I asked.

'Nothing,' the senior of the two replied. 'We were there eight hours and the fellows didn't budge. It's still as a tomb. They must be sick, breathing that foul air.'

I went on a recce again, dressed as before in chauffeur's clothing, walking all the way to the pond, looking at the rushes growing by it and the scum floating on top. Salt and Pepper had said that it was ten feet deep towards the centre, even in summer. It was three to four feet deep at the edges, and the bottom sloped gently towards the centre.

We'd have to avoid the centre, where most of the algae seemed to be.

There were birds' nests along the edges of the pond. We'd move into the pond just after twilight, under cover of the racket of the birds coming home. Their squawks of alarm at our sudden presence wouldn't be substantially different from their usual cries at returning home.

The numbers that could hide in that pond were limited. Eight men, perhaps ten at the most. Enough, with back-up right behind to barge in at the first sign that we'd been discovered.

Back at the command post I worked the plan through with Kelkar once again. 'We move at dark, into the reeds at the edge of the pond. We'll have cover there, unless they have a man watching all the time with NVGs.'

'You plan to go in early?' he interrupted.

'No. Late. We'll get into the pond at dusk and stay there. If we move in later we'll disturb the birds and they'll make a racket, which might warn them.'

'And when you get out of the pond, won't you disturb the birds?'

'Not as much as on the way in. We'll drive some of them away, and we'll only have to move from the fringes of the pond into the coconut plantation. Much less disturbance than moving all the way along the edge of the water.'

'How long do you plan to hang around in the pond? Will you be underwater?'

'We'll be at the edge of the pond, where you can see those bushes. We might not need to go underwater but we will if required. Breathe through tubes, and so on. We'll have to be there four hours, maybe five.'

'That's asking a lot, isn't it?' he asked, frowning. 'Spending that long motionless and then bursting out, I don't like that much. Only the snipers can do that kind of thing.'

'I'm not taking many men in,' I said. 'Ten can get into the pond without being noticed, I think, so that's the number of men going in. We'll have as many snipers among them as possible. And it isn't that they'll have to be motionless. A little movement now and again won't matter.'

'Ten's far too small,' he objected. 'If you want to make three prongs you'll need at least fifteen.'

'Two prongs. I had a good look at that tile roof. It's slippery, there's moss growing all over it. We can forget about vertical envelopment. We'll have one bunch to the front door, another to the back. The back-up begin their run in at the first noise from the house. They shouldn't take more than twenty seconds to get in.'

'How will you make sure the teams get into the house simultaneously?' he asked. 'One of them will have to leave early, the ones going in at the front.'

'Right. We'll have them acknowledge when they're in position. We'll have them go up to the building low—crawl up there and then get to the front along the walls, keeping below window height—unless there's a lookout visible. Since there hasn't been one so far I don't think we'll have one tomorrow.

'At the front door the team signal their arrival and then everyone moves in. Both teams should be past the door in three seconds, and by then the back-up can begin to move in, once the noises begin. Have the searchlights come on at the same time. Dazzle the bastards. Blind anyone who's using NVGs.'

'And once you're in?'

'We don't know enough about the inside of the house to tell for sure, especially the first floor. There's a big room as you enter along the front, then another, and past that a corridor, just before the courtyard. That's where Salt and Pepper say the staircase is. It's two rooms away from the kitchen. We'll have three from the front team and two from the rear go up the stairs.'

'And where do you think the hostages are kept?'

'Upstairs. And we'll have trouble getting there because the staircase is so far away from the doors. We'll have to blast our way in, which is why I want the searchlights on the moment the noise begins. To confuse them.'

'It's risky.'

'To use your own words, do we have a choice?'

'What about booby traps?'

'There's probably at least one. Remember, when I went up there Hairy Face opened the door, but didn't let us look inside? Probably because he didn't want us to see the lead for a trap inside—a trip-wire, or something that would be incongruous in that house. So it's a safe bet that the front door was booby-trapped, possibly with a Claymore. It might still be trapped, but I doubt it since after we deliver the ransom they'll have to move around, carrying stuff. So chances are the traps, if there are any, will be disarmed by the time we go in. In any case, we'll go in through the windows, which I don't think will be booby-trapped. And finally, if the lead team fail to make it, the back-up will, past the booby traps.'

He gave me a rare sidelong glance. 'You got that, did you?' he asked.

'Yes.' What he meant was that if we didn't make it we'd have to make sure the other side didn't either, so that the diaries would be destroyed.

'Will you go in with the lead team?'

'Yes. At the front door. Window, actually.'

'You're getting a little old for this kind of thing. Thirty-eight, aren't you? Make this your last.'

'Speaking from experience?'

'I am. I was in good shape at your age but I couldn't recover quickly enough from injuries. A blow on the head that you'd have got over in ten seconds three years ago will take you a minute to recover from now. If you go in there and bump into something you'll be disoriented too long to retain command if something goes wrong. You understand?'

'Yes.' I'd had the same feeling lately. A wrench, not entirely unmixed with relief.

'Still think your old friend the Grenadier did this?'

'More so. If not him, someone trained like him, to use whatever the land offers. Fairly sophisticated, painstaking, got an eye for equipment, got the training to use it. Who else could it be?'

There were plenty of men out of the three Para Commando units looking for work if you knew where to find them. They did their three-year stints with 1, 9, or 10 Para, and then reverted to their original units. Some of them took early retirement and went into industry, mostly in jobs managing large numbers of men. And then there were the officers who took the commando course just like that, without ever joining the Paras. It could have been one of those.

It could also have been a foreigner. A Pakistani? I doubted it. That trail would lead straight back to ISI and Gul wouldn't like that. He had his own serpentine way of doing things. He would have borrowed someone from an intelligence service, and there were many of those, the Libyans for instance, willing to lend.

There could be combinations as well. There could be a foreigner getting the idea of the ultralights and a local man doing the rest of it. That seemed the most likely. But there had to be someone behind these professionals. Perhaps it would lead all the way back to ISI after all, but there had to be someone in this country paying those guys off.

Who?

I called up the company commander, Major Ranbir Singh Arora, and the platoon commander, Lieutenant Nazir Rahman Bhuiyan, our sole Assamese, to pick the teams for the operation. Two teams of five men each, led by Bhuiyan and myself, would go in through the pond. Arora would wait in the wings with the back-up team. With Bhuiyan and myself, the total in the pond would be twelve, and the back-ups would number thirty. More would overpopulate the house.

The twelve in the pond would all leave the water together—at five-second intervals—to gather at the corners of the rear of the house. My group would then head for the front. When we were in position we'd signal the other group waiting at the rear of the house and then we'd go in. One man would blast the shutters off and move aside for the others to go in. The back-up team would begin to move in from the perimeter at the moment the windows were blasted, and Kelkar had organized for two huge searchlights mounted on trucks, and the headlamps of as many other vehicles as could be crammed into the area, to be aimed at the house when the back-up moved in.

I went over the plan twice with Arora and Bhuiyan, guilty at its sketchiness, apprehensive at sending them into something with so little knowledge of what awaited them, and then waited for the inevitable questions. The first came from Bhuiyan. 'What's the layout of the house? Where's the staircase?'

I pushed forward a scribble Salt had made a few days ago when I asked him the same question. 'Here you are,' I said, 'but it could have changed. There was some extensive remodelling done a couple of years ago and these guys don't know about it. So we're going on hearsay.'

'How come?' he asked.

'That building's been put together over a couple of generations, a room here, a wing there. It's pretty chaotic inside, if you get what I mean. There's a courtyard here, enclosed on all sides, but we can't get there without going over these tiled, sloping roofs.' I pointed out the corridor, and the bedrooms, the old granaries, and the staircase, and said, 'The bad news is that you'll have to keep your eyes open when you go in. We go in here,' I pointed out the window in the front room that would be closest to the door leading to the staircase, 'and here, the kitchen window, so that we can get to the top as quickly as possible. I'd say the hostages are on the first floor but we can't be sure. Make sure you check everywhere. We'll have six men—three pairs—go in on each floor.'

'What do we look for?' asked Ranbir.

'That's the good news. The hostages are both girls, pretty young things. Anyone else is a hostile. You disable hostiles, down them if you have to. No one must leave, but that's not your problem: the back-up team will take care of it, and the cordon that we'll put around the place.'

'How many hostiles should we expect?' This from Nazir. Keen, bright, very laid-back outside and very focussed inside. He'd been a tremendous footballer and then he'd given up the game to join the Army.

'I don't know. A minimum of four . . . maybe six. Not more than twelve in any case. Chances are that they'll be up when we go in, but they probably won't be expecting us.'

'What weapons do they have?' Ranbir again. Quiet, hard and unflappable. A bulldog.

'Expect sub-machine guns, grenades, explosives, booby traps. They might have mined the doors, that's why we go in through the windows.'

'How do you know they've mined the doors?' asked Nazir, pushing his thick hair off his forehead. He looked too young . . . No, not young. Too unlined. He didn't seem to have the mileage, but that was deceptive.

'Supposition. They know how to. They have reason to. They don't use the doors much. Only one guy has come out there yet. And they probably have an RPG-7D in there with them, though if they let it off they'll crisp everyone inside: them, the hostages, and us.'

'What about that other place in town?'

'Another team. That's why I called only the two of you in here. The other one's a simultaneous op with independent logistics.'

'Simultaneous?' Ranbir's eyebrows rose. During lectures and training sessions his superiors, myself included, had drilled it into him that simultaneous operations were murder. Now he was throwing that in my face.

'Afraid so. But that's smaller, simpler. When we go in here they go in there. Can you think of an alternative?'

He looked at the doodles and few briefing sheets in his hand and slowly shook his head. 'It gives me the creeps,' he said. 'All of a sudden I understand your lecture a whole lot better. It's more than a matter of synchronizing your watches and tally-ho the bastards . . .'

'Good,' I said, 'we'll leave it at that for the time being. But bear one thing in mind. I expect them to shift the third hostage in here some time before the deliveries begin. If they do, I'll pass the word on to you immediately and you can tell the men. You will then have a problem identifying the hostage. We have photographs of him the way he was before the kidnap, and made-up photographs of what we think he looks like now. We'll pass those around.'

'Right, chief,' they said in unison.

'One last thing,' I said. 'During or after this operation, if you come across a set of diaries, hang on to it. There are four volumes, with midnight-blue rexine covers, cheap-looking, large—A4 size—and thick, each about an inch thick. You know what they are. If you get anything that looks like those diaries, pick it up, stick it in your pack, and hand it over to me. If I'm unable to take it from you for any reason it goes only to General Kelkar. The men are not to hand them over to anyone else . . . At any cost. Clear?'

'The famous Mehta diaries,' Nazir said, grinning. 'Maybe I'll keep them. My retirement fund.'

I grinned back. 'The brass'll send me after you, then.'

He rolled his eyes in mock horror. 'Fifty-fifty, chief,' he said, raising his hands in supplication, 'and I'll do all the dirty work. All you'll have to do is sit at home and collect your weekly suitcase full of cash.'

Over the next ten minutes we went over the plan once again, this time reviewing the communication procedures.

'Enough,' I said, 'get out of here. I've got the other bunch to brief. Send Simon in as you go.' Simon D'Costa's was the other platoon here, and would take the second house. Simon arrived minutes later and his briefing was shorter and simpler. I had the plans unrolled on the table and he absorbed everything with no questions and when I was through, went happily off to pick six men to do the job with. Simon was unimaginative but reliable. You could leave something like this to him and forget all about it.

I looked outside and found it pitch dark. Night had come and I hadn't even noticed it. I was tired. All that travel, the meeting, the tiff with Sandhya. I tried to sleep and slept badly. I still felt uneasy about this operation. Uneasy and nervous. I'd read my share of fiction built around kidnaps and terrorists. Most of it was American and populated by supermen who could drink anyone under the table, lived on expensive cigarettes and black coffee, and yet on the crucial day, without the least preparation, they would blow their way into a building and get hostages out unhurt. I wished I could be like one of those men, but I'm small and compact and ordinary. And I was thirty-eight. A superman or two would really come in handy now, I thought sourly . . . I shouldn't have got into this at all. Should have continued as a simple infantryman and retired as a Brigadier with a modest pension, with no moral issues to ruin my sleep . . . And no Sandhya, either.

Nazir woke me at midnight. There had been movement about the house, he said. Hairy Face had just left. Did I want to stay up while waiting to see what the police said he did?

'No,' I said, 'he was going to fetch the other hostage here.'

There was no need for concealment now, so if anyone tried to stop him he'd use force. It would be wise to tell our watchers, if they were in contact, that they were to avoid confronting the man.

I tried to go back to sleep but couldn't. Half an hour later Nazir was back. 'He's brought the hostage, chief,' he reported. 'The police have a positive identification. You were right, they made no effort at concealment. The same car that he used last time, the white Maruti.'

'How many men does he have with him?' I asked.

'Two. That's Hairy Face, the hostage, and two others.'

'In that case you can expect at least nine hostiles in the building.'

'No simultaneous ops, chief,' he said. 'Do you want to talk to Simon?'

'Yes,' I said, 'fetch him in.'

Simon came, stolidly awake, prepared for anything. I told him his operation was cancelled, as expected, and his men would now be used for back-up. He was mildly disappointed but didn't show it.

I got a cup of coffee and sat back to think about this new situation. Interesting, there being only two men with the CJ's son in that house. Two men can't watch a prisoner round the clock and they wouldn't want the prisoner to be tied up all the time. In any case, physical restraints were clumsy—ergo, they had the hostage drugged, which meant some medical knowledge. They might have injected him with a sedative, or mixed powdered Nembutal or whatever in his food. They knew what to give him, and how much. Since they hadn't stirred from the house they must have arrived prepared for all that.

I totted up the pluses and minuses once again. The biggest plus of them all was that there wasn't going to be a simultaneous operation. To counterbalance that was the fact that there was a third hostage in the house and one whom we might find hard to identify. Of the two men who had moved into the site, one would join the defenders, which meant the odds against us were a little heavier now, since I couldn't increase the number of men on our side.

I spoke to Kelkar who had woken up. He agreed with me on the odds, yawned, said he was relieved about calling off the simultaneous bit, and went off to organize a police cordon about the house, now that we knew they wouldn't be going anywhere until after the delivery of the ransom.

The police cordon was one of the sore points that had evolved over the past two days. The SOF contingent wasn't around to cordon off the site to make sure no one got away. We didn't have the numbers for it. The Karnataka Police were asked to do it for us, but the idea of standing guard while we went in didn't suit them. They had finally agreed to the idea of forming the cordon, but only with much dissent. They were also supposed to turn the lights on when we went in but I doubted if they would do so with the kind of split-second timing we would have liked to have.

So now the area was sealed off except for the people who would deliver the ransom. We waited through the long, hot day, clouds overhead promising rain but delivering none. The cordon, visible from within the farmhouse, didn't seem to upset the kidnappers, who seemed to be utterly unflappable.

The booty arrived at half past six, a little before dusk. Dark, at this time of the year, came at a quarter past seven. Lights came on in front of the house as the truck arrived, an olive green Army Toyota. The driver drove slowly past the gate, stopped, and backed up until the rear of his truck was ten feet beyond the gate, as instructed. He jumped down from the cab and walked up to the gate, a slim young Lieutenant from a unit of the Madras Engineering Group.

When the driver was midway up the drive the door of the house opened and out came the first man we'd seen there since Hairy Face. He was slim, too, dressed, as far as we could see, in dark, sombre clothes, the shirt tucked neatly into the waistband of the trousers. He had a white scarf wound around the bottom half of his face, and another over his forehead and hair. I could see his ears through my field glasses and they weren't hairy. He was about five nine, the same height as the driver, and he wore shoes and gloves, and seemed very fit. There was no way I could tell his age but from his confident, quick stride he seemed a young man. He was also probably a runner, for his legs were long, and his ankles spring-loaded. And he was unarmed.

One of the shutters of the window next to the front door opened a couple of inches and from it poked a muzzle. A rifle muzzle with a cup-shaped attachment, meant for firing a grenade. It was pointed straight at the truck. Any funny stuff and all hell would break loose. These boys played rough.

In the back of the truck were laid suitcases, whole rows of them. Plain suitcases, all black, as the kidnappers had specified: no fancy armoured boxes. There must have been two dozen of them. They had made our job difficult. By asking for a mixture of currencies—all used—and bullion they'd made it hard for us to put chemical tracers on. It made it tougher on them as well, since it slowed down the counting process. I was pretty sure they'd do a random check and leave it at that: the government had said repeatedly that there would be no hanky-panky.

The masked man looked at the row of suitcases, then asked, in sign language, where the diaries were. The Lieutenant pointed at the cab of the truck and said something. The man signalled him to bring out the diaries. The Lieutenant opened the door of the cab, reached in and pulled out a black briefcase. He handed it over to the masked man, who tried to open it and failed. He handed it back to the Lieutenant, who inspected the combination lock under the handle of the briefcase, twiddled it, and got it open. Mask took it from him, looked at the contents, nodded, and moved off towards the house while the Lieutenant waited.

Mask disappeared into the house and emerged moments later, empty-handed. He walked up to the truck once again, signalled the Lieutenant to take one of the suitcases—he pointed it out—and made a follow-me sign. The Lieutenant carried it along until just outside the door of the house. Mask stopped him, took the suitcase, and indicated to him to get another suitcase from the truck. Only after the Lieutenant was halfway down the drive did Mask open the door, drop the suitcase in, and shut it again.

What did they have in there that they didn't want us to see? Or were they just skilled at keeping us nervous?

The Lieutenant came back with a second suitcase. Mask

took it from him, and as before, waited for him to go halfway down the drive before putting the suitcase inside the door. There was someone else inside taking the suitcases away to check their contents.

It was slow, but it worked, and it bugged the hell out of me. It became too dark to see and I swapped my field-glasses for NVGs but they were no use. A quarter past seven.

Time to move. There were already birdcalls from the pond.

I ran round to the back, sweating after an hour in my body armour, not liking the thought of waiting it out in the pond. I hadn't thought of it that way.

The twelve of us collected and each checked his buddy's equipment list—sub-machine gun, flash-bang and fragmentation grenades, ammunition, knife in a sheath on the calf, rope, bomb for the door, pouch of drinking water, NVGs, walkie-talkie, sidearm with its magazine full and nothing up the spout, fireman's axe. The stuff to be kept dry was in a separate watertight compartment that would be zipped open when we emerged from the water. Then we added on the one piece we were carrying for the first time—a facepiece of the kind used by skin-divers, with a breathing tube a foot long, to sustain us during our time in the pond. It interfered with the helmet so we carried that separately. The facepiece would be discarded as we left the pond.

General Kelkar appeared from nowhere. We went through the radio routine once again, and I could see the old warhorse responding. From this moment we were in his hands and I knew he'd keep everyone else off our backs until the back-up team went in. He shook hands with each of us before we left, uncharacteristically nervous, but said nothing at all as we slipped out of the command post to the wall at the boundary.

We ran out one by one, at ten-second intervals, from behind the wall to the pond. There was irregular ground between and we used it for cover, as we did the reeds and rushes. We slid smoothly into the water, invisible in blacks. They wouldn't spot anything but the movement even with NVGs and that too only if they concentrated. And the pond was the last place where they'd be concentrating right now.

The birds squawked in alarm as the lead man moved in. We were late. They had already settled in some ten minutes ago. I'd cut it too fine, watching the exchange. But there were some crows here, oddly enough, cawing loudly. There were more heading for the trees next to the house, also cawing loudly. They nested there. Their cawing would cover some of the noise from the pond. The birds squawked for each of us, their indignation growing. I sympathized with them, as I would with any householder who finds his territory invaded at bedtime. The squawks died down as we got into the water, picking a point among the reeds.

The water was slimy and choked with algae. We'd seen the algae floating on top but never imagined they would be so bad at the bottom. The ground was mushy and we couldn't put our feet down with any ease. There were small currents that shifted us sideways, movement that with a firm floor we wouldn't have noticed.

And then a water-snake stung me. Its teeth didn't get past the Kevlar and it wasn't really venomous, but it was a nuisance. If it bit someone on some exposed part of the body it would be disastrous. Salt and Pepper had warned us about these little snakes but we hadn't paid much heed. Now, standing in four feet of dirty water on a mushy mixture of vegetable matter and soil I wished we had. Any snake that could get its fangs past our combat boots or Kevlar deserved it, I thought irrelevantly.

The bird noises had started again. There must have been eggs in some of the nests in the vicinity. The females kept cawing and clucking and at one time I thought I saw one peck at one of our men.

The clouds gathered above. I wished for rain. The immersion wouldn't hurt the weaponry in the short run, but for a moment I wished for Austrian Aug sub-machine guns rather than our Ingrams, because the Augs could actually be fired from underwater.

In the blazing heat of a June day the clouds brought relief from the sun but now, at night, they just added to the humidity and made things infinitely worse. They trapped the heat, and in the water, in our body armour, we sweated copiously. The pouches of drinking water would take care of immediate needs but within half an hour of entering the water the idea of being in there for another three hours was already unbearable.

The Kevlar wasn't porous. We broiled inside it, sweated, and grew restless and edgy. Worst of all, we itched all over, and there is no way you can scratch yourself through Kevlar. And the filthy water seeped in, not through the Kevlar but through the gaps between armour and boots, through socks and through the ends of sleeves, until, crouching silently in the dark, I wished we had come in without the armour.

Time passed wearily by, the sheer discomfort of each second etched clearly and deeply on my mind. We should have gone in from the front. After what seemed to be a week had passed I lifted my wrist out of the water to look at my watch and found it was only three-quarters of an hour. It was getting serious now. There was no way we could stay in there for another few hours and be immediately effective afterwards.

Ten minutes later a strong breeze sprang up from the south and brought thunderclouds rumbling overhead. The heat eased for a while and when the wind decreased it rose again, and there was the smell of dust in the air.

Thunder crashed in the sky, and a great jagged blue-green tongue of lightning lit up the ground.

Time to go. I moved slowly over to a shallower part of the pond, unzipped my waterproof case and pushed the transmit button. 'Red One calling Homebase,' I whispered. 'Come in, Homebase. Over.'

The answer was equally soft. I almost missed it in a roll of thunder. 'Homebase to Red One. What's up? Over.' Kelkar at the command post.

'Red One,' I said, 'shall we go in with the thunder? More cover. Over.' The thunder might cover the bang of our entry, win us those few crucial seconds we needed to get to the staircase. An odd flash of lightning might well expose us to an alert lookout, but lightning flashes weren't long enough for someone to spot a camouflaged man. Best of all, they made NVGs useless. The lookouts wouldn't use NVGs now. Our own NVGs would be useless on the way in, but with eyes accustomed to the darkness we could see just enough to make our way. Salt had shown me the electricity meter and the mains, placed outside the house, and we'd turn the power off as we went in . . . This was the time to go. My adrenaline was on. Please say yes, I thought.

Kelkar answered in seconds though it seemed an age to me. 'Red One, I need to check,' he said, 'give me a minute.' I heard him speak to someone in the background, then to Ranbir waiting with the back-up team, and then he was speaking to me again. 'Red One, we have a problem. No searchlights, incomplete cordon. Repeat, no lights, weak cordon. Over.'

'Homebase, it's still worthwhile. Give me a green. Over.'

'Red One,' came the answer, 'you have your green. Go with the thunder. Back-up is in place.'

The wind strengthened once again, damp and cool. It would rain soon. I signalled the others to prepare to go, heard small splashes and bird noises once again as they moved to the edge of the pond. A large streak of lightning split the sky overhead and thunder boomed, and I heaved myself out of the water and splashed on wet boots to the cover of a small shrub twenty feet away. The others would also be moving now but I couldn't hear them. From far away came the noises of engines revving up as police vehicles ground into action behind the cordon that I hoped would be in place. I bent to leave the facepiece behind, put the helmet on and ran along the ground, along the edge of the pond, to the rear of the house, squelching through the mud, sliding in the wet, stumbling through the dark.

The NVGs were useless and they cut off peripheral vision, but the lightning saved us. It flashed only for a tiny fraction of a second but the image lasted long enough for us. I pushed the NVGs firmly up on my helmet and ran into the coconut plantation, the darkness of a tall palm looming suddenly up. Another dozen paces and I was at the next palm, and just three palms away was the overgrown area abutting the rear of the house. The white walls showed faintly and I felt a lot happier now that I'd got my bearings properly.

We assembled at the rear of the house, along the wall, staying low, out of sight of anyone looking out of the window. I led off again along the side of the house, on probably the safest leg of the journey in, and just three minutes after leaving the pond I was below the window we planned to blast through.

I crouched under the jutting eaves, breathing a little heavily, to collect my wits before going in. On my waist was a beeper. One press on a button would tell Ranbir and Kelkar that I was in position, two that I was moving in, and one long beep to tell them something had gone terribly wrong. One man in my own team had moved some five yards away, to the meter outside the house. The wires were sheathed in tubing but that wouldn't stand up to the axe my man wielded.

I pressed the beeper once, waited a minute, then pressed it twice, firmly. I moved away from the wall as my buddy stuck the explosive charge to the window frame and joined me on the ground.

Three seconds later the explosive went off, leaving the window frame hanging loose. At the same time the lights in the house went out and I leapt forward, caught the edge of the frame in my hand and ripped it off. It came away easily, and through the cloud of dust that the explosion had raised I led the way into the house.

We didn't need the NVGs inside the house. Though the power had been cut off the inverter ran two of the lights on the ground floor. As I went in I saw the corridor directly ahead. According to Salt's directions, the staircase was in the corridor, to the left.

A man appeared in the doorway, outlined against the light behind him. I fired a three-round burst from the Ingram that flung him out of the doorway into the corridor behind and then I was past him and at the foot of the stairs.

The staircase was an old wooden one with steps almost a foot apart, narrow and clumsy, full of shadows, almost a ladder. At the top stood another man raising a handgun to point at me. Another figure running in through a second door to the corridor distracted his attention for a moment and I shot him in the throat. The bullet should have knocked him backwards but he fell forward, onto me. I swerved out of his way and went up the stairs three at a time.

A passage on top, and a light on in one of the rooms, showing as a yellow line at the bottom. The sound of small-arms fire through the closed door, then the sound of a long-drawn-out moan.

We hadn't made it in time.

I kicked the door in and it swung open with a bang. There were two armed men inside turning to face me and the Ingram in my hands was already firing, almost as if programmed to do just that. They were firing too, and I felt two massive blows on the chest that knocked me down and back into the wall. I kept my hand on the trigger of the Ingram until its magazine was empty.

When I pushed myself off the floor and changed the magazine the men were on the floor, dead.

So were the girls. Both were dead, their throats slit. They had been shot afterwards; the bullet wounds weren't bleeding at all but their throats had bled dreadfully. There was more blood there than I thought would have flowed in the few seconds it had taken me to get up the stairs.

Someone had known we were coming.

More gunfire from behind, then the crump of a flash-bang grenade.

In a blind rage I turned and ran out of the door into the second of the rooms, where my buddy must have gone as he came up behind me. More carnage, and in the air the acrid smell left by the grenade. Three dead men on the floor—one helmeted and black-clad, a knife sticking out of the back of his neck, the others on their backs, shot to rags. My buddy was gone.

The man with the knife. He was still at large.

I took in all this in one long sweep of the room, then went into the third room on top. A table here, one man sitting slouched at the table. Piles of currency before him, neatly stacked. This man's throat, too, had been cut. On the far side of the man was something dark, on the floor. Another man, also dead, I didn't know how.

From outside, the sound of men moving in. The back-up team were on their way.

Out of the corner of my eye I saw movement. A cupboard door creaked open an inch. I stepped over to it, flung the door open wide. And there on the floor was a pile of blue books.

The diaries.

I picked them up and stuffed them into my pack.

I heard a noise behind me and turned and saw an SOF man in the doorway. 'I have the diaries,' I told him, 'the hostages are gone. There.' I pointed. He turned to check.

I looked down at the man on the floor, who had apparently been verifying the diaries. Why was he down? There was another sound from the doorway. Another SOF man, short and broad, somehow incomplete in his combat rig, looking for me. There were sounds from downstairs. The back-up team had arrived. Nothing more for me here. I bent for another look at the dead man, wondering why he had been killed. I only felt the single blow to the back of the neck that laid me out.

chapter nine

I came to in the ambulance, conscious of the jerkiness of its progress, disoriented and unable to tell where I was. I had a blinding headache and my chest was on fire, and my left ankle hurt. There was another stretcher in the ambulance that I could see if I turned my head as far as it would go . . . Why did it hurt so? Someone dressed in white leaned over the other stretcher. I must have moaned, for he turned around, and when he looked at me I tried to ask him for some water because my throat hurt, but no sound emerged. He bent over me and said, 'Just take it easy, sir, you'll be fine.' The voice was vaguely familiar. Luthra, the SOF medic. Why didn't he give me the water? I felt a prick in my arm and drifted off once again into the comforting darkness.

The next thing I knew I was in a white room. The ceiling fan swam slowly into focus in the grey light coming in through a window behind me and I saw I was in a hospital room. I heard the patter of rain on the roof. It was restful, that light and the sound of the rain, and I lay absorbing it for a while, then tried to sit up. A bolt of pain shot through my chest and I sank back, sweating. By the bed was an IV apparatus, a bottle upside down on top and a tube with a needle at the end, stuck in my right arm. They'd tied a splint to the forearm to keep it from moving around. A nurse in white marched in through the door, saw that my eyes were open, and left again. She returned seconds later with a doctor who poked and prodded me enough to wake me up thoroughly to the unrelenting reality of an aching chest, a throbbing head, and an ankle that seemed to be enclosed in something three sizes too small for it. I looked downwards and found my chest strapped up tightly, so tightly that I could breathe only shallowly. On the left arm was a light plaster cast. I glared at the doctor for having interrupted my rest but he ignored my glare and kept doing whatever he was doing.

'What's wrong with me?' I asked him, but he ignored the question. He finished his examination, said something to the nurse, and walked stiffly out of the door.

Now why would he do that? This was a Services hospital, I could see. They'd brought me to Bangalore, and I was alone. Perhaps he'd gone to call someone from the unit.

The nurse, meanwhile, took the needle out of my arm and wheeled the IV apparatus away. She came back in a minute with a white tablet and a glass of water for me. She showed me the switch for the bell on the bedside table, told me to ring for her if I needed anything, and bustled out. I lay back, the pain beginning to recede already. Those tablets acted fast.

The man who came in some minutes later wasn't from the SOF. He was a fortyish Major with Q branch and with him was a cold-eyed plainclothesman who introduced himself as Superintendent Padmanabhan of the CBI. 'Where am I?' I asked. 'And what's all this?' I'd been expecting the usual team of Intelligence men for a preliminary debrief.

Padmanabhan smiled briefly, with only his lips. His eyes remained icy. 'This is the Air Force Command Hospital, Bangalore. It is larger and better equipped than the Army establishment here. And let me be honest about why I am here. We are trying to get you in custody but the Army don't seem to want to release you so quickly. Otherwise you would have been under arrest. That's why I've come, to see if our action is justified.'

'What the hell for?' I said, trying to sit up, forgetting for the moment about the pain in the chest.

'Colonel, your raid ended in disaster. All three hostages died, as you probably know.' I didn't, though I knew the girls were dead. 'We also found the bodies of seven kidnappers. Five of the commandos who went in with you died, including Major Arora.' He paused for effect. 'And the diaries are missing. Not what you would call a successful operation, is it?'

His sarcasm bounced off me. 'But I got the diaries,' I said, 'I remember putting them in my backpack. I told one of my men I had them.'

'He told us.' Padmanabhan smiled again. 'He told us and died. We weren't sure whether he was dreaming. So you admit you had the diaries?'

'Of course I do. I just told you I had them in my pack. All four volumes . . . I checked only one of them but they looked right. The right size, the right colour . . . Didn't you find them in my pack?'

He shook his head. 'We found nothing in your pack that wasn't there when you started off. The diaries have disappeared. You had them, you say you put them in your pack, and they're no longer there. We didn't find them. None of your commandos has them. The kidnappers are all dead and as far as we know no one got out of the cordon. And we found no traces of the diaries in the remains of the house after it blew up. My men have picked out every single surviving object larger than a matchbox.'

'The house blew up?' I asked stupidly.

'Yes. Two of the men leading the back-up team died. It went up just as they entered. Didn't you know?'

I shook my head. All I remembered was that terrific blow to the head when I turned away from the door . . . And yes, there had been an SOF man there. 'I got knocked out before that,' I said, 'but I remember an SOF man there . . . Not the one I told about the diaries. He went off to investigate the girls, who I saw had been killed.'

'Did you have the diaries at this time, Colonel, when you saw this other SOF man there?'

'Yes,' I said, 'I remember thinking it was Subedar Kanwar . . .'

'Kanwar survived the raid. He was downstairs all the time . . . Colonel, I suggest you tell me everything that happened after you entered that farmhouse.'

'Before that,' I said, 'tell me how many men you found with their throats cut.'

'We found one kidnapper like that. One commando with a knife in his throat, inserted from the back. That was all.'

'The girls were killed that way, too. They were killed before the raid.'

'The bodies were too badly burnt for us to make out anything. They are with the specialists now, we will see what they say.'

'Do you remember the man who was knifed at Kabini? He died the same way.'

The doctor came into the room. 'Your time is up,' he said to the visitors. He stood beside me, felt my forehead and then my pulse. He called the nurse, who took my temperature, then offered me a tablet.

Padmanabhan waited until I'd swallowed the tablet, then said, 'Just a few minutes more . . . You know what this is all about.'

The doctor glared at him, then at me. 'All right,' he said, 'but if you're not gone in ten minutes I'll have my men throw you out.' He marched out again.

'You were talking about the man who was knifed at Kabini,' Padmanabhan said when the doctor had gone. 'What about it?'

'Same man,' I said. 'He did the same thing with the hostages and some of the kidnappers. And perhaps with my man, the one with the knife through his neck . . . And have you spoken to General Kelkar?'

'General Kelkar is in roughly the same position you are in, Colonel,' said Padmanabhan.

'You mean, you've got him locked up?'

'Not quite. But he's under house arrest. Confined to quarters I believe is the term. But we've more or less ruled him out since he wasn't involved in the raid itself.'

'I'd like to speak to him.'

'You can't, sir.' The Q Branch Major spoke for the first time. 'You're also confined to quarters. There's a guard at your door and an officer will keep you company through most of tomorrow until the order's withdrawn.'

'Will it be withdrawn?'

'We're working on it. The CBI have asked that you be taken into custody and the Army says no, so they worked out a compromise that'll keep you confined to quarters. The Advocate-General's branch are working on it. One of them will be with you tomorrow.'

'I'd much rather be under arrest. I can at least get out on bail.'

Padmanabhan laughed, a rasping, unpleasant sound. 'Not when we take you in. We're talking terrorism here, Colonel. No bail, no nothing. And we interrogate you.'

There was something terribly contrived about all this. 'Lay a finger on me,' I said for effect, 'and you'll be in trouble.'

He laughed again, bitterly. 'I wouldn't touch you, Colonel. In a day I'd have you in tears just speaking to you, asking you questions. Believe me.'

I kept shut. I couldn't get out of confinement except to

go to jail and there I wouldn't get bail. I considered trying to get a lawyer and gave up the idea. I thought back to the raid. So many people dead. It had been a massacre. The searchlights hadn't come on because I went in ahead of time and maybe someone had escaped; we never knew how many men there'd been.

'Are you willing to talk?' Padmanabhan asked.

'I'll tell you what happened during the raid, or before it,' I told him. 'I'll tell you the truth. As much of it as I know.'

'That'll do fine,' he said. 'Go ahead.'

'The doctor said ten minutes.'

'I don't care. If he throws me out I'll come back in here with a court order. Talk.'

'All right.' I reached out for a glass of water and my chest twinged. I couldn't move without evoking some protest from it. 'Give me some water,' I said.

He rose, poured out a glass for me. The Major seemed to feel a twinge of compunction. 'If you don't feel up to it, sir,' he offered, 'I'll see to it you're not disturbed until you're better.'

'Lying here worrying about it isn't going to leave me any better,' I said. 'If the Superintendent has the time to listen to me talking slowly he's welcome.'

The doctor returned. He'd swapped his whites for an Air Force uniform. He was a trim man with square shoulders, impatient and brusque. His shoulder flaps showed him to be a Wing Commander, equivalent to a Lieutenant Colonel, and the name-tag on his chest said

D.K. Bhowmick. 'Time's up,' he said, looking at Padmanabhan, 'want me to call the guard?' He looked tired and red-eyed and sleepless.

'I'm fine,' I said from the bed.

He glared at me. 'I suggest you leave medical judgments to me,' he said, then unwillingly added, 'sir.'

'What's the extent of the damage?' I asked. 'It makes sense for me to know.'

He hesitated. 'You've dislocated your left shoulder quite badly, you've got a cracked shoulder-blade, a cracked rib, a hairline in your left arm, concussion from a blow to the occiput, some lacerations and fairly comprehensive bruising over the chest and the back, mild burns on the right thigh, a sprained ankle.'

'I remember the blow to the head and the bullets aimed at my chest,' I said, 'but not the rest. How did it happen?'

'Impact damage. Probably after the blast. Something must have fallen on you. I thought at first that the concussion was also blast damage but it could have been inflicted earlier. Can't prove it either way. The pattern of bruising on your chest fits with your armour being hit by two small-calibre bullets on the left side. They'd have got your heart but for the armour.'

'Thanks,' I said, 'I'll talk to the Superintendent.'

He looked at me narrowly. 'All right,' he said, 'but stop the moment you feel light-headed. If your head feels worse, call me immediately. The sister will be in from time to time.'

'This is informal,' Padmanabhan said when the doctor

had left, 'but I can get a steno and everything else if you want to make a formal statement.'

'Any way you like,' I said wearily. 'I'll tell you what happened and you're going to get the same answers whether it's formal or not. But first, I want to get in touch with my wife. Tell her I'm all right.'

The Major looked at me unhappily. 'She's been informed that you're injured, that the injuries are not serious and that you're here . . . I'm afraid there's nothing more you can tell her.'

'I want to speak to her, dammit.'

He shook his head. 'I'll give her a note if you'll write it down,' he said, 'and 'I'll have to read it before I give it to her, of course. That's the best I can do.'

I shook my head in disbelief, and turned to the CBI man. 'All right,' I said, 'here it comes. The story.'

He nodded, settled back in his chair, and I told him. I told him first about the plan, about going in through the pond and not telling the Delhi Committee at first that we were planning to, fearing that there would be a leak. He interrupted me there. 'Why did you think there would be a leak?' he asked.

'The kidnappers seemed very confident . . . And knowledgeable. They wouldn't have been able to take the girls without prior information, and we had no indication that the source had been stopped. From that time on, everyone was suspect. And in the end our suspicions were borne out. If the forensic pathologists do their work well you'll find that the girls were killed in advance. They were probably monitoring our chats on the walkie-talkies. Did you find any equipment in the house? Scanners and such?'

'I'll ask the questions, Colonel,' he said.

'I thought this was informal.'

'It is. Otherwise we'd be recording everything said. Tell me, didn't you change the time of the raid? Advance it by two or three hours?'

'I did. It seemed right.'

'Why?'

'There was thunder in the sky, noise to cover our entry. There was lightning, which would make NVGs useless. And we were uncomfortable.'

'You thought it was better to go in then despite the fact that your back-up wasn't fully ready, and the lights weren't available, and the cordon wasn't foolproof?'

'I knew about the lights. The back-up was ready. I didn't know how weak the cordon was.'

'The lights were crucial, weren't they? An important element of your raid. Yet you took off without them. Entirely your idea. General Kelkar says he thought it best to rely on your judgment and gave his permission.'

I blew up. 'It was bloody hard, waiting in that pond,' I told him. 'Try sitting neck deep in dirty water in body armour on a warm day in the dark with snakes around you and you won't ask fucking moronic questions like that.'

'Don't talk to me like that.'

'I'll give you the respect you earn from me, and so far you've got none.'

The Q Branch man interrupted. 'Take it easy, sir,' he said, 'we can come back later.'

'If these guys are going to behave as stupid as this I'd much rather you didn't come at all,' I said, still on a slow burn.

'I can't help that, sir,' he said, 'they do what they like.'

'In that case,' I replied, turning to Padmanabhan, 'I'm going back to sleep. I've had it with you, barging in here and threatening me with all kinds of stuff, refusing me information that I'm too weak to use anyway. You ask questions and refuse to listen to the answers and then expect me to help you out. You must be out of your tiny bloody mind.' I rang the bell on the bedside table and the nurse appeared in under a minute. 'I'm tired, sister,' I told her, 'and my head hurts. Please call Dr Bhowmick. Right away.'

Bhowmick arrived in minutes, on a very short fuse. He took in the occupants of the room from the doorway and stopped in front of Padmanabhan. 'Outside,' he said, raising an arm to point at the door.

Padmanabhan lifted his hand in a peace sign. 'Listen, doctor, I can get back in here with a court order . . .'

Bhowmick exploded quite spectacularly. 'Come back in here without my permission and I'll have you put behind bars for trespassing on Air Force property. Talk of court orders again and I'll make sure you don't get to speak to my patient for the next six months. Understood? Now get out before I have you kicked out.'

Padmanabhan left glaring but with no further protest

while the Q Branch man looked unhappy. To hell with them, I thought, they could get their answers elsewhere. But the only way to clear myself was to find out what had happened. Those kidnappers had known we were coming. Someone had told them. It had to be someone at that table in Delhi.

The girls had been killed in advance, which meant that they'd never meant to leave them alive. God, it was a mess. I'd have to find out what had really happened and who was behind it. But I was stuck in this hospital and couldn't do much even if they let me out, not for the next couple of weeks.

I looked around the room. There was the bed, a standard hospital bed on a white-painted metal frame. By the bed was a small metal locker, the top of which was the table. On it were a lamp, a jug of water, a glass tumbler and bell-push. There was a drawer underneath. I stuck a hand in and found four strips of tablets and colourful capsules, the labels of some of which made some sense to me. Diclofenac sodium. A painkiller. Methocarbamol. A muscle relaxant. Remnants of years-old training stirred in my mind. Lectures in a classroom, from a fiftyish Medical Corps surgeon with gentle hands and burning dark eyes. 'You will have to learn to handle pain, gentlemen,' he had lectured, 'and I will tell you how to get the edge off pain. Enough so that you can function. Flee or fight.' He had talked that afternoon about NSAIDs—non-steroidal anti-inflammatory drugs—and made us memorize brand names and generic names, his voice droning on as we rested for a route march coming up that night. 'You should be able to procure supplies of these in any drugstore anywhere in the world, gentlemen,' he had said, 'otherwise all this is useless.' And finally, something on the nature of pain. 'When you break bones, it's the soft tissue around the break that hurts. Inflammation. Cramps. Bruised cartilage. That's what hurts. Not the broken bone.'

More memories stirred. 'A tablet will take time to get to your bloodstream. If you're in a hurry, buy liquid painkillers used for children. Drink half the bottle. Or use Alfapsin, an enzyme. Put a tablet under your tongue. Five minutes.'

Useful after I got out. I wouldn't be able to see a doctor there.

I put the medicines back in and tried to pull the drawer out of its slot. Nothing doing. It was flanged at the end and wouldn't come off unless I could get a couple of rivets off. In a corner a piece of metal glinted. I looked at it closely, found it a rectangular metal frame used to hold a mosquito repellent coil.

I tried the locker underneath. The door creaked open and inside were my watch—a gift from Sandhya, a digital multifunction watch that told the date and time and had a compass besides—and my old brown wallet. The watch was running, the wallet more or less as I'd left it, containing a couple of hundred-rupee notes and some change, a photograph of Sandhya and another of Kiran, and a card with my name, address, telephone number and blood type written on it. The watch said a quarter past six.

There was nothing I could use as a weapon if I needed to get out.

With more apprehension than I'd felt in a long while I looked at the darkening grey outside the window. My headache was getting worse again and I could feel my pulse pounding in my head. I remembered Bhowmick's instructions and rang the bell for the nurse. She seemed to have been just outside my room for she arrived in seconds with no signs of having hurried. 'Yes,' she asked, 'What is it?' In her eyes was the same weariness there'd been in Bhowmick's, and she sounded harassed despite the crispness of her uniform. They must have brought the casualties here.

'My head hurts,' I explained, 'and Bhowmick told me to call you as soon as my head got worse.'

She found a strip of tablets on the table by the bed, took out one and handed it to me with a glass of water. 'You were supposed to have that earlier but I didn't give it to you because you had visitors . . . And then I forgot. There's been so much to do.'

'They brought everyone from Mysore here, did they?' I asked.

'Yes, there was a burn case who died . . . Another with eighteen fractures. Dr Bhowmick worked on him for three hours in the OR.'

'Which unit?' I asked.

'Yours,' she said, 'first battalion.'

'What's his name?'

'Lieutenant Bhuiyan. A boy.'

'How is he now?'

'Stable. But still serious.'

'Is Bhowmick the Director of the hospital?'

'No, that's Air Vice Marshal Shastry. But he had been working without rest for too long so he went home to sleep. Dr Bhowmick will stay until AVM Shastry returns.'

I had friends in the Army Medical Corps but these Air Force doctors were strangers. I couldn't expect anything better from them than neutrality unless the police became egregiously accusatory. I realized all of a sudden that my bladder was full. I began to swing myself off the bed but gave up the movement less than halfway because of the overwhelming pain surging through the chest and shoulders. I lay back grimacing with an acrid taste in my mouth. The nurse, watching, understood why I'd tried to get up. She knelt, reached under the bed, and brought out a bedpan. 'Use this,' she said severely, 'you're not allowed to get out of bed. In any case I don't think you can, and even if you do you'll find it hard to walk because of your ankle.'

She turned busily away while I used the bedpan. 'Anything else?' she asked when I was through.

'Yes,' I said, 'can you get me the newspapers? For the last three days, if you can. I want to catch up.'

'We can't give you anything besides what's required medically,' she said. 'I'm sorry, but the Director's orders were quite clear.'

'Why?'

She shrugged. 'I didn't ask,' she said sarcastically. 'Do you want anything else? I have other work to do.'

I nodded dismissal and for an hour or so after she left experimented some more with my limbs. Slowly. I could move my right arm slowly and carefully without too much effort. Moving the left arm around produced much more discouraging results. The slightest jerk sent pains sweeping through my chest and upper back, thanks to the fractured rib and shoulder-blade. The dislocated shoulder felt all right, except for a dull ache, probably due to torn ligaments. I experimented with my left ankle and found I could move my foot around without too much trouble. The right side, my stronger side, was more or less functional but there were injuries all the way down my left side.

By the end of the exercise session it was really dark and I was bathed in sweat and my head was beginning to throb again. I rang the bell for the nurse. She bustled in and turned on the light and when she saw the damp bedclothes her earlier anger melted. 'Why didn't you call me earlier?' she asked. 'Is it hurting?' When I nodded she poured a glass of water and handed it to me with a tablet.

I swallowed it and looked woozily at her. Time to use her sympathy. 'Look,' I said, 'I can't just lie around here doing nothing. Get me a magazine if you can. An old one will do.'

She gave me a look that started off steely but softened a little by and by. 'I'll try,' she said, 'an old magazine or something. You must act as if you found it in the locker.' I nodded weakly. I'm not a good actor but there was no need to act. I was weak as a kitten. 'I go off duty at eight. Your dinner will be ready by about that time. I'll bring it to you with your dinner . . . Are you sleepy? I can get you dinner earlier, if you like.'

I shook my head. 'Eight is fine. And what time will you come after that, on your rounds?'

'The night nurse will come whenever you ring the bell,' she said, 'there will be someone on duty twenty-four hours. The night nurse will also check on you at midnight, and once again at four, when she goes off duty. Maybe more times, but only if there's medication to be given or if there is anything life-threatening.'

'And the doctor?'

'He'll come once, unless you call. Generally they do a round at night but the emergencies are all over and they're resting. I don't think he'll come at all. If he does, he'll come after midnight.'

Between dinner and midnight, then, I'd be left more or less alone. 'What can I do if the aches and pains get worse?'

She pulled the drawer open and took out the strips of tablets. She held out one, the only white strip in the bunch. 'Take one of these, with water. It'll make you drowsy very quickly. The effect will last for some time, an hour at least, I think. Don't take too many, not more than two in any case. If you have two you'll certainly go to sleep. But check with the nurse as well. That's what we're here for.'

'Thanks,' I said, 'and don't forget that magazine.'

She gave me an odd look. 'If you're in pain you won't be able to read. Maybe I shouldn't give you the magazine. You might strain yourself.'

'I slept through most of the day,' I told her, 'I need something to keep me going through the night. Please.'

I inspected the strip of tablets after she'd gone. There were eight left. A whole strip would have been preferable but I didn't dare ask for more. I knew how quickly the tablets worked, otherwise the timing would have been awkward. Timing was everything.

Under the sheets I tried moving my right side once again. The dull familiar pain returned and I knew I could handle it.

When I moved my left arm the pain was much stronger but that too was familiar and perhaps faintly less intense. If I had two tablets to take the edge off, I'd be a going concern for a very short while, until sleep overtook me. A shaky concern, liable to topple any moment, but going all the same. Enough.

But what would I do outside? I could call Sandhya. I had enough money to do that, to make a long-distance call to Delhi. And after that? And how would she help if the police were after me, as they surely would be when they discovered I'd left the hospital? Calling her would leave me broke and still helpless. And by morning they'd be watching her because she was one of the people I was likely to go to after breaking out of hospital.

If I got out of hospital I'd have to lie low for a few days, at least two or three. I'd have to hole up in a hotel and I'd have to see a doctor, maybe get some treatment. I had to have more money. I had very little, and no credit cards, no ATM cards, nothing . . .

I'd call my brother Gopi. He was in America, in Santa Cruz, across the bay from Monterey, where he worked part-time with a computer software manufacturer and spent the rest of his time experimenting with gadgets. Three years younger and infinitely brighter than me, he'd been in the US for nearly fourteen years now, working for eleven of those years in good jobs. He had all the money I'd need for now, and more if I needed some to chase Hairy Face and Co., but he had no way to deliver it to me, not here in Bangalore. He had no friends here and there was no way he could send it to a bank in my name.

I had no idea what to do with my freedom even if I got it. I lay back, feeling useless, beginning to sweat again.

I took a tablet off the strip and swallowed it with water. The nurse had left the tumbler full, covered with a coaster, thinking I wouldn't be able to pour it on my own. I tried it, to see if I could, and nearly dropped the jug, but managed it and set it back in place with a feeling of triumph. I stuck the strip under the mattress and lay back again. The tablet began to act and in the resulting wooziness came an idea that might not have occurred if I'd been thinking straight. I'd call that girl, Urmila, the hostage who had been released. I'd understood her, given her a prop, told her to contact Sandhya if she wanted to. She owed me.

The nurse brought my dinner on a tray at eight. Clear vegetable soup, a leg of chicken, slices of tomato and cucumber and onions, and a roll, with a cup of fruit salad for dessert. Better still, under the tray she held last fortnight's copy of *India Today.* A good thick magazine, of over a hundred pages. She asked me if I could eat on my own or if I needed help. I said on my own, and thanks for everything, and she put the tray on the bedside table and left, telling me as she did, not to strain myself.

I tucked into dinner with an appetite that had risen quite suddenly and unexpectedly. Ten minutes later I was gnawing on the chicken bone when the new nurse, who'd just taken over, walked in to check. She looked at the tray, found I'd polished off everything, nodded her head in approval, as if she'd expected to find the dinner half eaten. 'My head is beginning to hurt again,' I said.

'When did you last have a tablet for that?' she asked.

'Long ago . . . I don't remember.'

She looked for the strip of tablets on the table, didn't find one, then looked up a chart at the foot of my bed. She clucked indignantly, and went out to fetch another strip. When she returned, she took one tablet off the strip, and gave it to me along with some water, putting the rest of the strip in her pocket. Hard luck, I thought. 'The man on guard at the door,' I asked as I handed back the glass, 'is he Army or police?'

She gave me a strange look. 'Police,' she said. His presence obviously irritated her. 'Stupid man. He sits there and checks everything that we bring in here. As if you could get out even if he wasn't there at all. And I have to give him his dinner, and if he wants to go to the toilet he expects me to stand guard while he's gone.' She flounced indignantly out of the room, leaving me grinning inside at the strange mixture of maternity, authority and sentiment that nurses have.

After she left I examined the magazine. I rolled it up as tight as I could and hefted it experimentally. Lessons learnt under a hot sun—a permanent memory of a Marine Commando trainer squinting at a bunch of prospective SOF officers, demonstrating that bricks could be broken with a magazine. A magazine rolled up properly is heavier than its own volume of wood, and as hard. A blow on the head with one would certainly knock the guard out. What I had in my hand was a short truncheon. I was grateful the guard was a policeman, not an Army man: I'd have hated to hit a defenceless colleague, but a policeman was a different matter altogether.

I hefted the club in my right hand, then swung it down. The best angle, I calculated, would be if I were sitting up and the policeman kneeling beside me, offering his head or the back of his neck. I swung the club harder, ignoring the instant, intense protest from the region of my chest. No, I wouldn't be able to swing it hard enough without medication.

There were other things to do. I looked in my wallet for something I could use as a screwdriver. I found a small coin, an old round copper one-paisa coin that had been out of circulation for decades, a coin older than I was. I'd found it on the ground somewhere years ago, when it was already out of circulation, and had kept it because it reminded me of childhood. The milled edge was worn from the handling it must have taken in the four decades it had existed, but it was still in good shape. I tried it on the slot of the little screw on the back of the pendant switch for the bell and found it just too big to fit. I tried with my fingernails, but they were all trimmed to the quick and my fingers just slid off.

With the beginnings of panic I looked around for an alternative, and with a faint resurgence of hope, found one. The little frame of the mosquito repellent. I'd have to get out of bed to get my hands on it. A useful bit of practice for walking about once I got rid of the guard, I thought. I raised myself slowly, the pain in the chest quietened by the painkillers, and a minute later was sitting up straight, some of my weight resting on my right arm. I took a deep breath, waited for the pain to subside a little, then swung my right leg sideways off the bed. The bed was high, and my feet didn't touch the ground. I used my right arm to move my body closer to the edge until my foot was solidly in contact with the cold floor.

Another break. I was sweating again, from the pain and the exertion, and breathing heavily. Just breathing hurt now. I collected myself, swung the other foot down onto the floor. Then, slowly, I straightened up, all my weight on the right leg, holding on to the foot of the bed with my left.

The left ankle wouldn't support any weight, as I found out moments later, the hard way. I put some weight on it and had to hold back a gasp as a sharp lance of pain burst its way right up my leg. That little bit of metal looked unutterably far away. And I'd have to bend down to pick it up when I got to it.

I bent, and holding on to the bed with my right hand,

tried again, with similar though not identical results. It hurt less.

Not much less, but noticeably less, maybe only because I was better prepared for it. I let go of the bed, gingerly took one experimental step, and found with considerable delight that I was still on my feet.

From there on it got easier. The end was in sight and I made it in three steps to the frame. I caught it between two toes of my left foot and lifted it up into my hands. Turned to get back into bed, almost fell, saved myself with a hand on a chair-back.

Back in bed I waited for my breathing to return to normal, feeling the chill of drying sweat, smelling like a pig. I fit the edge of the frame in the slot on top of the screw and turned it with something like exultation.

That blasted frame was a total failure as a screwdriver. It bent and the screw didn't move. I bent the frame in two and tried again, and again it bent. I straightened it out, the pain beginning to show up again in my left arm, and bent the frame twice, into three layers. This time I held my breath as I applied it to the screw slot with trembling fingers, for yet another fold would make the thing too thick to fit into the slot.

It turned a quarter turn before sliding out of the slot and I breathed out loudly in relief. I tried again, and this time with the screw loosened a little the frame stayed in position for a full turn. The head of the screw was now no longer flush with the surface of the switch. I inspected my fingernails, found one that wasn't cut quite to the quick and applied it. It worked.

A minute later I had the wires exposed. I pulled one of them right off and put the cover back on the switch, not bothering to tighten the screw fully. I lay back in bed, exhausted, my hospital issue clothes soaked through with sweat. But the switch didn't work any more, that was what mattered. I tried the bell to make sure, listening for the faint ring. Nothing happened. I waited ten minutes for the nurse to turn up. She didn't.

Tablet time. I'd already had two in the past hour and a half but the exertions of the last half hour had more than nullified any effect they might have had, and driven away all traces of sleep. My watch showed half past nine. I swallowed two tablets together. Five left now.

Ten minutes later I was feeling remarkably detached from the assortment of aches and pain that had bothered me so much. My head dropped back on the pillow and I had to force myself awake. I raised my left arm six inches and some of the pain returned and with it wakefulness. I rolled up the magazine, getting it as tight as I could, until there was no slack at all. 'Guard!' I called weakly. Nothing. 'Guard!' I called again, slightly louder. There was a stirring outside and a uniformed policeman stood in the doorway, his head cocked to a side. 'What?' he asked.

I gestured to the switch on the table. 'I need a nurse,' I told him, 'the bell doesn't work.'

He eyed my sweat-soaked clothing with some trepidation. 'I can't leave my post to call the nurse,' he said. If I were genuinely ill and he refused to go he would be in trouble.

I sat up slowly to let him see that I was really wet all over. He took a step into the room and the apprehension on his face deepened. 'That's all right,' I told him reassuringly, 'don't go. Take a look at the switch. If you can make it work then there's no problem.'

His face lightened in relief and he stepped up to the bedside table. The switch was on a short lead and he had to bend over to examine it. I had tucked the end of the wire back into the switch so the problem wasn't apparent. As the guard bent, the light above cast a shadow over the switch. 'Kneel on the floor,' I said, 'otherwise you won't be able to see clearly.'

He knelt then, with his back towards me, the back of his neck exposed. Now.

I shifted, moved a little closer to the edge of the bed. I'd have just this one chance and if I missed it they'd make sure I never got another. I hated to do this to someone who was basically an innocent bystander, but had no real choice. I picked up the magazine, raised it high, and brought it down on that thin neck, just where it joined the skull, with as much force as I could muster.

I don't know what made him turn but turn he did as the magazine descended, without getting up. He took the blow on the side of the neck, a little early, and crumpled to the floor, dropping the switch with a clatter as he did. The sidearm in his holster, strapped to his belt to prevent anyone else taking it off, slid partly out.

I nearly fell off the bed myself, lost in the tidal wave of pain that the blow provoked. The swing itself hadn't hurt much but the impact jarred every nerve in my body and the magazine slipped from my hand as I collapsed, helpless, speechless with pain, the scream dying in my throat.

For a minute I lay there, gasping and retching, hoping he wouldn't recover first. He didn't. He lay still, his face strangely peaceful, as I struggled to regain some control over a body that seemed to have gone on strike, waiting for the black spots that floated in front of my eyes to disappear.

By and by my breathing returned to normal and the pain receded to the extent that I didn't have to gasp each time I tried to move. The black spots in my eyes settled down. I looked down at the guard lying on the floor with the magazine lying next to him and felt a stab of compunction. Well, they'd take care of him when he woke up. I swallowed another two tablets because the first two seemed to have worn off. There wasn't much time but I waited five minutes before getting out of bed. I retrieved the *India Today,* which had come unrolled, and rolled it up again to give the guard another dose if he happened to wake up before I left. I hoped he didn't, for my sake as much as his, because hitting him would hurt me almost as much as it would hurt him.

He was taller than I was but no thicker, so he looked much thinner. I knelt on the floor beside him and began taking his clothes off, starting with his shoes, cheap black leather shoes a size too large for me. I got his shirt buttons off, then his belt, and then unzipped his trousers. Then, with an effort that revived all the agony that the tablets had managed to quieten, I got his trousers off. I hadn't anticipated this to be so hard; I had to lie on the floor awhile to get my breath back.

If getting his trousers off had been hard, getting his shirt off almost defeated me. I had to lift his torso off the floor and with my chest protesting loudly I propped him up against the locker and somehow managed it. If he had come to at that time I wouldn't have been able to do a thing to him.

When I was done I couldn't raise the strength even to get off the floor, so I lay there beside him for a while, the sweat pooling on the floor. The guard, the shirt and I, all three were in a mess on the floor. Time passed, and when the pain became bearable I looked at my watch again. Five minutes past ten. My chest hurt so much I couldn't breathe deeply any more and I wondered desultorily if the cracked rib had been knocked out of position, then decided to ignore the pain.

A substantial part of fatigue is fear, fear of overtaxing one's body, fear of doing permanent damage. Lying on that bare cold floor, when I stopped caring about the possibility of doing myself further damage, some of the fatigue went away and then I picked myself up off the floor, undressed, and put on the guard's clothes, buckling on the belt last of all. The sleeves of his full-sleeved shirt were too long, as were the trousers, but no one expected a guard to wear well-cut clothes. The sleeves were folded up to the elbows but I unfolded them and found that they covered the cast on my arm. After dressing, inch by inch I pushed the man under the bed so that no one who peeped casually into the room would see him lying on the floor in his loud red underwear.

By the time I got the man under the bed I was sweating again and it showed on the uniform but with all the exertion my ankle was actually bearing up better. I stood by the locker and drank two glasses of water to replace some of the fluid I'd lost. I picked up the rolled up magazine, since leaving it behind would mess up the helpful nurse's life, then walked slowly and steadily to the door, managing without much effort to keep a fairly straight line, pushed the curtain aside, and walked out into the deserted corridor. The first step into a fragile freedom that would certainly be more restrictive than any form of imprisonment.

chapter ten

The staircase was barely twenty feet away but in the harsh glare of the tubes overhead it seemed a mile off. The lift was closer but at this time anyone moving around would more likely use the lifts, so I took the stairs. If my room had been on any floor higher than the first I would have risked the lift.

As I reached the landing between floors I heard the soothing patter of rain on the windows and hoped it would draw the men in the hospital compound into shelter. The handgun at my waist was no reassurance: if at all I had to use it I'd be better off turning myself in.

Half past ten, said my watch. An hour and a half, ninety minutes, to the next check, and during those ninety minutes I had to find myself a place to hole up. No one saw me on the staircase, but a medical orderly in the ground floor corridor looked curiously at my sweat-stained uniform and the stubble on my face. I glared at him and he looked hastily away. If he were questioned later he'd remember me but by then I would hopefully be long gone.

I walked past the Air Force sentry on guard in the porch, who looked rather contemptuously at my police uniform and then turned away. The drizzle was increasing in intensity but I didn't want to hang around so I walked out onto the driveway and let the rain cool me off. Only one more hurdle to go, the main gate with the sentry box next to it. I hoped the rain would keep the guard inside that box.

He was sitting inside, watching me curiously as I entered the lamplight around the gate. He didn't get a good look at my face but uniforms are reassuring and when I walked straight-backed past him he, too, turned away. I stepped out onto the road, looked left and right, and crossed the road to the shelter of a tree.

I was free.

It was another matter that I didn't know what to do with my freedom. I stood in the shelter of the tree for a minute and seeing no traffic began to walk away from the gates in the general direction of what I thought would be MG Road, the centre of town, trying all the while to get my bearings. I knew I was somewhere on the way to the airport but not exactly where, and hoped for a signboard somewhere that would have something to tell me.

I had to make a telephone call. When they came looking for me they'd have my description out and if I called from a manned public telephone they'd have me in no time—getting hold of the number I called wouldn't be a problem. Unless . . . Unless some of the old crossbar exchanges were still in use. The electronic exchanges had seven-digit numbers and the crossbar exchanges six-digit numbers.

And if I remembered right, there were some six-digit numbers in this area. The thing to do then was to look for an old coin-operated telephone, and confirm before calling Urmila that it had a six-digit number.

I walked away from the hospital, towards the airport, and a hundred metres on saw a light in a shop. I asked the shopkeeper in Hindi where the nearest public telephone was and he pointed towards the airport. He looked at me curiously. A Karnataka policeman speaking Hindi when he could as well speak Kannada was a rarity. 'I want an old telephone,' I said, 'a coin-operated one. Is there one like that nearby?'

He must have thought I was mad but the uniform kept his suspicions at bay. 'I think there is one that way,' he said, pointing in the same direction, 'near those shops. Near Hundred Feet Road.'

An old front-engined autorickshaw chugged towards me, one almost as battered as the ones I saw in Delhi. There was a passenger inside but I stuck my hand out all the same and the autorickshaw stopped right in front of me. I didn't know why it had stopped until I remembered the uniform. The driver, who in the faint lamplight looked as broken down as his vehicle, looked questioningly up at me.

'Hundred Feet Road,' I said. He responded in Kannada, saying perhaps that he had to drop the other passenger off first, and I nodded and climbed in. The other passenger, a drunk lolling back in his seat, looked apathetically at me and I sat back with relief that lasted only as far as the first bump on the road.

The chill, wet wind blowing in through the open sides of the little vehicle soon drove away all the fuzziness brought on by the medicine. I sat straight on the seat, not daring to lean against the jolting backrest. For a while I raised my bottom off the seat, resting on my good hand, but that position was too difficult to sustain so I lowered myself back onto the seat and clenched my teeth, hoping the nightmare would end soon.

The other passenger got off two minutes later. He paid the driver and stumbled off into the rain towards an apartment block that loomed darkly by the side of the road. The driver muttered something under his breath and started off again with a jerk. I put my hand on his shoulder and told him in Hindi to go slow. He looked at me oddly, and I added that I was ill. He slowed down after that, guiding his old vehicle gently past the potholes on the road, and I was grateful for the delicacy of his touch on the controls.

Everything was closed down now, except the restaurants, which typically closed at eleven. A quarter to eleven now. The rain had driven everyone to shelter. Another bump, another explosion of pain in my chest. I was on the verge of giving up. I dry-swallowed a tablet from the strip in my pocket, then stopped the auto, about two hundred metres before the junction of Hundred Feet Road. I paid the driver off—something he apparently didn't expect, for policemen rarely if ever pay—and went looking for a public telephone with a directory.

Ten minutes to eleven. They'd find out that I was missing

in a little over an hour and they'd come looking in all the hotels in the area. Since this was a case that involved the highest in the land they'd probably have my face on TV on the first news bulletin of the day . . . When was that, I thought vaguely. Maybe at six, or half-past, perhaps. Getting into a hotel would be suicidal.

I walked on in the drizzle, shivering, walking slowly but still better off than I'd been in the auto, and found a coin-operated telephone outside a small shop selling cigarettes and sweets. The man at the counter had a directory, and there was only one man ahead of me and he was already speaking. I fumbled with the directory, found Urmila's father's name, with the man running the stall looking at me all the time. I looked in my pockets for a one-rupee coin to make the call, and didn't find one. The man at the counter offered me change, and I took five coins from him. When the man ahead hung up and moved away, I dialled, hoping that whoever picked up the phone would find Urmila instead of telling me to go jump in the nearest lake.

The phone rang for a long while before anyone picked it up, and then a fresh young voice tinged with irritation said, 'Hello?'

'Urmila?' I asked.

'Yes,' she said, the irritation gone. 'Who is this?'

'Raja,' I said, 'Raja Menon. Remember?'

'Raja?' she said, trying to place me. Then she remembered, and said with a gasp, 'Oh, you mean Colonel Menon! Hi there, you sound terrible!'

'Keep your voice down,' I said, 'don't let anyone hear this. I'm in trouble. Big trouble . . . I shouldn't be asking you this but could you help me?' I didn't want to say the next word but it was dragged hoarsely out of me: 'Please.' The man at the counter was still staring at me but the man who'd just got off the phone was talking to him in rapid fire Kannada so he couldn't concentrate on eavesdropping and I was talking softly anyway.

'Of course,' came the reply, and I sagged at the knees in relief. 'What can I do for you?'

'Did you know about the raid in Mysore? We hit the kidnappers and tried to get your friends out.'

'It was in the papers,' she said, 'and on the news. It was terrible . . . They're both gone now, Priya and Mallika, aren't they?' Her voice began to crack. 'The papers said you were hurt. That you were in a hospital in Bangalore with several broken bones and a concussion.'

'I was,' I said, 'I broke out. I can't explain on the telephone. They say I was involved with the kidnappers and the police wanted to put me in jail so I had to break out of there. They had a guard on me but he was pretty lax because I'm injured and they thought no one with this kind of damage would try to escape. I knocked out the guard and got away.'

'They must be crazy to think you're involved!' she exclaimed. 'Where are you calling from?'

'From a public telephone outside a shop on the way to the airport, a kilometre from the Air Force hospital. Look, I need to hole up for a while, and get better. Then

I need to call my wife, and I need to find out who's behind all this.'

'Do you have money?' she asked. 'And do you need a doctor?'

'I've got a couple of hundred rupees,' I replied, 'and I don't need a doctor right away.'

'Look,' she said, 'I can raise some money, that's not a problem . . . But I can't come out and give it to you. I'll call my cousin and ask him to come out to see you and help you out. Is that all right with you?'

'Not if he'll hand me over to the police when he finds out who I am.'

'Of course not!' she said, shocked and hurt. 'He'll do as I tell him to. He listens to me.'

'How old is he?' I asked.

'Twenty,' she replied, 'but he's nice.'

She'd probably twist him around her little finger. Seventeen-year-olds, when they're not behaving monstrously, can be extraordinarily persuasive. 'All right,' I said, 'get the lad.'

'Give me your number and I'll call you back.'

I looked at the man staring at me through the glass and knew I wasn't going to wait here for her call. 'No,' I said, 'I'll call again in ten minutes.'

'Okay,' she said, 'I'll be ready.'

I walked out into the street again. The uniform was soaked and water dripped off the peak of the cap onto the tip of my nose.

I hurt. God, how I hurt! I found a dark spot where the

street lamps didn't shine and sat down for five minutes. Then I got up with an effort and returned to the telephone outside the shop, managing to raise a grin for the man. I sagged against the wall as I dialled Urmila's number.

She picked it up on the first ring. 'Raja?' she asked.

'Yes,' I replied. Even to myself my voice was dangerously slurred.

'Hang on, Raja,' she said, 'hang on. Are you all right?'

'No,' I mumbled, 'but I'll make it.'

'You're in luck,' she said, 'Nicky—that's Nikhil, my cousin—is alone in his house. His parents are off at their coffee plantation in Coorg and he's got the house to himself. They took their live-in servant with them so there's no one else in the house now. He's got money, and a credit card. You can stay with him as long as you like. He'll pick you up in fifteen, twenty minutes, depending on how far away you are. Can you sit on the back of a bike?' I thought of the auto ride and almost said no but eventually managed a yes. I told her exactly where the telephone was, described some of the shop signs that I could see. She said, 'Oh! That's not far away. He'll be with you in ten minutes. He'll be on a big black bike, an Enfield, and he's tall—like six two—and he's got curly hair and a helmet with white stripes along the side.'

'Tell him to look for a wet policeman,' I told her, 'I'm in uniform. And tell him I'll be twenty metres away from the shop, between street lamps, in the dark.'

'Why?'

'I don't want to be seen with him. Not here.'

'Oh,' she said, and understood. 'Okay. And one more thing.'

'What?'

'I called your wife a couple of days back and she helped me sort things out. It helped. Do you want me to call her again?'

'Yes,' I said. 'Tell her I'll call her tomorrow morning. Tell her I'll call her at Deepak's place, Deepak Kulkarni's. And tell her not to tell anyone, not even this guy Deepak. Tell her to be there, okay?'

'Right,' she said, 'I'll see you tomorrow.'

I hung up and walked the edge of the pavement and kept going, stopping twenty metres away from the front of the shop. The boy arrived on his iron steed in ten minutes, as promised, at a speed about twice the legal limit, the engine thudding loudly, audible half a mile away. He braked to a halt in front of me. The helmet's visor was down and I couldn't see his face. 'Colonel Menon?' he asked, beginning to get off the bike.

'Nicky?' I responded. 'Don't get off.' I held out, with some effort, my right hand for him to shake. He put out a gloved hand, shook it briefly. He turned around in his seat, unstrapped another helmet like his from somewhere behind, handed it to me, and gestured me to climb on. 'I've got a couple of injuries,' I told him, 'take it easy over the bumps, please.'

'Sure,' he said, his voice muffled by the helmet, 'Urmila told me. Don't worry, sir.'

I checked my watch as I climbed on. Ten past midnight.

They'd have discovered the guard by now.

As it turned out I didn't have to worry about the bumps. Nicky drove slowly and carefully and very, very smoothly, and I sat behind him looking at his broad back, holding on to a large, firm shoulder whenever I felt I was going to fall off the bike. After what seemed an age but wouldn't have been more than twenty minutes we stopped outside an apartment building. The sign above said 'Golden Heights'. The watchman opened the gate, and we thudded quickly into the basement parking area, stopping neatly by the lift. 'Get off here,' Nicky said, 'I'll join you after I park the bike.' There was a chair next to the lift door, for the watchman to sit, and I slumped into it while Nicky went off to park behind a half-dozen cars.

I must have blacked out for a minute because the next thing I knew he was shaking me by the shoulder. The left shoulder. I straightened up, grimacing involuntarily, biting back a moan, and he stood back. 'You're in bad shape,' he said. 'Let me give you a hand.' He held out an arm to support me.

'Stay on my right if you don't mind,' I said, 'the damage is mostly on my left side.' He came obediently across and put a large hand under my arm, and lifted me. I got up a little light-headed, swayed, and he corrected me without effort. A strong lad, I thought, and reliable. Good for him. The pain and the relief all together were making me woozy and I found my eyes wet.

His flat was on the second floor. We got out of the lift and into the flat without being seen. He led me straight to a bedroom with a single bed in the middle, its white sheets inviting. I took off the helmet and he had a good look at me and his face went still with shock. 'The guest room,' he said, 'you'll be all right here.' He guided me onto the bed and I sat on it, guilty about soiling the sheets with my wet uniform.

He opened a cupboard and brought out a lungi and a shirt several sizes too large for me. 'Get into these . . . Would you like a drink?'

'Yes,' I said, taking the clothes, 'a brandy would be fine.'

'I've got something better,' he said. 'Back in a minute.'

He was back before I finished changing clothes. He waited while I wound the lungi around my waist and lay down before handing me a glass with four fingers of a dark brown liquid in it, and four or five cubes of ice. I took a sip. It was scotch, with something stronger still, something sweet that tasted of almonds. 'What is it?' I asked.

'Johnnie Walker and Amaretto. Fifty-fifty. It's good.' He grinned. 'From Dad's private stock. He's cool about it because I don't steal much from it. I did pretty well in my exams so he's let me have my way around here.'

The drink was excellent. I finished it in ten minutes and lay back. The topmost button of the shirt was undone and the plaster on my chest showed, as did the cast on my arm. 'Let me have a look,' he said.

I unbuttoned the shirt and he looked at the plaster and the bruises on my chest and shoulders, now at their most colourful, and he whistled. 'Broken ribs?' he asked.

'Rib. And shoulder-blade. And arm. A sprained ankle.

Concussion, and bruises.'

He whistled again. 'Pretty heavy,' he said at last, 'I don't understand how you got out of hospital.'

I told him about the switch, about knocking out the guard with the magazine, and walking out of the hospital in the rain. He shook his head, then picked up a copy of *India Today* lying around, rolled it up tight, and hefted it. With an expression of surprise he said, 'You're right. You can knock someone out with a magazine. I'm a medical student. I have some years to go before becoming a doctor but I can tell you for sure you've made things much worse for yourself. Medically speaking, that is. What medicines have you been taking?'

I couldn't get up. I pointed at the trousers lying on the floor and he picked them up and felt in the pockets, finding what was left of the tablets. He looked at the strip. 'This is a mild painkiller,' he said. 'How many have you had in the past six hours?' I told him. 'That's far too many. But I suppose you would have had to have those quantities to get away.'

'I won't have any more tonight,' I told him, my words beginning once again to slur, 'I'm going to crash now.'

He bent over me. 'You do that,' he said. 'You do just that if you can. I'm a light sleeper so if you have trouble in the middle of the night just yell. Don't hesitate. I have enough influence with a drugstore owner to get you anything you might need.'

'Okay,' I said gratefully.

'And I'll get a doctor friend to see you tomorrow.'

'Thanks.'

'Good night.'

I went under almost immediately and woke only at half past six, with the sunlight pouring in through the window and the chirping of birds. I opened my eyes, coughed, closed my eyes and grimaced when something began to come adrift inside my chest. When I opened my eyes again Nikhil was there, large and reassuring. He smiled. At this hour he was ready for the day, bright and bushy-tailed, dressed in a blinding orange T-shirt over blue jeans. 'I heard you cough,' he said. 'I've called my friend, I can see that you're in trouble.' He handed me a tablet and a glass of water. 'If you feel as bad as you look, I can get you a toothbrush and a basin here, and a bedpan.'

I lay still in bed, not wanting ever to get up again. The doctor friend, who arrived at seven, turned out to be not a full-fledged doctor but a student at the end of his house-surgeoncy, a serious-faced boy two or three years older than Nicky who introduced himself as Prakash and poked and prodded me mercilessly, clucking his disapproval when Nicky told him of the wetting the plaster had received the previous night. He asked about double vision and headaches and floaters in the eye and at the end prescribed painkillers, calcium, a tonic, a broad spectrum antibiotic to ward off infections, paracetamol to take care of the fever that had come up after last night's wetting, and a cough syrup to soothe my chest. And total rest for two weeks.

Nothing doing, I said about the two weeks, two days should be more like it. We argued for a while and I noticed he didn't protest too much; Nicky must have told him what I'd been up to. 'All right,' he said eventually, 'you'll do what you have to do, I suppose, but keep to bed until at least the concussion wears off.' Nicky went out to fill his prescription and after he returned we watched the news at half past eight.

The follow-up on the kidnap was still the lead item and my escape from hospital was mentioned right at the beginning. The newsreader said I'd knocked out a guard and broken out of hospital and that the police wanted me very badly to help with their investigations into the kidnap and subsequent murder of the PM's granddaughter. Anyone giving the police information about me that led to my recapture would be suitably rewarded. They added a warning that I was not to be approached independently since I was a trained commando, was armed and would probably react violently. Then they flashed my photograph on the screen, an old one, retouched by a photographer to add the stubble and medium-long hair. They flashed another photograph, this one without the extra hair, and said I might also look like this.

'We'll have to do something about you before the maid arrives to clean up,' Nicky said. 'They've shown you with a beard and without one so we'll leave you with something that's in neither photograph, a moustache. A drooping one, Franco Nero style.' When I said I couldn't shave myself without setting my chest afire, he didn't bat an eyelid. Instead he offered to do it for me, and he made a good job of it, too, leaving a moustache on my face that made me look like a small-time hood in a bad Tamil movie. While I bathed, he saw Prakash off, and started breakfast, which he brought me in bed when I was ready. When I said his hospitality was beginning to get me slightly guilty, he grinned and said I was to shut up, that Urmila had told him I was real cool, and that she would be in shortly to see me. While I ate breakfast he produced clothes for me, a pair of jeans—his own, discarded long ago—cut off at about the right length, and a T-shirt, also his, that hung on me like a raincoat. 'Can't have you hanging around here looking like a camel's breakfast,' he said.

I drifted in and out of sleep that morning, thanks largely to the medicines prescribed by the doctor-to-be. I woke up once at about eleven hearing Urmila's voice somewhere nearby. My arm was under me and had gone to sleep and when I turned over to free it all the pain came back and I couldn't hold back a groan. That brought Nicky and Urmila running. 'Hi,' she said brightly when I'd more or less got back in control. 'You were passed out when I called at half past nine so I called your wife and told her you'll call her at four in the afternoon, same place. I told her you had crashed, like Nicky told me, and not to worry, and so on. You will call, won't you?'

'I will,' I promised, a little overwhelmed, 'I sure will. Thanks for everything. I don't know what I'd have done if you hadn't decided to help me.'

She grinned healthily back. The change in her was dramatic. She glowed, fizzed with energy. 'Daddy found out a little about you from some friends he has, and he told us some of it. About your parachuting into a house in Whitefield year before last, and so on. To tell you the truth, we're all pretty impressed, Nicky here more than anyone else. Though right now you don't look like much, if you don't mind my saying so. And that moustache doesn't suit you.'

I saw the signs of hero-worship, which always makes me uncomfortable, but there was nothing to be done about it and nothing to drive them away from possible adventure, so I asked instead if I could make a call to Gopi, my brother, in America. 'What for?' she asked. 'How can he help?'

'Money,' I said, 'and brains. He's one of the brainiest people I know. Thinks like a chess grandmaster. He's got half-a-dozen patents on electronic stuff already.'

They brought me a white cordless telephone from the living room. Gopi was fast asleep in his Santa Cruz apartment when I called, and an answering machine took the call. After the beep I said who I was, gave Nicky's number, asked him to call, and was about to hang up when he cut off the machine and picked up the phone himself. 'Raja, what the hell is going on?' he said. 'Sandhya rang me up to say you were in shit upto your eyebrows and she didn't know what to do and so on.'

'I am in shit,' I told him, 'and I need help.'

'What kind of trouble? She didn't tell me anything . . . She was crying all the time, not making sense, so I just heard her out.'

'I can't explain on the phone, Gopi.' I hesitated. 'Can you come over for a couple of weeks?'

'Right now?'

'Yes, right now. Take the next flight out to Bangalore. And . . .'

'And what?'

'Bring money. As much of it as you can.'

'That bad, is it?' he asked musingly. 'I've got your number. Let me talk to the airlines, then I'll get back to you, in about fifteen minutes. I'll have to wake some people up but that's all right. And Raja, this sounds like heavy duty stuff. Have you gone and killed somebody?'

'Worse,' I replied. 'Just get here.'

He hung up. I knew he would come. He hadn't taken a vacation in three years and he put in sixteen-hour working days. His employers wouldn't object to his taking off at short notice. In any case he only worked part-time. If they didn't let him off for these two weeks he'd be willing to leave them for good. Most of all, he had money to spare, coming in from royalties on one patent he'd taken three years ago. He'd offered me some from time to time, telling me to clean up my lifestyle, but I'd always had enough for myself, and had told him each time to bank it instead. Now I knew what I'd do with it.

The youngsters had left me alone to speak to Gopi and when he called back I picked it up at the first ring. 'I'll be in Bombay thirty-six hours from now. Then a four-hour wait for the next available flight to Bangalore. That'll fetch me up there early morning on the day after tomorrow. Is that all right?'

'Yes,' I said. 'I'll try to have you picked up at the airport. Don't check into a hotel anywhere on the way. The police are looking for me and it's possible they might just react to finding your name in a hotel register somewhere.'

He was silent for a while, then said, 'Raja, this is killing me. What have you done?'

'Tell you when you get here. Look for a tall young lad with a black crash helmet at the airport.'

'Can't you come?' he asked.

I explained to him about the doctor-to-be's orders. He thought about it for a while, then said, 'Raja, with your talent for trouble I'm surprised you've stayed alive so long. What you need is a bloody wet nurse. Right. I'll be there.'

I slept again after a light lunch of rice and vegetables, aided by the painkillers and an alprazolam tablet my new doctor gave me. Urmila woke me at five to four. 'I'd have let you sleep but you have to call Sandhya,' she said. 'I know she's terribly distressed.' I lay on my back while Urmila fetched the telephone from the living room. I dialled Deepak's number. He was out at work and his wife picked up the phone. When I asked for Sandhya she handed the phone over immediately and a moment later Sandhya came on the line. 'Raja?' she asked, her voice husky with anxiety.

'Hi,' I said.

'Raja, what kind of a mess are you in?' I could hear the tears in her voice. 'Why did you run away from hospital?'

'Not much I could do there. It looked as if there was someone determined to get me out of circulation. It looked like someone's built up a case to the effect that I caused the mess in the first place. Collusion and all that crap.'

'You should have stayed there and cleared it up in court.

Martial or otherwise. Running away points at guilt.'

'That might not have got me cleared,' I explained. 'Courts martial are a little different from the civilian stuff you read about. And after that I'd have to face charges in a civil court as well. Take months, if not years, to sort out. Enough time for whoever did it to get away.'

'What's the matter with you,' she asked, 'must you always run towards danger? Haven't you any sense?' A sniff and a silence. Then, 'How badly are you hurt?'

'I was fit enough yesterday to knock someone out,' I said. 'A few days in bed and I'll be fine. Then I'll work on getting those diaries back.'

'What are you going to do now?'

'I haven't decided but I'll need money and some time . . . I've asked Gopi to come down. He'll be here the day after tomorrow and we'll take it from there. I'll stay in bed until then, get fit by the time Gopi gets here.'

'Raja, the papers say you had several broken bones and concussion . . .'

'Hairline fractures. They heal fast. You know.'

'Okay.' She didn't sound wholly convinced. 'What do you want me to do?'

'Lie low. Get out of there. Go to Calcutta and live with your parents until this thing blows over. Keep busy.' Her parents were retired and lived in a suburb of Calcutta. They'd be happy to have her and overjoyed to have Kiran with them for a while. 'If the police come asking you questions tell them you don't know where I am.'

Suddenly she was in tears. I could hear her sobbing. 'I

can't take this,' she said eventually. 'It's not fair. You lose out on everything. You get shot at and blown up and beaten up and everything and at the end of it they blame you for it and want to lock you up.'

'It's not all that bad,' I said, 'and everyone's not involved. There's just this one guy at the centre of it and I have to get rid of him . . .'

'I don't know about that, Raja, and I don't know if I can live with this. I really don't know.'

'We need to talk. Give me time.'

'Yes, yes, I wasn't threatening to walk out on you . . . But we do need to talk.'

'We will. Take care. Love to Kiran. Go to Cal, and don't get worked up if I don't get in touch. Bye.'

That night I didn't sleep. The rift with Sandhya was widening. I could not afford to lose her. I refused the painkillers Nikhil offered, the pain having died down to a dull ache as long as I didn't move around. I lay awake in bed and strategized, trying not to think of Sandhya.

I had just one slender lead, the Grenadier. Rawat. Another chat with Basappa at the guest house would help confirm it either way. I couldn't forget Rawat's walk or his mannerisms or his unmistakable intelligence. Maybe that alibi was false: colleagues could always be persuaded to tell little lies. I knew where he worked and where he was based and that was it. I'd go to Kabini first, talk to Basappa, and then move in on Rawat if Basappa confirmed it was him. I'd have to scare Basappa to get him to speak. I remembered him cowering in his chair when I spoke to him. There'd been something fishy about him. The police hadn't threatened him with more than a beating or two but he had been terrified. Had Rawat threatened him? Sent a frightener after him?

I kept drifting in and out of sleep till the painkillers wore off and it became impossible to sleep. For a while I thought about what I'd like to do to the Grenadier when I got him. It didn't work. The pain raged on and I shifted restlessly in bed. It wasn't only the pain, I discovered. There was something else on my mind, something nibbling at the far edge of my consciousness.

It took my mind off the pain and I chased after the fugitive memory with a vengeance. Bits of it surfaced irregularly, each bringing with it the lightening that accompanies fresh discovery.

Something had happened during that raid. The second SOF man, the thickset one, whom I'd seen just before being knocked out . . . Something about him didn't fit. We had been issued four grenades each for the raid. There'd been no grenades in his harness, but I'd heard only two go off before I saw him. So he couldn't have had more than two at the beginning—clearly he wasn't on the team. Who was he, then?

Hairy Face. Had they got him? The newspapers said nothing about him. Padmanabhan had said that seven kidnappers had been killed. If one had gotten away with the diaries, that made a total of eight. Six in the house, two with the CJ's son. With three hostages, and the counting and verification of the ransom to be done, that didn't seem to be enough. Had more than one man escaped from that farmhouse?

I should have waited, I should have waited for the searchlights. Then no one would have got out and even though the raid would have failed anyway, the consequences would have been far less damaging.

But where had those guys hidden?

The answer came out of the blue, at half past four on that wet pain-wracked morning. For all our training, when we are in houses, we rarely look carefully above eye level. Most of the threats in those situations are lower down. The man who got away, he must have hidden above eye level. I'd noticed vaguely that there were lofts in some of the rooms. Perhaps they had been big enough to accommodate a man. There'd been no time to search them . . . It couldn't have been an ordinary man. Only a gymnast could do that sort of thing, or perhaps a rock-climber, used to putting his weight on his fingertips. Since he'd taken only a few seconds to get up there he had to be a man with some training. There weren't so many men around with that kind of training and those instincts.

The next thing I knew the rain had stopped and bright sunlight was streaming in through the windows. The clock at the bedside said half past nine. I felt refreshed, better than at any time since leaving the hospital, which wasn't saying much, but a noticeable improvement nevertheless. I raised a smile for Nikhil when he came in to check on me and made it under my own steam to the bathroom—without aspirin, even—and managed to brush my teeth without a grimace and to shave myself with only two cuts. I had two leads now, both tenuous, both extremely hard to chase, but better than nothing.

Urmila came in the afternoon, managing to raise my spirits further with irreverent banter about my appearance and the colours of the bruises and so on. Nikhil kept me informed about what was going on on TV—the messages had now spread to the private channels beside the government-run ones—but there was no progress. The police had nothing new on me. As best I knew, the trail would have stopped at the coin-operated public telephone. And the build-up to the regular election campaign was on. The ruling party didn't let anyone forget that the PM's granddaughter was dead. They made it sound as if she had been sacrificed for the good of the country and it only evoked revulsion in me, reminding me of what Sandhya had said about the kind of people I worked for.

I dozed through the night, sinking easily into a healing slumber. Gopi called early in the morning to say he'd be in by an earlier flight from Bombay and Nikhil went off to the airport armed with a bit of cardboard on which Urmila had written 'Gopi Menon' with a red felt pen. They turned up together at a quarter past nine, Gopi having sat on the back of Nikhil's bike all the way from the airport without falling off.

I almost didn't recognize Gopi when I saw him. He'd always been a bookworm, a couch potato, pudgy and double-chinned, a confirmed hater of all forms of exercise. Now the extra weight was gone, and so were the spare chins. His belly was flat and there was a bounce to his step. He grinned and stuck out his hand for me to shake, and sat beside me on the bed. 'I can see what you're thinking,' he said. 'I started jogging, then karate lessons.'

'How come?' I asked. 'You hated anything physical.'

'A girlfriend—we parted ways last year—started me jogging. After a while I got to like it enough to run away from her. Then, a couple of years back, I got mugged one night in San Francisco. Some junkie held me up with a flick knife and took four hundred bucks off me. The day I got back to Santa Cruz I looked around for a taekwondo or judo class and found this guy who taught karate so I joined that instead.'

'Did you get a chance to find out if the lessons were worthwhile?'

'Yeah, sure,' he replied easily, 'I got mugged again. This time in Detroit.'

'What did you do to the mugger?'

'Nothing. This time he got only eighteen bucks. The karate guy taught us to keep a spare wallet with some money in it, twenty, thirty bucks, like that. When you get mugged, he said, hand the spare wallet over. You need to get the money right. It's got to be enough for the junkie to get his next fix of whatever he uses: if he's got that much he doesn't really care. If he gets less than that he might cut you up in frustration.'

We hadn't met in nearly five years—he hadn't been able to make it to my wedding and hadn't ever met Sandhya—and while we'd talked several times on the telephone we'd never got used to communicating at a distance. There had always been affection between us, but rarely words. Urmila and Nikhil left us to ourselves as we talked. Catching up took ten minutes, maybe less. After that it was down to serious business. 'All I know about this trouble of yours is what I read in the papers. They say you killed the big honcho's granddaughter and stole some diaries, and the police are after you now.'

'They are.' I explained to him about the kidnap, the raid, and the disaster, and the nature of the diaries.

He whistled when I told him of the diaries. 'Whoever's got those little blue books rules this place. Boy, oh boy! So what do you do now?'

'Someone got out of that farmhouse with the diaries. That someone also killed the hostages and some of the kidnappers . . . I want to find him and take him in. Otherwise I'm finished for good.'

'Do you have any leads? Whom to follow, what to ask?'

'Yes. There was a cook at Kabini whom I need to talk to, about a possible villain.'

'Who's he, this villain of yours?'

I told him about the ex-Grenadier. 'He had the skills,' I concluded. 'The description matched. Not all the way, but enough. I suspect the cook didn't tell us all he knew because he was more afraid of the kidnappers than of the cops. So I've to try and scare him some more.'

'And how will you do all this, with the police after you?'

'Anyone can go live in that lodge. It's open for business now. I'll change my appearance a little, maybe get hold of platform shoes to make myself look taller. We'll spend a day there and I'll talk to the fellow.'

'What do you want me to do?' he asked, after a long silence.

'Double-check my thinking,' I replied, 'provide me a front man when I need one, or back-up. And run sensitive errands.'

'Right,' he said, 'I'm game. But how are we going to do all this while you're in bed? That outsize doctor says you'll have to be in bed for weeks.'

'I'm much better now,' I said. 'The concussion seems to have eased off, and the shoulder's fine. I can walk. It's only the cracked rib and shoulder-blade that I have to watch out for. And the shoulder-blade doesn't really count, it's not an essential bone. I guess painkillers should keep things under control long enough.'

He looked me all over, shook his head in wonderment. 'You're nuts. But I'll go along with you just because if you try all this on your own you'll get yourself killed. When do we move?'

'We'll have to check at the office of the lodge,' I said. 'That's somewhere off MG Road. We can do that now.'

'I'll go,' he said, 'you stay in bed.'

'Test drive,' I replied bleakly. 'If I can't make it as far as MG Road today the chances are I won't be able to make it to Kabini tomorrow.'

While Gopi ate breakfast Nikhil called up a taxi service. I trimmed the moustache Nikhil had left on my face, stuffed myself with painkillers and put on dark glasses that covered most of my face. At ten we went down to the white Ambassador waiting to take us to town.

The Bangalore office of the lodge was on the first floor of a crowded commercial complex opposite the Army parade ground. The staff were surprisingly efficient and courteous, considering that it's a government enterprise. The man at the desk told us that while nothing was available for the next day there was a room available the day after that, and while we conferred he pressed dull black-and-white brochures on us. What were the options, Gopi asked, and the clerk said there were none: they had one package and that was it. Roughly two thousand rupees per day for Indians, a hundred dollars a day for foreigners. Two to a room.

Gopi paid for the reservations and the clerk told us to make it a point to get to the lodge by noon, because the package was a noon-to-noon one. 'If you reach there early,' he advised, 'you can have an early lunch and a nap before you go on the jungle trail in the afternoon . . . The road is very bad, very bumpy. You will be tired when you reach there.'

'Have you had many cancellations lately?' I asked.

'Yes,' he replied ruefully, 'there was a kidnap there. It was not our fault but people blame us. Everyone says that the Kabini lodge is not safe any more. But it is not true.'

By the time we got back to Nikhil's house I had a headache and the pains in the chest were again making themselves felt, but now I knew I could take it so it didn't bother me. I went straight back to bed to let the healing process continue and Gopi did exactly the same to get over his jet lag. We awoke late in the evening and found Urmila watching TV in the living room. 'Nikhil's gone out,' she explained, 'and he didn't want to leave you two alone so he told me to stand guard.'

Outside it began to drizzle and as evening crept wetly towards night Nikhil returned with his house-surgeon friend in tow. 'Just want to make sure you're all right,' he grinned. 'Your brother doesn't seem to think you can look after yourself.'

This second examination was a great deal more thorough than the first had been. 'I'm not sure what I'm doing,' he explained, 'without X-rays to tell me what the damage is. I can only guess at where the breaks are. From what you say you seem to be better but a minimum of two weeks is what the books recommend for damage like you've sustained.'

I nodded. 'That's not the problem,' I told him. 'I'm beginning to smell. This plaster around my chest has been soaked in sweat and rainwater and God knows what else and if you can't get rid of it or at least change it, I'm going to take it off.'

'It'll be painful,' he warned me. And it was. By the time the clean white plaster was wound around my chest my head was drooping: I had felt every tug and every squeeze and every little jerk and the pain just went on and on. Gopi was looking studiously away and Urmila blinked away tears when I straightened up at last.

'That should hold for a few days.' The young doctor-to-be hesitated for a while. 'Look, if you get into bad trouble . . . I'll give you a few ampoules of a fast painkiller. You'll have to inject it into yourself, though, if you're not near a doctor.'

'Tell me,' I said, 'I've done it before. I'll use diclo, or fortwin. Ketorol hurts.'

'Where'd you learn that?' the young man asked, surprised.

'Part of our training,' I whispered, fighting a surge of pain.

'Oh, training,' he said, now puzzled. 'Anyway, just remember that if you want to give yourself an intra-muscular injection, do it in the middle of the thigh. On the outside. You have a lump of muscle there, and fewer blood vessels. Remember to aspirate the syringe before injecting yourself.'

Gopi and I rested through the night and through most of the next day. In the evening Gopi went out and fixed it up with a taxi hire company to pick up the two of us early in the morning at a hotel in town to go to Kabini, paying cash in advance. The rest made all the difference and when Gopi and I set out in an Ambassador taxi at five the next morning I made it all the way down the stairs on my own and without painkillers. We reached Mysore in three hours and a half, slowed down by intermittent rain, heavy traffic, and an accident just outside the city. We halted in Mysore for me to recover, with the help of alprazolam and breakfast.

We set out again at half past nine in a grey drizzle with

headlamps on, and very soon the road degenerated to a muddy track with a ragged strip of tar down the middle. The monsoons hadn't arrived yet and there was still dust in the air but enough rain had fallen to turn the road into mud. It was humid and through patches in the clouds the sun blazed down. Every bump on that scarred surface sent stabbing pains through my chest. Six times Gopi looked at me with concern and six times he told the driver to take it easy over the bumps, and with the driver following instructions we took close on four hours to cover those last eighty kilometres to the lodge. I was grey with exhaustion when we finally drew up outside the lodge at one in the afternoon. It had begun to drizzle again and an attendant turned up with an umbrella to keep us dry on the way to our room. The driver was willing to fend for himself the one night we were to stay, and as the attendants carried our baggage—two overnight bags—Gopi said he wouldn't mind extending our stay here. They led us to a room at the end of a long row, a room with an extra window and a view of the lawns and the scrub in which monkeys sported. I saw one of them amble up to a tap, open it, drink his fill, and shamble away contentedly, leaving water pouring out all over the lawn.

The staff at the lodge were concerned, too. Gopi told the manager that I had acquired a terrible migraine on the ride, and arranged to have my lunch delivered to our room. I ate in the room, soup and fried rice and a fruit salad for dessert, served by a uniformed attendant who waited, after I had finished, for a tip. Gopi returned from his lunch in the dining hall at a quarter past two, smelling strongly of beer, praising the view of the river. He forced some more tablets into me, drew the curtains and in that darkened room I drifted off to sleep.

I came awake at four, to a hammering on the door. The attendant stood outside, tray in hand, asking whether I wanted tea or coffee. I chose tea. Gopi had left a note for me, saying he'd gone out on the package tour and would be back in the evening. The attendant hung around, pretending to make the bed while I sat at the window sipping the unbearably sweet tea. It seemed a good opportunity to get some information, so I asked the attendant about the kidnap.

'Very sad, sir,' he said, shaking his head. 'Very bad for lodge. No one come now. They think lodge is not safe.'

'What happened?' I asked.

'Those men, they come at night and kill all the bodyguards. Five men they shoot.' The body count had gone up as the story spread. 'They come in special planes, they land here.' He made a sweeping gesture with his arm. 'They come with bombs and rockets and machine guns. They take the ladies, then they go away. The security men, they are no use. They take three ladies, Prime Minister's family.'

I had my opening. 'How did they know when to come, and where?' I asked. 'They must have had someone here helping them out. Otherwise they would have had to spend time searching, and the bodyguards would have done something to stop them.'

He'd heard the gossip, seen Basappa being dragged off by the police, and perhaps spoken to him after he'd been released on bail. He looked around and lowered his voice to speak confidentially. 'Yes, sir, one man here is helping them. Basappa, one of the cooks. Useless man. He only wants to drink. And he likes women, sir. He goes after women in Mysore. He is borrowing money for that and not returning it. That is why he is in trouble.'

'Why? What did he do?'

'Don't know, sir. The police, they take Basappa, then they release him on bail.'

'Does he still work here?'

'No, sir, enquiry is going on. He is under suspension now.'

'So where is he now?'

'He is living in his wife's house. And he is having a little money, buying liquor regularly.'

'I'd have thought he'd run away.'

'No, sir. Where will he go? And he is going to the police station every day to see the constable. In the evening he is at his wife's house in the village.'

The power went off. It wasn't warm but the drizzle had made it humid and I began to sweat. Soon I began to itch, and I went inside the room to take off my shirt and perhaps scratch as best I could. The attendant watched with interest. 'What's your name?' I asked him as I tossed the shirt in a corner.

'Viswanath, sir,' he replied, 'I am living here only. In quarters.' He pointed. 'Sir, what happened to you?'

'Car accident. I was discharged from hospital only five days ago.'

'You should not come here, sir, with injury. You cannot see anything. Why you did not postpone your trip?'

'I should have but there was no time. My brother lives in Guwahati, in Assam, and he finds it hard to get leave. He fixed up his travel programme two months ago. The day before yesterday someone told us about this place and he wanted to see it, and I came along because I didn't want to spoil his vacation. I had no idea the road would be so bad.'

'Yes, sir, road very bad . . . More tea, sir?'

'No, thanks,' I said. 'I'm curious about this Basappa guy . . . Why did the police let him go? They should have kept him in jail until they found out who was behind the kidnapping.'

'Sir, he is suspended from service, he cannot go anywhere because he has to report to the police station every day, and he has no money.'

'But you just said he had money.'

He laughed. 'Yes, sir, he was having money but it is all gone. He show everyone the money and the shopkeepers come and take it from him. What is left he is spending on liquor. Basappa cannot keep money. They say his wife is beating him every day.'

I grinned at the man. 'Poor guy. What does he do for money then?'

'Nothing, sir. He is coming here in the evening and trying to tell everyone that he is involved in big case and he is trying to get drinks from them. It work in the beginning but now nobody listen to him.'

'I have nothing to do here,' I said, 'I'd like to meet this guy. You said he comes here in the evenings.'

'Yes, sir, but now the Director is telling not to permit him to come. Now he is in village all the time. I can call him . . .'

'No,' I said, not wanting to sound at all eager to meet him, 'I'll see him only if I feel like it, and at a time that is convenient to me.' This last was true. I had to catch him alone to put the screws on him.

'His wife's house is in the village, sir, he might be there now. You want to go now? I find out.'

'No, Viswanath, forget it. I'm tired now, otherwise I'd have gone with my brother. If I feel like seeing him later I'll go down to the village and see him. Otherwise, who cares? But tell me, where does he live? How can I get there?'

He gave me directions, with much gesticulation, and I understood eventually that in the village was a big banyan tree, and by that a temple beside which was a small, dark alley, and Basappa's house was the last one in the alley. I tipped Viswanath twenty rupees, which he accepted with much bowing and scraping, and sent him off to his work.

Gopi returned at a quarter past seven, thirsty, tired, dusty, and very happy. 'Hey, man!' he said. 'This place is terrific. We saw a leopard, and four different kinds of deer—barking deer, spotted deer, nilgai, sambar—and then the driver took us to within ten feet of an old bull elephant down by the river. Whew! That elephant was big! He could have turned the jeep over just like that!'

'Just one elephant, was there?'

'No, there was a whole herd of them. At least four cows, a couple of calves, one kind of half-grown. They form up into a circle, with the calves in the middle. Just like they say in the books. Great, man, great . . . But there aren't too many birds. The guy showed us some drongos, but that was mostly it.'

'Do the animals go anywhere near the village?'

'I asked the guide about that. He said no. He said they might do it in summer, when there's no water, but otherwise they generally avoid human settlements. Except monkeys, and sometimes a hungry leopard at night. We saw one on the way back, in the twilight. We were going along and all of a sudden the guide shone his torch at the side of the road and there it was! It crossed the road and climbed up a tree and disappeared. The guide said it might raid a house and carry off a chicken or a goat or something. An elephant got into the village some years back to steal booze. Can you imagine it? An alcoholic elephant?'

It raised my spirits, the sight of my kid brother excited and happy like a seven-year-old. There was room for simple joys in life. I was glad he was with me. 'Hey, when are you going to the village?' he asked.

'After dinner.'

'Do you know where to go?'

'Yes, I found out while you were gaping at the bloody elephants. And look, Gopi, lay off the booze. And the beer, okay? And don't eat too much at dinner.'

'Spoilsport. Why?'

'We'll have to look around, maybe climb a fence or two, keep a lookout for leopards. And this is the snake season, the rain drives them out . . . You don't have to come along, of course.'

'Are you kidding?' he laughed. 'You stick me in the first real adventure in my life and expect me to stay out of it? No way!'

'Get ready, then, and finish your dinner as fast as you can.'

He groaned. 'You don't give a guy a chance to relax, do you? I'd hate to have you for a boss!' He stomped towards the bathroom in mock anger to shower and change. I watched him and wondered how I'd grown old so fast. Though he was only three years younger than I was he didn't look much older than Urmila and Nikhil.

I looked out of the window and saw that it was raining again. Gopi came up behind me. 'Lovely weather,' he said, 'I just love the rain.'

'I know,' I said, 'I've had to pull you out of it enough times to last me the rest of my life.' As a little boy he had loved to play in the rain and I smiled at the sudden unbidden memory of him at the age of five or six, splashing in puddles, dancing in the rain.

'I hated you then,' he said, 'you used to seem to do it just to bug me. Big brother Stalin.'

I took a swing at him and he ran to the door, leading the way to the dining hall. We went down the path, paved with round stones, through the lawn to the office building and past that to the dining hall at the riverside. I wanted to eat early and set off for the village while the attendants were still busy with dinner. When we finished it was a quarter to eight and most of the others were just moving in, many of them carrying their drinks, to sit and chat before eating. Viswanath asked if anything was wrong, and I smiled and told him no, that everything was fine, that I was still a little under the weather, and could he make sure I wasn't disturbed through the night. He nodded and smiled and we moved on.

We slipped out of the gate unseen at a quarter past eight, while the man on watch was relieving himself in the bushes some twenty yards away. The village was less than a kilometre up the road, a small, dismal collection of huts with a few brick houses here and there, most of the people being associated with the resort in one way or another. I followed Viswanath's directions and found the banyan tree and the temple next to it. There was a single street lamp between the tree and the temple and in its light we saw the opening of the alley in which Basappa's wife's house was. We had just reached the mouth of the alley when I sensed someone behind us. I turned just in time to see an indistinct figure in black duck behind a tree. I grabbed Gopi's hand and we turned away from the alley, taking cover in a doorway where in our dark clothing we wouldn't be noticed. As we watched, the man in black emerged from his cover, looked around, and began to jog towards the banyan and then into the alley, where we lost sight of him in the dark.

The man in black moved fast, whoever he was. I got an

impression of squat power. I edged out of the shelter of the doorway, with Gopi at my heels. When we caught sight of him again he was levering himself over the wall of a house at the end of the alley—Basappa's wife's, going by Viswanath's instructions—and even as we watched from the corner, he dropped off the wall and disappeared into the compound.

He emerged less than two minutes later, climbing easily over the wall. He landed outside on his toes and ran as he hit the ground. This time he didn't look around for pursuit: he headed straight for the exit from the alley, straight at us. He hadn't seen us there and he was running full tilt at us when I nudged Gopi. 'Get the bastard,' I said, and as the man came level with us I stepped out into the street in front of him.

I underestimated him quite terribly. He was faster than I'd imagined, and incredibly strong. As I reached for him he evaded my hands with a swerve and a twist of his torso and in the same movement hit me on the left side with a vicious two-handed blow that knocked me down and put me out of action with an overwhelming pain lancing its way through my chest and shoulders and head from the point where he'd hit me. In a haze I saw Gopi emerge from shelter and aim a kick at the man's head. Without skipping a beat the man ducked, and while Gopi was off balance got close in and threw him over his hip and on to me. Gopi landed heavily across my legs as I rolled desperately away to avoid him falling on my chest. My right hand came down inches from a stone and as Gopi fell I lobbed it at the man in black running without a backward glance. More by chance than by design the stone struck him on the back of his head. He stumbled and tripped, but recovered very quickly indeed, long before Gopi got anywhere near him. He turned, saw Gopi closing in on him and me trying to get to my feet, and with a burst of speed disappeared into the dark.

I'd been wrong about not being traced.

The police hadn't traced me but someone else had. Who? This guy looked like Hairy Face, or the stocky man in SOF uniform, the impostor.

Gopi came dispiritedly back to help me to my feet, and we stood there for a minute, getting our breath back. Then we heard a woman's scream from the direction of Basappa's house. The man in black must have killed him. His wife had found him. His widow, actually.

If we were seen anywhere in the area we'd automatically be suspects, and at the first brush with the law I'd lose my cover. I grabbed Gopi's hand and tugged him away. 'What the hell are you doing?' he asked furiously. 'We should go back and help that woman!'

'Forget it,' I gasped, 'the man's beyond help and the neighbours will get there in no time. We have to get back to the lodge, pick up our stuff, and get out and disappear.'

'Why?' he asked, slowing down to let me catch up. At every step my ribs hurt and I couldn't sustain the pace for long.

'Explain later,' I panted, 'I can't keep up with you. You go ahead, get to the room, shut the door. Pack all your light stuff, papers, cash, anything that might tell them who you are. Pack my stuff as well. Put it all in my bag and wait for me. Pretend to sleep. Leave the bathroom door open. If anyone comes say I'm in the bathroom.'

Gopi ran on ahead and I slowed to a walk. I wished I'd been fit. That would've given me, with the help of the element of surprise, a chance against that man in black, Basappa's murderer. He'd done the job quickly and smoothly, like a professional hit-man . . . Who could he be? He certainly wasn't Army-trained. Too unconventional, and far too well trained. In the Army we concentrated only on killing the opposition, without too much attention paid to incapacitating or handicapping them . . . And why had this man waited till I arrived here to kill Basappa? He could have done it before . . .

The pain overwhelmed me. I sagged by the road three hundred yards from the lodge gates, a little over a kilometre from the temple. My sprained ankle was almost healed now, and it was bearing up much better, but that blow to the chest had probably torn something adrift, and hadn't done the dislocated shoulder any good either. I wished I'd had the foresight to carry the painkiller with me, but I had no way of knowing in advance that my fishing expedition would turn into a massacre.

I managed to get back to my feet, then in desperation lapsed into some of the basic rhythms that had kept us going on those sixty-kilometre forced marches in battle order with a twenty-five kilo pack. But no battle pack ever put a knife between your ribs at every step. I found the rhythm, finally, synchronized my steps with my breathing, found the agony controllable, and walked on, concentrating on not letting my head down.

Past the gate now. It was still unmanned. Security was lax here, being oriented towards keeping poachers in check rather than kidnappers or other criminals out. Good for me, I thought dizzily, no one would mistake me for a poacher. The pain was biting deeper now, bringing on waves of nausea and a coppery taste in the back of the mouth. I couldn't afford to stop here and throw up, it would be too noisy and take too long. I held it back, took a deep breath, kept going, off the road, towards the building that now loomed up less than fifty yards away.

It had taken me well nigh thirty-five minutes to cover that distance of a kilometre and a half, and it had very nearly defeated me. I reached the rear of the building, saw the bathroom door hanging open right at the end—eight rooms, some one hundred feet away—and made it, knees beginning to give way, breath coming rapidly. Inside the bathroom I held on to the door and it slammed. Gopi heard the noise and came running to drag me in. 'You took so long!' he said. 'I was thinking of coming after you.' He would have made that distance in seven or eight minutes at most, nearly half an hour ahead of me. He helped me into the room and to the bed. I collapsed, sinking into the soft mattress.

'I need to take it easy for an hour or so,' I said, 'and some medication. We'll lie low for a while, then decide what's to be done.' Gopi brought me the painkillers and a glass of water and sat next to me on the bed.

'Why can't we stay right here?' he asked. 'No one saw us go out, everyone knows you're ill. They won't suspect us.'

'That they might not, but the police might come asking questions and there's no way we can hide our identity from them for very long and then I'll be back in hospital, or worse, in prison. We have to get out of here, and we have to do it soon.'

'But where will we go?' he asked. 'If we take the car they'll trace us.'

'We walk out of here,' I said, 'we jump the fence and disappear into the jungle.'

'But what are we going to do in the dam' jungle?' he complained.

'It's not so hard getting along in the jungle if you know how to,' I smiled weakly. 'It's been part of my training, living off the land.'

'You mean that commando shit you went through? Rambo-type crap?'

'Not quite,' I said. 'We'll be there only a couple of days. We'll carry our food, or buy it someplace, or go without. It might be only one day.'

'But why?'

'Someone's chasing behind us,' I said. 'That's why they sent that guy in black out there to get rid of our friend Basappa, to get rid of him before I talked to him. So now we get into the swamps and emerge somewhere far away from here, and chase my other lead.'

'How do you think they traced you?' he asked. 'In Bangalore you were pretty sure they hadn't. You said something about crossbar exchanges and stuff that I didn't understand and I just swallowed it. And who are they? They wouldn't be the cops, of course.'

'I don't know how they traced me unless they've been watching me all the time, and I don't know who they are except that they must be in some way connected with the kidnappers. And I think they traced me because the timing's a bit close. I come here to talk to Basappa and just then he goes and gets himself killed. Unless you believe in coincidence. Strange . . .'

'What is?'

'There are two sets of people after me,' I said slowly, 'and the extra-legal ones have a good network of their own . . . if they've been watching me all along, they have a network.'

'That's obvious,' he said. 'What else?'

'Strange things happened during that raid. Like I found the hostages with their throats cut. They'd been killed even before we ran the raid. They'd been shot as well, but afterwards. I could make out that much. The other thing was that I found a kidnapper—one of their gang, anyway—dead, with his throat cut. And there was a man in there dressed in SOF combat blacks. I saw him and thought he was one of us but something looked out of place, and then I figured it out. We all had four grenades on our harnesses but he didn't have any, and I'd heard only two of them go off before I saw him. In the heat of the moment I didn't realize but later I did.'

'And now they're knocking off their own people as you get close to them, right?' he said, his eyes glazing over: a sign of intense thought.

'Yes,' I said.

'And this raid of yours, you said you threw the timing. You went in ahead of schedule.'

'Yes. A couple of hours or so.'

'Okay,' he said, 'tell me once again what happened when you went into that house. No, start earlier. From the time you positioned yourself for the raid.'

I told him the lot, from the time we got into the pond to the time I got knocked out, from behind.

'Are you sure that thickset guy was masquerading? He couldn't have used up his grenades some other way?'

'No. I'd have heard.'

'In that case they knew when the raid was coming. He wouldn't have spent all his time dressed up like you guys.'

I hadn't thought of that. 'Exactly,' I said, 'so what does all that tell you?'

'It was meant to be hijacked, this kidnap.'

'Hijacked how?'

'The hostages were meant to get killed. Whoever planned this would have set it up so that a small group—one man, max two—would have got out with the diaries, leaving the other kidnappers in the house with the dead hostages. That means you wouldn't have got the hostages out alive, or the diaries.'

'Explain,' I said.

'Some of them were ready for you when you went in, others weren't. Is that right?' I nodded. 'There you are, then, there were two groups. One that knew you were coming, another that didn't. None of them was really ready at the time.'

'Okay,' I said, 'but they were preparing for it. Otherwise I'd never even have laid my eyes on the diaries.'

'Right. There might have been more than one of the kidnappers dressed like you guys. You don't know. But you could assume that all of those men dressed like you were meant to survive.'

'Right.'

'You said that when you went in your back-up team were going to train searchlights on the place. Light it up good. Right? They would have known that, the group that was meant to survive, if they knew the timing, and were taken a little by surprise only because you went in early, without those searchlights from your back-up team.'

'Yes.'

'They planned to get away just before your raid, leaving dead hostages and the expendable members of their own bunch behind.'

'All right.'

'And it was hijacked again.'

'Meaning?'

'Meaning that you got your hands on the diaries, which was not what they wanted, and then someone else took them from you during that raid. That someone else was not someone who they had planned would get the diaries. So the bunch that were after the diaries in the first place are after you now.'

'What for? I lost the diaries and that's public knowledge.'

'They might not believe you. You've broken out of hospital, right? So what they're doing is following you around in the hope that you will lead them to the diaries. If you have stashed them away somewhere you'll have to pick them up some time, and they'll be waiting. If you don't have the diaries, as they probably know you don't, they expect you to lead them to whoever has them. They're looking for whoever's got the diaries, and they're following you as well.'

I sat quiet for a while. Then, knowing I was wrong, said, 'That sounds too far-fetched.'

'Does it?' he smiled. 'Can you find another explanation that fits?'

I tried and didn't find one. 'Okay,' I said, 'anything else?'

'Yes. You explained about some ex-Grenadier or something who you thought was involved in this thing. The chances are he is. They probably knew Basappa would put you on to him and offed him to stop him doing that.'

I knew that and it was good to have one's thoughts confirmed. 'Why?'

'They don't want you going for any of their own men. They want you to go for the guy who stole the diaries. They'll stay behind the scenes and let you do their work for them, lead them to the diaries. Don't you see why they waited this long to kill that Basappa? They've made sure you remain on the black list of the law men. The police will find out you were here, enquiring about Basappa the night he was killed. The only way you can prove your innocence now is by finding those diaries. Clever bastards.'

'We can check that out. I'm going after the Grenadier anyway: I don't have a choice. If they knock him off before I get to him it'll confirm what you said. But then I have another lead.'

'Who?'

'The guy whom Rawat—the Grenadier—worked for. I don't see how his boss could escape knowing he's such a shady guy. By implication the boss too is shady.'

'Leaping at conclusions, aren't we?'

'Better than nothing.'

'Yes. And . . . that guy in black. He's not going to kill you.'

'That I knew. He could have gotten both of us in that alley.'

'That's it. Give me some more time for it to simmer. Shall we move out now? Do you feel up to it?'

I didn't, and the painkillers were getting to me now, making me light-headed and woozy. I wouldn't be able to concentrate. Besides, we were all right for the time being: I could afford a catnap. 'Wake me in fifteen minutes,' I said, 'I need it.'

When Gopi woke me fifteen minutes later the moon had disappeared behind clouds and the dark had almost solidified. I hefted the torch we'd kept with us in case we needed it, and Gopi carried the single pack in which we'd stuffed whatever I thought would be just enough to see us through a day or two in the forest—two bottles of mineral water, a change of underwear, Gopi's passport and tickets and my wallet—along with all the money Gopi had brought—some twenty thousand dollars worth of currency and traveller's cheques, and forty thousand or so rupees that he had left from what he had changed at the airport.

In the rain we sneaked out of the bathroom door along the back of the lodge and towards the gate. There was some light, from the lights other guests had left on in their bathrooms, from the faraway round lamps on the lawn, from the street lamps on the roads within the complex, but all of it was too faint to be of any real use on that night. We bumbled through the opaque darkness without using the torch, which someone might have seen. A quick look at the gate confirmed that we would not be able to get out of the complex unnoticed: two men were in the guard house and they checked every now and again to see if the rain was letting up.

The eight-foot high barbed-wire fence started at the gate and we broke out of it a hundred yards away, forcing a path through the hedge inside it. Another ten yards and we were on the road back to Mysore. I had a large-scale map of the area, courtesy the Karnataka State Forest Department, acquired in Bangalore before we left for Kabini. One of the basic skills we had been taught in the Army was map-reading, and I had a compass in my watchstrap. We wouldn't get lost, that was for sure, but I had no idea where to go.

We stopped a kilometre from the gate and in the dark

I switched on the torch to look at the map. Four adjoining sanctuaries were marked on it clearly: Kabini, Nagarhole, Bandipur and Mudumalai. We were close to the edge of Kabini, and south of us was Nagarhole and Coorg. We would head south, I reckoned, emerging from the forest in Nagarhole, heading then for South Coorg and then Wynad and Calicut, or we could move towards Mudumalai and end up somewhere in Tamil Nadu, heading then for the border near Bangalore, probably Hosur. From there I would once again pick up the trail of the Grenadier.

The road wasn't hard to follow. The undergrowth along the sides of the roads inside the sanctuaries had been cleared, to make it easy for tourists to spot animals as they searched for water in summer. We got off the road some three kilometres from the lodge, getting into the forest and heading due south.

My major fears were snakes and leopards. Snakes, being cold-blooded, prefer to sleep out the hot day in cool places and hunt at night. This area was full of cobras and vipers, and a few kraits, and the rain would have driven them out of their burrows. The leopards, being good tree-climbers, would have taken shelter in trees in this kind of weather, lying in wait for prey. If disturbed, they could get aggressive, and since they are, pound for pound of body weight, the strongest of the cats, could be formidable. I knew that they fear fire, but in this weather, trying to lie low, there was no way I would light a fire.

I figured we had a lead of at least a couple of hours, at most seven hours. Assuming that Basappa's widow or the neighbours retained enough sense to report the murder to the police immediately, it would take them at least half an hour to get to the scene. They wouldn't immediately connect the murder with the guests at the resort—though eventually they were bound to—and would further bring in the CBI, since Basappa had been let loose on bail from CBI custody. By the time they got to Viswanath and thence to us and the empty room we had left behind, it would probably be early morning. And since we had made it out of the resort without being seen, and the rain would probably wash our tracks off, we'd be safe at least until late in the morning.

If, on the other hand, the police weren't told immediately, they'd arrive and take statements and with every passing hour the trail would grow colder. But they would definitely get to us by morning, when the attendant was supposed to bring us tea. At six in the morning, Viswanath had told me. He would notice us missing, raise the alarm, and that would be that. But Viswanath would also tell them about my injuries, which would put them off the track until they used the injuries to identify me . . .

We could bank on the police not even getting on to our trail by early morning. They would find the cab still around, and perhaps interrogate the driver. The trail would end there because he'd picked us up at a hotel, not at Nikhil's house.

The drizzle would help. Gopi said that some of the guides were good trackers, and we'd left a trail that an experienced tracker would be able to follow without much trouble. The rain would hold off a good tracker by a few hours, no more. On this terrain, short of sleep and food, slowed down by aching bones, we'd average at best two kilometres an hour at night, even with the torch to light our way for us. If we had four hours we could get eight kilometres away. From there we'd have to find our way to a road some place and take a bus. Walking cross-country would otherwise drain both of us too quickly.

We should have stolen a vehicle and dumped it somewhere to put them off the track, I thought, and bought ourselves a few hours. But neither of us was comfortable stealing cars, though I did know how to get a Maruti's door open without a key, and could hot-wire it from inside. Besides, I didn't want to leave my fingerprints behind: they were on record at Army Headquarters and would be available to the police without delay.

And all this was only as far as the police were concerned. We had no idea where the man in black was, but I had no doubt he'd be behind us. I had the pistol I'd taken from the guard at the hospital stuck in my waistband. If the man in black turned up I'd not hesitate to shoot him if I got the time.

Two kilometres into the jungle. I held the tension back and kept an easy pace that taxed me little and Gopi not at all. I had to tell him several times to take it easy, not to make noise, to be patient, and all the time he hurried and ran on ahead like a dog on a leash. We changed direction now, turning due east, walking through a small stream to break the trail, wetting our feet and getting ourselves thoroughly uncomfortable.

Two hours out of the resort, I guessed we were three to four kilometres into the forest. We had crossed two streams, both generated by the rains that seemed to have fallen steadily in these parts. I was running out of steam once again, the chill combining with wet feet to give me a cold in the head. I sneezed twice, the involuntary tightening of the chest leaving me gasping in pain. Time for a break. I looked for a spot where the undergrowth was thinner, where we could see the ground, and found one. I brought a bottle of water out of the pack and swallowed a tablet, while Gopi just sat back and shut his eyes.

The attacker came out of the dark. Gopi heard nothing at all and I was half asleep from the painkillers I'd taken. When he came, it was with a slight rustle of leaves that I sensed at the fringes of my consciousness: it broke the pattern of the sound of raindrops dripping onto the leaves. I saw him blurring out of the edge of the small clearing, silhouetted against a small patch of night sky. I rolled away with a yell that brought Gopi awake. Gopi, not quite fast enough on the attack, made a grab at the attacker's leg, slowed him down enough to let me get on my feet and face him as he turned.

The man in black himself. The rain, I noticed, had stopped, and the clouds had moved on a little. In the starlight I saw something in the man's right hand. It looked like a vicious six-inch blade, but it didn't gleam in the faint moonlight. The barely visible blade shifted and weaved as he switched to a throwing grip and I crouched instinctively, swaying away to my left, and then Gopi exploded into action from the man's unguarded side. Gopi was fast but not as fast as our man, and nowhere near as powerful, but he managed to throw a bough at the man, who saw it out of a corner of his eye and brushed it almost contemptuously away with his left arm and whirled to face Gopi, changing his grip on his knife once again.

The knife artist. The one who liked to cut throats.

Anger boiled up within me and before I knew what I was doing I had taken two steps towards him. He turned again, unsure of whom to deal with first, hesitating visibly. Gopi's offensive had taken him by surprise.

And then I saw how he had managed. He had NVGs on, bulging out of the front of his face like a frog's eyes. He'd be able to see movement, silhouettes and flashes, but not contrasting colours. Gopi and I were about the same height and build and in those green goggles we might look the same to him. Hence the hesitation.

Which meant he was after one of us. Which one?

Gopi swayed closer and aimed a kick at his right ankle, not with any hope of connecting but to draw him out into an attack that would leave him off balance for me to retaliate. As Gopi closed, he went down on one knee to block Gopi's swinging leg and go for his groin. And in that moment I went for his NVGs. Without them he would be blind for a few short seconds and between the two of us, charged and angry as we were, Gopi and I could demolish him. So I thought, anyway, and feinted with my left arm and went in with my right, feeling fabric, feeling the straps give way as the goggles came away in my hand. The straps slid off his head and I flicked the goggles to my right and spun away from him, helpless with pain.

He came after me then but he was blind in the dark and that left the way open for Gopi to kick him in the kidney from behind, twice. I heard his breath escape in a whoosh and he turned violently to face Gopi. Then he seemed to change his mind about attacking and without breaking the rhythm of his movement slid away into the forest and was gone even before I could get anywhere near him. I did pick up the bough for a shy at him but only managed to hit him on the arm and he dropped his knife and kept going.

Gopi sat down with his back against a tree trunk, breathing heavily, and I collapsed on the ground. 'We should get moving again,' he said when he had got his breath back, 'that sonovabitch will be back any time.'

'Not tonight he won't,' I said. 'If he does come again we'll take him.'

'How?' Gopi almost shouted. 'We've faced the guy twice and both times he could have taken us with ease.'

'He was using NVGs—night vision goggles. I saw them on his face, and ripped them off. I chucked them somewhere that way and he didn't wait to retrieve them when he left. Without those glasses he won't risk attacking the two of us in the dark. And if we find the NVGs and if they're still working, he won't stand a chance. We must hunt them up, they'll enable us to get along faster without using that blasted torch to tell everyone and his brother where we are.'

It took us fifteen minutes of weary searching to find the NVGs in the bushes. They had fallen on a sapling and the straps had snagged on a branch. On the ground by it, was a mask: not really a mask but a bandanna like the ones the kidnappers had worn whenever they'd come out of the house. I picked it up and found that it was made of strong, fine silk and weighted with steel balls at the corners: not a kerchief but a garrotte, the traditional weapon of old-time Indian thugs.

And ten minutes later, searching with the NVGs, we had the knife as well. The blade was six inches long, as I'd guessed, double-edged, and black . . . No wonder it hadn't gleamed. A knife British commandos had used during the Second World War, banned now in Britain. It came with a sheath that could be worn on the leg, but the man had taken the sheath with him.

'Why didn't the motherfucker just move in and cut our throats?' Gopi asked.

'He's only after one of us, not both,' I explained, 'and in the dark, with NVGs, he probably couldn't see which of us was which. Otherwise he'd have had no trouble finishing us off. Did you notice, he hesitated when facing both of us, just before I got his goggles off?'

'No. I was too busy looking to save your ass and mine. Hey, let me have a look through those goggles.' I handed them to him, and I showed him how to control the brightness. He looked through them, and exclaimed, 'Yeah, now I see. He wouldn't have been able to tell us apart. In that case, he was going after me, not you.'

'Right. Perhaps to force me into the open. He must be afraid he'll lose me in the forest.'

'I'll buy that. Since we've got the bastard shaken, I intend to get some sleep. Not one more step without a snooze.'

I woke him at half past four. The clouds were back but it wasn't drizzling. Gopi put on the NVGs but it takes some practice to get the hang of using them. Ideally, you should use them for a while on terrain that you know, so that you can figure out how they distort reality: Gopi hadn't had a chance to do that. So I put them on, and with another painkiller swallowed, we set off again, a little faster than before, as the weak light of dawn seeped into the sky.

chapter eleven

The maps and the compass in my watch turned out to be the most useful things I had as we headed south into the sanctuary. We startled the occasional barking deer or the spindly-legged spotted deer, which took off with incredible speed before we got within a quarter-kilometre of it. We saw a herd of elephants by a waterhole, a temporary one that would dry up by February or March, and saw traces of their progress—great steaming spheres of dung, branches ripped out of trees, soup-plate-sized spots on the ground where their feet had been. We went a long way around them, and the old bull of the herd trumpeted mildly and raised his trunk as he smelt us pass by.

We collected leeches aplenty and at every stop we had to pull three or four off our legs and feet. There were also cuts and bruises, due to clumsiness and thornbushes. I looked for cobwebs to put on the cuts, and basil, but found none. But the worst part was the dirt. We didn't have a change of clothing and in the humid warmth of the day we sweated, except when it was raining, and then we got wet—and stank. I had just got used to it when I went undercover in Uri, but Gopi, fresh from the US, complained mightily.

We covered eight kilometres that second day by my reckoning. And we ate nothing at all.

I didn't have much of an appetite but by afternoon Gopi's face was drawn with hunger. 'We'll stop here for the time being,' I said a little after noon, 'then we'll turn back.'

'What the hell for?' he exploded, standing with his arms akimbo. 'We just took all that trouble to get away from there and now you want to go back! Are you nuts?'

'Do the unexpected,' I said calmly. 'Our friend in black saw us heading south and east. There's not much choice by way of routes when you strike out in this direction and they'll be waiting for us, watching all of them. So we go back, but not the way we came. We'll take a parallel route back.'

'What about Madras and all that stuff you were talking about?'

'We'll have to go into that once again, won't we?' I answered wearily. 'Look, Gopi, we have to keep them off balance, keep them guessing. And the only way to do that is to keep changing our patterns of movement. It means extra effort but also extra safety.'

'And where will we head?' he asked, calming down. 'We can't go back to that resort.'

'We'll head for Mysore, and from there . . . from there we can go anywhere. I don't know yet. We're heading for Bombay, to catch Rawat, but we could do that from Bangalore or Calicut, or wherever.'

We slept the rest of the afternoon, taking it in turns to stand watch—extremely boring for someone who's not used to it—and Gopi woke me at dusk. 'I wouldn't mind if it'd rain,' he said, 'I wouldn't mind the hunger so much if there were water splashing down all around us.'

'You'll catch pneumonia, more like,' I said, 'so shut up and get moving.'

'Always the big brother.' He grinned. 'The trouble with you, young Stalin, is that you never learnt to enjoy yourself. Try it one of these days, fooling around in the rain. Great feeling!'

I aimed a kick at his bottom and we set out. We made far better progress with the NVGs than without. For all the exertions of the past couple of days, the pains in my chest were decreasing, and the ache in my shoulder was gone: perhaps my body was beginning to cope with the punishment. By now hunger was the big problem. I'd managed to stuff a couple of bananas into the pack before we left, and I gave them to Gopi since I'd had recent practice of going hungry for a day or two, but by nightfall Gopi was desperate. I could see nothing to eat—no berries or wild fruits like in the *Jungle Book*, and no animals to shoot and roast over a fire—and we had to live with our hunger until morning, when, exhausted, we reached the road.

Just half an hour later we were at a bus stop, with a small shop by it. Gopi stuffed himself with peanut brittle and bananas, and tea to wash it down with, and ten minutes after we finished, we flagged down a bus headed for Mysore.

We slept through the bumpy ride, waking up only in Mysore, where the conductor saw us off with a curious look.

At a shop close to the station we bought essentials, clothes and another bag before checking into a small hotel nearby which had two rooms free where we could lie low comfortably for a day or two. While Gopi attacked a steaming breakfast I shaved and showered and dressed in dark trousers and a T-shirt. 'Where are you going?' he asked, sipping coffee.

'Phone calls.'

'Will you get in touch with Urmila and Nikhil?'

'No.'

'Why the hell not?'

'How do you think our friend with the knife got on to us?'

'Oh,' he said, 'I missed that. What about Sandhya?'

'I'll call her father. Ask him to tell her to be at a friend's place where I can speak to her. She'll be out of her mind now.'

'Must be hellish for her. How can any woman take it?'

'She's got her own work as well. That helps.'

I got through to Sandhya's father at the first try. He didn't sound too happy when I told him who it was, but that was only because I was in trouble. His endless faith in me, and his wife's, shamed me. I broke in on his greetings. 'Tell Sandhya to be at Deepak's place at five,' I told him.

'Yes, yes,' he said, 'but how are you? Where are you? Do you want money? Can we do something for you? Would you like to come here until it is settled?' The questions poured out of the old man and behind them I could sense his barbed anxiety for his daughter, who'd had a rough deal out of life so far.

'Nothing now, thanks,' I said. 'Just give her this message. I'm sorry to involve you in something like this.'

He cut me off with the beginnings of offence sharpening his voice. 'How can we not be involved?' he asked. 'After all, you're family now. Nothing will change that.'

'Thanks,' I said, 'that's enough for me for the time being.'

'Don't worry,' he said, 'call me any time, for anything. I can come there if you want. I know one of the old DGPs here. I can talk to him if you think that will help.'

'Not just now,' I said, 'I'll let you know if I need anything. Just give her the message. Tell her to be there.'

'She will be there, don't worry,' he promised, and hung up.

Gopi was asleep when I got back to the hotel so I went out again to book two tickets on a commercial flight to Bombay, from Calicut rather than Bangalore. When I asked the travel agent how to get to Calicut, he smiled and said that there were buses, buses of all kinds, deluxe buses, ordinary buses, anything. He got me two places on a bus but the flight to Bombay was another matter altogether. With a little pleading I got the agent to call a friend of his at Calicut's Karippoor airport, and got him to promise to put us on the flight when it took off next morning.

Back at the hotel Gopi was irritated. 'We've shaken them off,' he grumbled, 'take it easy for a day or two and then we can get after them. Try to heal before you chase.'

'Gives them time to find us,' I replied. 'We've got none to waste.'

'They're not all over the place,' he said.

'As long as it's only the man in black or the police, that's all right. But having both of them on our tails is a different matter altogether. And I'm afraid they might go after Sandhya . . . Or her parents. I have hostages to fortune, and don't you forget that.'

'Why haven't they already gone after her?'

'She's in SOF quarters in Delhi. Not the easiest place to get into. Besides, she's useless to them unless they can take her and get word to me that they have her. Getting their hands on her is no use if they can't use her as a lever.'

'Do you have an Internet account? A PC at home, with a modem?'

'I don't, Sandhya does. She got into it last year.'

'We'll buy a PC, a notebook with a modem. Use my Internet account. Then we can communicate securely.'

'We need a base for that. Forget it. We'd have to have access to a telephone. Plus extra baggage to lug around . . . Not worth it. All I want is for her to get out, go to Kathmandu or Paro or some place and stay there until this thing blows over.'

'You can't do that,' he said. 'If she's not in contact you won't be sure whether she's safe.'

That I wouldn't. For the first time I felt a terrible, tearing anxiety for someone, a feeling I'd never had before. I couldn't let anything happen to Sandhya and Kiran. She couldn't ask for police protection, not with her husband a fugitive. As long as she didn't move out of where she was she'd be all right. But even there she'd have to face some kind of ostracism. And before long they'd ask her to move. I reckoned she could stay there another week, until the paperwork caught up. As far as the Army was concerned I was still not proven guilty, but AWOL—Away Without Leave—after the operation. 'I'll tell her to continue where she is,' I said, 'maybe ask Harkishen, my batman, to keep an eye on things. He's pretty good.'

'And this Rawat guy is the only lead you have now?'

'Yes. And maybe his boss, whoever that is. I'll take them both if necessary.'

He looked at me strangely. 'I've never seen you like this,' he said finally. 'You're harder. You're talking calculated violence now, and it's in your mind all the time.'

'First direct threat to my family,' I explained. 'I never felt this before. I never had to think of non-combatants behind me at risk and without protection.' I don't know if the explanation satisfied him. I myself didn't think about it till much later, when it was all over and I wondered at all the hard and incredible things I'd managed to do.

When I called Sandhya later that day at Deepak's place, she was there, and composed by this time. 'Raja,' she said, 'your friend Mankekar called. The old man. I've been getting feelers about moving out of here but he called to say that there was no need to do that until this is settled, and to call him if anyone tries to force me out. And he gave me a number, his private number. He told me to give it to you if you got in touch, and to ask you to call him if he can help.'

Kelkar's work. For the first time since leaving the shelter of Nikhil's house in Bangalore I felt a moment of warmth and safety. 'Stay right where you are, then,' I said, 'and ask Harkishen to stick around. He'll keep an eye on things for you.'

'He's already around,' she replied. 'He won't go away. He arrived the day after you disappeared and he just won't shift. And he's told me a dozen times to tell you that if you get in touch and want him to do anything for you he's game. He's got leave due, he told me, so he can come whenever you like . . . And he said not to worry about money either, for the time being.'

Harkishen had been my batman ever since I joined the SOF, a Pahari from the Terai, a tall, lugubrious, sombre-eyed man who had little to say to anyone. For some reason known only to himself he had appointed himself my protector and, when I'd got married, Sandhya's as well. 'No problem, then,' I said, 'you just relax at home. I'll call from time to time. Expect nothing for a couple of days.'

'All right,' she said, 'I don't have a choice, do I?'

'I'm afraid so,' I said gently, 'but this is the last time. I promise you that.'

'What do you mean?' she asked.

'I intend to quit when this blows over. Start again, from scratch.'

She was silent for a few seconds. Then, 'You're serious, aren't you?'

'Yes. We'll talk about it later.' On that conciliatory note I hung up, cheered for the first time since that sneak attack in the forest, relieved that Kiran and Sandhya were out of it.

I boarded that evening's bus to Calicut with more twinges in my chest than I'd have liked. Gopi had managed, by dint of his American accent and a wonder-struck druggist, to get me supplies of painkiller without benefit of a prescription. I swallowed two and passed the six-hour ride in a state of middling discomfort and semi-somnolence. After a six-hour rest in Calicut the flight to Bombay was more of the same, and I arrived in passable shape at the Airport Plaza hotel where Gopi insisted we go instead of heading for a better hotel in the city.

It was drizzling when we checked in, but at this time of the year—the third week of June—I'd have been surprised if it hadn't been raining all the time. At noon I called the offices of Wesco's airline subsidiary to get in touch with Abhay Rawat, formerly of the Grenadiers. The receptionist who responded to my call treated me to five minutes of tinny strings playing 'Jingle Bells' and other inane tunes. A voice then put me on to a woman with a British accent who told me haughtily that Major Rawat was no longer with the Wesco group. 'Where can I contact him, then?' I asked. 'He must have left a forwarding address.'

'That's right,' she said, 'he left a box number to which we send all his mail.'

'And who might you be?' I asked.

'I was his secretary,' she replied, 'but only for about three months.'

'So who do you think might know how I can get in touch with him?'

'You could speak to the present security chief, Mr Deshpande, but I don't think he'll be able to help you, either.'

'Do you have Rawat's residential address?' I asked.

'He was given a flat by the company while he was with us,' she replied, 'but he moved out of there two weeks ago.'

'He must have left in a hurry.'

'Yes,' came the answer. A pause, then, 'If you'll excuse me, I have to get back to work.' She hung up. Just one way out now, I thought, call old man Mankekar.

I dialled the number Sandhya had given me. It rang about twenty times before the creaky, rolling, old man's voice responded. 'Yes?' he said.

'This is Colonel Menon,' I said, 'you told my wife I could call you if I needed help.'

'Yes,' he replied, not sounding at all surprised, as if he'd been expecting my call. 'You see, Colonel, Kelkar backed you up, his story matched yours. There seemed to be some inconsistencies in what the CBI reported after your raid . . . Too many loose ends for my liking. Afterwards, when that man was killed, at Kabini, it didn't seem to be your style, but could be the kidnappers'. What's happening has the flavour of a witch-hunt in which you're the witch. As I see it, at worst you were incompetent, and at best you were betrayed. So I offered help. Not for you but because my friend the Prime Minister deserves to know the truth.'

'Why don't you tell your pal the PM to call off the search, then?' I asked.

He was silent for a moment, then said heavily, 'Why don't you turn yourself in and let the police do what you're doing? Same reason.'

'I'm not going to tell you where I am,' I said, 'nor will I make long calls I don't want the number traced.'

'Young man, I didn't ask you where you were.' The voice snapped now. 'And I don't make a habit of betrayal. Do you understand me, young man?'

'Yes, sir,' I said, taken aback at the vigour in him.

'All right . . . Let me tell you, I'll inform the Committee that you have been in touch with me.'

'Why?'

'If they find out that you've been calling . . . I can conceal what we've been discussing, but I have to tell them you've been in touch.'

'All right.' He was a tough old man. There was no harm in his telling the Committee that I'd been in touch.

'Now what do you want me to do?'

'Trace a man. Abhay Rawat, ex-Army, used to be security chief with Wesco until recently. He resigned a few weeks ago, disappeared without trace. I want an address.'

'The name is familiar,' he said, 'I'll have him in twelve hours. Why do you want to trace him?'

'I intend to talk to him. I tried to talk to the cook at Kabini but someone killed him minutes before I got to him.'

'They said you had killed him. The police traced you as

far as Kabini and lost the trail. You must have gone into the forest.'

'No comment. I'll call you tomorrow morning at half past eight. Will you be there?'

'Yes. No one else takes this telephone. If I'm not here an answering machine takes over. It's in my study, you see, and no one ever comes in here except the maid, to clean, and only in my presence.'

If I'd been given a chance I'd have been after Basappa and Rawat much sooner. But I had one advantage now. I didn't have to stick to the law. I was willing to beat the truth out of the man. I'd get into wherever he was and drag him out and break the man.

When I talked to Mankekar the next morning, the aches and pains had subsided. I had been for a short, slow jog early that morning, and the protests from various muscles that had been unused until then drowned out the pain from the injuries. I breathed deeply for the first time since waking up in hospital. Mankekar picked up the telephone at the first ring. 'Colonel?' he asked even before I could say 'Hello'.

'Yes,' I said, 'you could call me Raja.'

'Raja,' he said easily, 'I found your man, though not without trouble. He resigned without notice from his company and was let off even though he is supposed to give three months' notice. I heard he was told to quit, but I don't know why. Perhaps the company didn't want to keep a man with a past like his. When you started checking on him they must have done some digging of their own.

another look, walking past the house again in the opposite direction, pretending to be searching for an address written on a scrap of paper I carried in my hand. The outer wall was solid, but not high enough for real security—only about four feet, with iron fenceposts planted in it and three feet of fencing above. With a little stretching I could get onto the outer wall and thence a sunshade, and from there the balcony was within reach, if I stretched a little more. It would take some doing but I could do it.

I'd never looked at houses from the point of view of breaking in silently and wished for a passing moment that I had been a burglar. With some tools and a little practice getting into these houses would be a breeze.

The rain intensified. I unfolded the umbrella and walked past the house once again. The watchman ducked into the back of the house and emerged wearing an old khaki raincoat, leaving his place only for a couple of minutes. He was far better than the average watchman, I could see, but in his bearing and manner there was little sign of the Army. He looked like a goon. Where had Rawat got him from, I wondered. This guy with his greasy medium-long hair and dirty nails and bad posture wasn't disciplined enough to be out of the Army, at least not recently.

Back at the hotel I told Gopi what I planned to do. 'I'm going into that house,' I told him, 'and I need some hardware before I do that.'

'What kind of hardware?' he asked suspiciously.

'Hooks. Something I can use as a grapnel. Preferably rubber or plastic coated, rustproof and light enough to

He's just moved house. I'm told his children are away holidaying somewhere, and he hasn't had the time to get a proper establishment going. I have his address here . . . Will you note it down?'

'Yes,' I said, 'could you continue to check on the man? Who let him off the job? Who took him on?'

'I can tell you that straight away. The Managing Director, a man called Saifuddin Ahmed. He hired and fired Rawat.'

'Anything more on Ahmed, then?'

'I'll search. Call me again.'

'Tomorrow morning. Same time.'

He agreed and hung up. The address gave me no clue to where Rawat's house was. Back at the hotel I asked the receptionist where it would be and she said it was near Andheri. 'The Lokhandwala estate is quite well known, sir,' she said, 'it's close to Seven Bungalows.'

'What kind of a place would this be?' I asked.

'It's a bungalow, sir. They built those bungalows in the early eighties . . . They'd be far too expensive now. You won't have any trouble finding it.' Where had Rawat got the money from to buy a bungalow in Bombay, where real estate was among the most expensive in the world? His connections, while powerful, wouldn't have got him lumps of money all of a sudden.

I wished he'd been in an apartment building. The layout of a flat is easy to find out, and a couple of days' observation is enough to find out the patterns in peoples' lives. Watchmen like to talk, besides, about weird habits of people who live in the apartment blocks they guard. A few hundred rupees and I'd have known what to do. A bungalow is a slightly different proposition.

The Lokhandwala estate, I discovered, was not too far from the hotel, by Bombay standards. It was across the tracks, up the western line a couple of stations to Andheri station, and four kilometres from there. The auto driver knew exactly where to go, and after he dropped me off at a corner within the estate, by a shopping complex, I discovered that Rawat's house was only about hundred metres further up the road.

I bought an umbrella from a shop in the complex and stepped out into the rain. Most people on the street wore raincoats and rubber shoes, some carried umbrellas—almost totally useless in the wind whipping in from the sea—and had their feet wet in any case.

The bungalows were small, with handkerchief-size lawns, some with a couple of flower-beds. Two storeys, most of them, showing signs of alterations made by owners wanting to be different from the others in the row. All had grandiose names, all typically upper middle class.

Rawat's house stuck opulently out. It had been done up, repainted recently with expensive enamel that would hold off the corrosive effects of being so close to the sea. The window and door frames were all new, and the front door was carved and looked solid enough to hold off a tank. There was a satellite dish on top—unnecessary because there were dozens of cable operators in the area—and potted plants in the small veranda and in window boxes.

And a watchman at the gate.

There was a small wooden sentrybox inside the low gate, and the watchman lurked inside. I had a good look at him as I walked by. Bombay's watchmen, typically Gorkhas, are paid to stand and watch and raise the alarm if required. They are never armed with anything more than a cane with a thong at the end of it that they loop around their wrists, and most of them have little idea of how to use it to any effect. But this one was different. A giant of a man, hard-faced and heavily moustached, with swelling shoulders and heavy, tattooed arms, thick wrists and large, beefy hands. Long fingernails, I noticed, and black. His paunch drooped over his wide belt but it didn't look as if it would slow him down at close quarters. An ugly customer. He carried the standard cane with the loop around his wrist. As I passed by he turned away from the gate and looked into the house at a dog barking from a window, and as the fabric of his trousers stretched I caught sight of something in his hip pocket, something that would have been eight inches long and about an inch wide. A comb or a knife? He stuck his hand inside his pocket and palmed it: it was a knife, all right, and he probably knew how to use it.

Two obstacles, then—the watchman outside and the dog inside the house. From the sound of its bark—high-pitched and piercing—the dog was a small one, perhaps a Pomeranian or a spitz or something of the kind. It wasn't a Rottweiler or Dobermann, though it was in its way as dangerous: that bark would wake anyone up.

There was a small balcony on the first floor with two doors opening off it, probably to two bedrooms. I took throw. Some good nylon rope, preferably steel-cored. And a small backpack to put all this stuff in.'

'Go to a climbers' shop.'

'I don't know if there are any here. Nothing in the yellow pages. I looked. I'll get ordinary stuff and modify it if I can. It's only for one use anyway.'

'How will you get into the house?'

'Knock out the watchman. Get in. Talk to Rawat. If I can get him to talk right there, nothing like it. From what I remember, the man's not too strong, despite his appearance. He'll crumble.'

'I'll come with you—' Gopi began.

'Nothing doing,' I said, 'you stay right here, handle anything coming this way and be ready to help. Have a taxi on call. If I don't get back to you, get to Delhi. Go to Sandhya. We'll take it from there.'

'Balls!' he said, getting off the bed. 'You need a bloody wet nurse. A shrink first, to debug whatever's going on in your spaghetti-brain, and then a nanny to make sure you don't get yourself killed.'

'Stay out of this, Gopi,' I said, 'so far I've been on the defensive and now it's clear defence isn't working. Now I'm going on the offensive and I don't want you caught in the crossfire. I intend to go out there and break some laws and some man's spirit, which might not be pleasant, and I don't want you involved in any of that. If we get caught you run the risk of years in prison and misery after that.'

'How about rough stuff, then?' he asked angrily. 'You're in no shape for a real fight and if your soldier type or his watchman come at you they'll chop you up into little bits.'

'They don't know the dirty tricks I do,' I said. 'And I'll keep the Llama—the pistol I took off the guard at the hospital—and the knife we got from the man in black. I'll also take the NVGs which will give me a hell of an advantage in the dark. Then I can cut off the electricity and find him in the dark.'

'Look, there'll be others in the house. His wife, if he has one. Maybe kids. A maid. If he can afford a watchman he'll have a live-in maid for sure. How are you going to keep all of them quiet?'

'His wife'll be there, that's all. They don't have a live-in servant right now, just a woman who comes in to cook and clean and leaves in the evening. His children are away vacationing in the south. He's just moved house and he hasn't had the time to set things up like before. I checked. And remember, he won't be expecting anything like me.'

'What do you mean?'

'He might know I'm on the loose but he thinks I'm a wimp—some scrap we had once in Kashmir when he was drunk and juvenile and I kept my cool. He wouldn't expect me to break in at two in the morning.'

'That's when you intend to go?'

'I should go later but around here people wake up by five or so and I might be seen if I delay things too long. I'll try to get there by about one-thirty and if there's any lightning or thunder I'll make use of that.'

'And if you have to lug him away?'

'I'll manage. Knock him out, pour a bottle of whisky over him and shove him in a taxi. If the driver makes trouble I'll knock him out, too—I can manage that even in my present condition. Then I'll drive out of the city and talk to him there.'

'Can't you just hire a car?'

'Not in this country you can't,' I explained. 'At least, not with the papers I've got. Or you, for that matter. They'll be onto you in hours if you try anything of the kind.'

'I don't like it,' he said. 'You're leaving too much to chance.'

'What else can I do?'

'Use me. I'll hire a cab and hang around somewhere there. I'll have the driver go by that house every now and again. Or something of the kind. We have to work out a set of signals. If there's a problem I'll come down there . . .'

'No need for that,' I said, 'your presence in the area won't help one bit. If you're here I can just call you and you can come belting down in a cab. At that time of the day it'll take maybe fifteen minutes from here: no big deal. So you stay here at the ready.'

'Raja,' Gopi said quietly, looking directly at me, 'this going on the offensive business . . . you talk so casually about knocking out all those guys. Sure you can do it?'

I didn't answer and he let it be. This was not a question I was going to ask myself.

We went out after lunch to pick up several lengths of nylon line, a length of pipe, a black bag and a hook—I eventually got a clunky iron hook from a hardware shop—

and I fashioned a mask for myself out of a strip of black cloth. I showed Gopi Rawat's house, and gave him comprehensive instructions on how to get there in a hurry. Then I napped, had a cup of coffee instead of dinner. Food, especially when one is ill, tends to slow one down in body and mind and I wanted to be as alert as possible. At half past eleven I walked out of the hotel, wearing a raincoat although it wasn't raining, to hide the bag. I took a roving taxi from near Vile Parle station and got off near Four Bungalows, a kilometre from Rawat's house. It had started to rain by now, a weak downpour. By ten past midnight I was a hundred yards away from Rawat's house, skirting puddles in the light of the yellow street lamps.

I walked past it in a drizzle with the collar of the raincoat turned up and the hood pulled down low over my eyes, noting the street lamp thirty yards away from the gate, noting the outline of the watchman, the same large man whom I'd seen earlier, hunched up inside the sentrybox, noting the wet and slippery walls. I'm no acrobat and if I couldn't get a grip on the edge of the wall with my fingers, I wouldn't make it. The situation wouldn't improve even if it stopped raining because there was no sun to dry the water. The rope and grapnel would help but I'd have preferred not to use them at all. I cursed and kicked my way through a puddle, and two passersby took care to keep at least five yards away to avoid getting splashed.

Further on I looked for dark spots in which I could hide. Cover on the way out, if I needed any. If I went in and he was out, or if I had to leave in a hurry for some other reason, it would be better to have at least one escape route marked out in advance. A garbage dump a hundred yards from the gate, between street lamps and therefore in the shadows, provided one shelter. Twenty yards further was a small ditch by the road, and beyond that a small culvert behind which I could duck if the rain continued.

And of course there were the apartment blocks. There were dozens of them, all surrounded by four-foot walls, all providing some dark spots in which I could take cover. The best plan, I thought, would be to run for it from building to building. Pursuit, if any, would have to check every building along the path I took.

I took up position in a corner, behind the outer wall of a block of flats, out of sight of passersby. By half past midnight there was more traffic on the roads, which surprised me till I remembered that the people on the streets were returning from the last movie show of the day: the English movies, none more than two hours long, would have finished at about midnight and the Hindi and other Indian-language ones would go on for another half-hour or so. There'd be some traffic here until half past one at the latest. After that there wouldn't be a soul on the streets.

Nearly another hour to go. The rain was chill now and the cold brought on aches in my chest. I swallowed a tablet, hoping it wouldn't interfere with my functioning later. The lights in Rawat's house winked out one by one, the last being in one of the rooms on the upper floor, a dim one, probably a bedside lamp. The rain eased a little and the watchman came out of the guard house and stretched and shone his torch at a puddle just outside the gate in which a scrap of paper was floating. The watchman from another house, four houses away, came to chat with Rawat's watchman but apparently didn't find common ground for he left soon, without even smoking a beedi with the man.

Rawat's dog barked continuously at everyone who passed. There were three other dogs in buildings nearby, all bigger, with deeper barks, all barking at passersby. No one would bother about a barking dog unless it went on and on, but I had to make sure that the creature wouldn't get to me while I was on the wall. I could see its round shadow as it ran around in the tiny compound and the small veranda, staying out of the rain but braving it if someone passed by.

A truck came down the road, its headlamps higher and brighter than a car's. I ducked under the wall and waited for it to pass even though I doubted if anyone would see me unless they looked closely. A couple walked by, both wearing raincoats with no caps, huddled together under an umbrella. Young lovers hurrying back to the comfort of a home.

I waited another ten minutes, then took off my raincoat, rolled it up, and stuffed it into the corner. Then I stepped out to tackle Rawat's watchman: there was no sign of thunder in the sky and I wasn't about to wait any more. The rain came, though, swirling down, driven almost horizontally by a brutal wind coming off the sea from the direction of Versova, and I was soaked in seconds. Visibility dropped in seconds to fifty yards, and the street lamps seemed shrouded in a thick fog. All the better for me, except that the damned NVGs wouldn't work until I got into the house, out of the rain. I took them out of the pack, put them up on my forehead.

Dealing with the watchman turned out to be easier than I'd expected. He was huddled in an armchair in a corner of the veranda, the dog beside him. I went right up to the gate and beckoned him over and the dog came along, yapping mildly. He tried to shush it but it kept barking and he hunched into his raincoat and got out of the veranda and took the two steps to the gate. 'What do you want?' he asked, in good Hindi, squinting into the rain, considering with interest the peculiar glasses on my forehead.

He wasn't a Bombayite, his Hindi was too chaste for that. From UP, or perhaps Bihar. 'Could you tell me where this place is?' I asked in the same language. I held out a bit of paper on which an address was scrawled.

He did what I'd hoped he'd do. He brought out a torch and shone it at the paper, which was already soaked, thereby cutting off his night vision. In the dark I swung at him, aiming for his head, with the bit of pipe, an improvised cosh. The impact of the blow sent a tingle up my arm and into my chest. I nearly dropped the pipe, but managed to hold on. The watchman collapsed on his side, in a puddle on the concrete just inside the gate, the dog barked hysterically, the torch fell in the same puddle and went out.

And then, incredibly, he rose. His skull must have been an inch thick for him to take a blow like that and regain consciousness so soon. He grabbed the torch but it wouldn't come on and the next thing I knew the man had thrown the gate open and was charging me with his head down. His eyesight was gone and his reactions were blurred and the dark made him misjudge, otherwise that bull of a man would have had me that night. I hit him again, on the charging head, and then again in the kidney and on the head a third time. This time he stayed out. But I had no idea how long he'd be out, especially with the rain pouring down as it was.

The dog, meanwhile, still barking furiously, ran through the opened gate to nip at me. It was a small, pathetic creature that shrank as it got wet. I held out the pipe to it. It got the pipe between its teeth and I hit it on the head with the pistol.

The whole thing must have taken a quarter of a minute, from my first swing at the watchman to the knockout blow to the dog. I looked around. No one in sight. I hopped over the gate and tied and gagged the guard. I didn't know what to do with the dog so I forced its mouth open and tied a length of rope through its mouth and around the back of its head, knotting it tightly behind its ears. I wasn't sure if this would incapacitate the dog: all I hoped was that this would keep it quiet for a few minutes if it happened to resurface while I was around.

I dragged the watchman behind the sentrybox—getting him into it would have required some delicate manoeuvring for which I didn't have the strength or the time—and then the dog. I clambered onto the top of the wall just behind the sentrybox, to a side of the house, and walked along the top to where there was a sunshade over a barred ground-floor window. The balcony had a wooden railing and I had to throw the hook only about three feet to snag it on the railing. My chest was on fire now but I managed to swing onto the rope and haul myself over the railing into the balcony. Then I tried the handle of the closer of the two doors.

The first discordant note. The door opened silently. I pulled the NVGs down onto my eyes and looked into the room. It was empty except for a bed in the corner, just a bare bed with a mattress on top, no sheets, no pillows, obviously unused. Wrong room. But a door on the far side, opening out onto a landing, was wide open and I could see the banisters of the staircase beyond the landing. I turned back out onto the balcony and tried the handle of the other door.

That one, too, opened silently. There was a faint sound, like a gasp, but there was no one awake in sight so I thought I'd imagined it. On the double bed against the wall were two people, both motionless, sound asleep . . . and I noticed dark stains on the sheets. They lay in unnatural positions.

I took a step closer and then I saw. They were dead. They had both been murdered, their throats cut. They had bled onto the sheets . . .

That gasp or sneeze. It meant the murderer was still around. I whirled and as I did there was a flash behind me that would have blinded me if I'd been looking at it, and a bang that left me with a buzzing in the ears. With the bang I ducked instinctively, turning again as I did so, saw a cupboard door open and a man erupt into the room. Black clothes, mask, NVGs, as before. A stocky figure, as fast and powerful as before. He ran for the door leading out onto the balcony, coming at me from the side. I sidestepped his charge, swung my pack at his face, and when he twisted his torso to evade it, kicked him on the shin.

It was like kicking a lump of iron. I almost broke my toes inside the rubber shoes but it seemed to have no effect at all on him. He slowed a little, went into a crouch. There was a tiny click and a knife gleamed in his hands.

I knew that crouch.

In a straightforward scrap I didn't stand a chance against him. A knock-down-and-drag-out fight was the last thing I wanted. With Rawat and his wife—I presumed the corpses were theirs—dead there was no point in my hanging around any longer. I didn't wait to see what the man in black would do. I feinted an attack at his legs and when he swayed away before his counterattack, I broke and ran for the door.

The buzz in my ears was beginning to clear up and I could hear voices below. There must have been watchmen around in the other buildings. Anyone familiar with the place would toddle along and call for the watchman here, who was lying face down on the wet concrete behind the sentrybox with the gagged dog beside him. If they found him I was in trouble.

The rope was still where I'd left it. I went quickly over

the railing, the NVGs now useless in the rain. I caught the rope, and without bothering about the sunshade slipped down to the ground not far from the prone guard. I ran to the back of the house and over the wall, ran along the top of the wall to the house on the left. No dogs there, I knew, and a large, comforting pillar-box outside. Behind me the watchmen were already beginning to yell, so I ignored the shooting pains in my chest and made for the street behind, parallel to the one on which Rawat's house stood. No trees in Bombay, but enough dark corners in which to take cover on a dark rainy night. The man in black must have made his way out, for I heard a second shout go up, and thought with a flicker of satisfaction that he would have a harder chase than I would.

I hoped they'd catch him. That would take the heat off me for the time being.

I knew what he'd been trying to do. He'd wanted to murder the couple, take me by surprise, and leave with all the evidence pointing at me having committed the murders. If they knew enough about me to do that they knew where Gopi and I were staying. I had to find a telephone, tell Gopi to get the hell out of that hotel before they caught up with him.

I was near the road to the station now, jogging steadily when I heard the jeeps come in. Two police jeeps with lights flashing and engines roaring at high revs screamed past, then turned right into the street where Rawat lived. I ducked behind a gatepost as they went by, then jogged away towards the station. The rush of adrenaline was fading now and the pain became more oppressive, intensified by the cold. About a kilometre further up I found a taxi, an ancient Premier dawdling my way. I stuck out a thumb and the taxi stopped. 'Andheri station,' I told him.

'There are no trains for an hour,' he told me in Marathi, 'you'd better take a taxi all the way otherwise you'll fall ill.'

'That's all right,' I told him in Hindi—I understand Marathi but don't speak it—'but what I need is shelter from the rain and a place to make a telephone call.'

'There is a hotel near the station from where you can make your call,' he said, switching to Hindi. 'It's not expensive. If you have money I can even take you to a good hotel in Juhu or Bandra.'

'The cheaper place,' I told him.

An hour later, Gopi had joined me. He came in a taxi that he'd hired outside the hotel, after checking. He'd left no traces of our presence in the Airport Plaza. I'd told him to pack and leave, and he'd done just that. 'What happened?' he asked. 'You sounded out of control, mad.'

'The man in black. He was waiting for me.'

'Shit!' exclaimed Gopi, 'Are you all right?'

'Yes,' I replied, 'this time he didn't have the time to inflict major damage. Both of us were in a hurry to get out of there and I think he sneezed so I had a tiny bit of warning. He couldn't catch me off balance. The honours were more or less even this time, but now we're in trouble.'

'What kind?'

'He killed Rawat and his wife. They were lying there with their throats cut when I went into the house. I had to knock out the watchman and the dog, but this guy seems to have got in past them . . . I don't know how. He got in ahead of me, killed them, and was waiting in a cupboard when I climbed in. He let off a flash-bang grenade but I was facing away at the time so I wasn't blinded. We had a little confrontation and I left because people around had heard the grenade and the watchmen were coming in. I made it out of the house in time and this guy was just behind me.'

'Do you think our friend got away?'

'Oh, yes. He's far too fast and tough and inventive for a bunch of watchmen to get their hands on him. Unless I'm mistaken he'd have had a vehicle waiting for him. He had a fresh set of NVGs, by the way, and a new knife.'

'Why do you think he was there in the first place?'

'We'll get back to that afterwards. First we take a cab to some hotel in town that has a twenty-four-hour coffee shop and we park there.'

We got another cab without much trouble and found our way eventually to the coffee shop at the Oberoi, with a view of the sea, unobtrusive service, and lots of space between tables. We took it by turns to go to the toilets—unoccupied at this hour—to change clothes and when we were more comfortable I ordered coffee and sandwiches for both of us and took up the conversation where we'd left off.

'I don't know. If he wanted to kill me he could have done it with no trouble at all. It's more likely he was trying to keep me there long enough after his getaway to have me caught and held for those murders. But . . .'

'He could have killed both of us there, and he didn't,' said Gopi. 'He could have killed you at this guy Rawat's place and he didn't . . . Remember what I told you about this earlier, about why they're letting you go? Making you a spearhead for their search?'

'Yes.'

'They were afraid that if you found out Rawat was involved you'd be more or less in the clear.'

'And?'

'If you took Rawat to the cops, and he talked, you'd be officially clear. The hunt for the diaries would then have become a joint matter between you and the cops . . . In which case he might have found it hard to take the diaries off you when—and if, of course—you did find them.'

'What bugs me is, how did they know where we were?'

'They must've been following you all the time. Or maybe they knew that you could exit that forest only at a fixed number of points, and watched those points. I don't think that's so difficult if you have someone to do the leg-work.'

'Could it be that they never lost track of us?'

'That would mean they were watching the hospital. Did you notice a tail when you broke out of there?'

'Not really . . . But I wouldn't have noticed in that state. They must have had the hospital watched . . . Otherwise it would take too many people to do it. Which means they're surely on to Urmila and Nikhil. We can't go back there.'

'So what do we do now?'

'We try to shake the tail . . . I don't know how, I'm a soldier, not a spy, so if the guy following us is an expert it might not work. Nothing to stop us trying, is there?'

'How?' Gopi asked. 'We couldn't shake them off in the swamps. How the hell do you expect to shake them off here?'

'In the forest I wasn't expecting anyone on our heels, that's why I didn't do anything to find out.'

'What would you have done? Kept looking over your shoulder?'

'At night, yes. In the day I'd have looked for alarms.'

'What alarms?'

'Go past a series of birds or monkeys or other animals that'll make noise as you go by. If they repeat the series of noises after a while that usually means there's someone taking the same route you did. In country where there are no tracks, the only way it could happen is if someone was behind you.'

He looked at me bug-eyed, and subsided. 'All right,' he said, 'you know. So how do we shake them off now?'

'We hang around in a hotel, one with a twenty-four-hour restaurant, until six in the evening, and then we go to the railway station and take a train out. The most crowded one possible. No reservations.'

'Why train? Air's quicker, safer, more comfortable.'

'Travelling without reservations in summer, in the vacation season, is the easiest way to get lost. And we'll do our waiting in public places. Railway waiting rooms. Places like that, where we'll notice anyone who stays the same length of time as us. They'll have a hard time following us around . . . but in the meanwhile I have to get some supplies. We might not be able to take the next train.'

'What supplies?'

'More hardware. Weapons. Two flak-jackets, if possible. Walkie-talkies so we can communicate. Some explosive, detonators and fuses . . . Timers. I'm beginning to get ideas.'

'What kind of ideas?'

'If the guys who took the diaries have an organization like the one that fixed the kidnap, we're not going to be able to face them without something substantial to protect ourselves with. We have to, if their average bloke is like that fellow in black. The other idea is, they must have a base in some city, Delhi, Bombay, Madras, maybe Bangalore. And they have contacts in the police, in government.'

'So? You're only making our job look harder.'

'I have one more faint lead, no more. I'm going to follow it up as carefully as I can, and I won't tell anyone what that lead is. I'll talk to old man Mankekar about the equipment and if he can't get it I'll acquire it some other way.'

'Raja,' he said, his voice full of worry now. 'You're talking of doing things for which you need a small army. You can't do it alone. You're nuts. Is all this even possible?'

'Nuts I might be but I know what I'm doing. I'll have to revive some of my old contacts . . . Go down south. I know some guys in the LTTE who might help if I tell them who I am. They won't turn me in because they know that if they do I'll go after them. They'll give me equipment and maybe even people.'

'You mean you can just walk into their safe house and tell them you need their help?'

'Sort of. We'll see when we get there.'

'Where?'

'The safe house. Nagercoil, near Kanyakumari.'

'Raja, are you sure you want to get into bed with the LTTE? Those guys are terrorists. Only they operate in someone else's territory.'

'I don't know, Gopi. If I have to have weapons I'll get them from wherever I can.'

'Can't you try smugglers?'

'It costs. It costs a helluva lot.'

'How much?' he asked. 'I've got money.'

'I have an order for at least three different weapons for different purposes. A high-powered rifle—an old Lee Enfield type will do—and an assault rifle, like an AK-47, some plastic explosive, Semtex or RDX, fuses of different types, timers . . . You're looking at a hundred thousand rupees for each rifle, plus ammunition. A total in the region of half a million rupees. Say seventeen to twenty thousand dollars. I don't have that kind of money to spare.'

'I do.'

'What!' I did a double take.

'You told me to get all the money I could lay my hands on and I did just that. I liquidated the accounts I'd set up in your name, sold some of my stocks and bonds, and ended up with something like forty-five thousand dollars. I've spent nearly five of that, so I've got thirty-five thousand left. And about twenty thousand rupees.'

I could have hugged him. 'I didn't know you had all that money,' I said, 'you must be rich!'

'Raja, I've got a job that pays me well over a hundred thousand a year, stock options, the lot. And I don't spend much. No vacations, no partying, no splurging. A steady girlfriend who's utterly independent . . . Money in the quantities you're talking about is no problem.' Thirty-five thousand dollars, he had said. At current rates of exchange it was roughly what I earned in six years . . . He must have read my thoughts, for he continued, 'Look, Raja, I want you to come out to the States. You'll be able to find work over there and I can stake you out in the beginning. You did that for me. I've got money there, I can raise another hundred thousand without serious pain: that should be enough for you to get by on until you get something going. I wish you'd taken it up earlier. I wish we'd talked earlier, before this goddam mess happened.'

'We can still talk,' I said, 'Sandhya and I have been fighting about my job and I can see her point of view. Not that that makes it any easier for her.'

'Great,' he said, 'one more reason to bury those diaries once and for all.'

It was getting on for four in my watch. I planned to call Mankekar about eight from a public telephone somewhere in the vicinity of Victoria Terminus.

I'd ask Mankekar first for the hardware I needed. I could get in touch with the LTTE, down in Nagercoil, for the guns, but getting anything from them would compromise my future. Besides, it would take too long: I'd have to find my way down south in the first place, and then come back up north. The LTTE dickered over everything, and that would cost me another day or two. They'd take another day or so to check me out. And delivery would take another couple of days. Another week, at least.

I didn't want to use my contacts in the north, like the former terrorist who'd guided us to the hostage near Uri. That would take as long, and there was an additional danger: word might leak back to ISI that I was involved in shady deals and god knows what they'd do with that information. There were small dealers in Gujarat and Bengal as well, dealing in arms coming in via Kutch in the west and Bangladesh in the east, but I had no contacts among them so I'd have to invest time in building them up.

No, that would take too long. I'd try Mankekar. His bodyguards carried SMGs, I'd noticed. It wasn't too hard for a VIP to get licences for one of those. I was sure he'd have the contacts to get whatever I needed, except perhaps the plastic explosive. But there was no harm in asking him.

If Mankekar agreed to get it, I could always pay afterwards, with Gopi's money; but how would I take delivery? A friend of mine lived nearby, in Colaba. I could have the stuff delivered to his house, but that would endanger him and his family . . . No, I'd have to work out some other way.

Gopi dozed off. We'd both stuffed ourselves in the coffee shop—I found that eating a lot helped me get back to normal after something like the encounter with the man in black—and in the cool, quiet, coffee shop I felt a dangerous warmth creeping over me as well. There were people around, though not close enough to hear our conversation, and the man in black wouldn't be able to get in here without us knowing. But I ordered more coffee to keep myself awake, because that man was horrifyingly competent at what he did. Man to man, on level ground, I was no match for him. And as for Gopi's brown belt, the man would probably make him eat it.

We left the hotel at seven, on foot, after over three hours in that hotel. Gopi was fresher for his sleep but I had a headache and a foul taste in the mouth from too much coffee and no sleep at all. My wet clothes were in a polythene bag inside Gopi's backpack, and I carried a sling bag on my good shoulder. Not enough luggage to slow us down substantially if we had to run for it. I stopped at a small shop selling paan and cigarettes and odds and ends and bought a newspaper, a copy of the Bombay edition of the *Times of India*. And there, on page one, was my face.

chapter twelve

Not my face the way it was now, with the Franco Nero moustache, but as it had been six months ago. They'd used a mugshot of me in combat uniform, in a forage cap and with a Colonel's insignia—the Ashok Chakra and two stars—on my shoulder flaps. I never wore collar tabs except on formal occasions, having learnt during my tenure with the IPKF that they mark you off as targets to the more enterprising snipers. It was a nothing face in that photograph, clean-shaven, short-haired, an average shapeless kind of nose, a medium chin, expressionless dark eyes set deep, a little gaunt about the cheekbones, but otherwise utterly ordinary. I looked in a plate glass window nearby as we walked past it, and was grateful for the blandness of my features: the moustache that Nikhil had recommended I wear, improvised soft plastic cheek pads that filled out my face, and the dark glasses were enough to give me an air of ferocity that would prevent anyone recognizing me from that photograph.

The story accompanying the photograph said that Major Abhay K. Rawat (Retd), formerly of the Grenadiers and more lately of Wesco Holdings, had been murdered in his house near Andheri by some person or persons unknown. His wife, Pramila, who had been in the house with him, had also been murdered. The watchman of the house had been found knocked out in the sentrybox, the dog at his side. Rawat and his wife had been shot, and before they died, their throats had been slit. An unusual knife of American manufacture found on the premises was probably the one used to cut both throats.

Also found on the premises, probably dropped by the killer, was a pistol that had been identified, from its serial number, as the one that Colonel Menon had stolen from his guard in the course of his escape from the Air Force Command Hospital at Bangalore. Rawat's neighbours had heard nothing except for a loud bang in the wee hours, and the watchman of a house nearby had seen, at the same time, a flash in one of the rooms on the first floor of the house. He had raised the alarm and one man had been seen making good his escape. Some nylon rope and a hook had been left behind. Meanwhile, Rawat's former employers and several of his friends said that Rawat's death was a shocking crime and couldn't be allowed to go unpunished.

I gave the paper to Gopi. He read the story carefully and quickly, then said, 'That fucker did exactly what he wanted, didn't he?'

'Some of it,' I said. 'He set me up for this.'

'How about the pistol? I noticed you have one in your bag.'

'I never dropped it. They must have got hold of the serial number on that guard's weapon, bought another like it, and faked the number well enough to put the cops off for a short while. But it won't last. You can't mess around with the serial number on a firearm well enough to fool a lab. The cops will find out soon enough that the number's been faked, and that'll help clear me.'

'Why won't it clear you completely?'

'Because I'm perfectly capable of faking it so that they think I'm innocent. In the meanwhile, it warms things up for us.'

'How so?'

'They have cops among their pals, and maybe some Army men as well. It wouldn't have been all that easy getting hold of that serial number, or etching it onto another weapon. They never lost track of us: it takes a couple of days to acquire and prepare a weapon the way they did. They're making sure I can't go to the cops. You were right.'

'Are they pointing you somewhere?'

'They're telling me where not to go, that's all. Using that bloke in black to guide me along.'

'I'd like to get my hands on that man,' he said, 'I'd just love that.'

'He could do you plenty of no good,' I said, grinning.

'Yeah,' came the reply, 'but not if I have a .45. I'd cut pieces off the bastard, and if he tried anything funny, blow the shit out of him. Like in those spaghetti westerns. Shoot his kneecaps off, shoot him in the gut, that kind of thing.'

We were near the Fountain by this time and I saw a

phone booth opening. This was a downtown area and at a quarter before eight in the morning, things were just beginning to stir before the offices opened. People were trickling in from the railway stations and bus stands, and early birds in their cars had already begun to take prime parking slots. I went to the phone booth while Gopi parked himself at an Irani restaurant thirty yards away. I dialled Mankekar's private number. The old man picked it up on the second ring. 'Raja,' he said, 'it can't be anyone else. Where are you calling from?'

'Bombay,' I said, 'phone booth near the Fountain.'

'Have you seen the papers?' he asked.

'I didn't knock off that guy, I swear,' I told him. 'Someone else did it and dumped the evidence. Follow up with the police—put some pressure on them to check the pistol out properly at the labs in Delhi—you'll find it's been planted there.'

'I believe you,' he said, sounding very tired. 'I believe you without all that. Killing that lady, that you wouldn't have done. I said this to the others but they don't believe me. And you're right about the pistol . . . The police said there was something fishy about it and the labs said that the number had been filed off and a new one brazed on. They caught it easily. Your credibility went up that much.'

'Thanks very much,' I said. 'But I called you because I need something from you.'

'What?' he asked warily.

'Weapons. Ammunition. A flak-jacket, body armour, some plastic explosive if you can manage it, Semtex or

RDX. A dozen detonators of different kinds. Fuses. Walkie-talkies.'

'What have you got there, Raja?' he asked. 'It sounds like a small army.'

'Nothing like that,' I said. 'Just me, stocking up.'

'It seems excessive. Are you sure you aren't going to indulge in a massacre?'

'I'm not. Will you get me this stuff?'

'What will you do if I don't?'

'Go to the LTTE. I know how to get in touch with them. Or to my contacts in the north, in Kashmir. But that would be costly. Not because I don't have the money but because I'd be obliged.'

'Yes,' he said, 'I'm glad you think that way. Give me a list.'

I recited it to him. Two sub-machine guns, preferably Ingrams, with a dozen magazines of thirty rounds each, a silenced .45, a sniper rifle with a folding stock, a telescopic sight and a silencer—in case I needed one for sniper work—with a hundred rounds, two sets of body armour, two flak-jackets, two kilos of plastic explosive, dets, fuses, time pencils.

'All right,' he said, 'I'll try to get what you want. When do you want it?'

'Tomorrow would be fine.'

'I'll get it as soon as I can. Where do I have it delivered?'

'Here in Bombay, Churchgate station. Or anywhere else I tell you. I might change my mind.'

'My bodyguards carry sub-machine guns, I think, perhaps AK-74s, and one or two of them carry pistols. All these I can get you without trouble. A bullet-proof vest also is no problem: I have one to spare right here, at home. They tell me to wear one but I'm not going to. An old man like me should be allowed to live in peace . . . I'll send my bullet-proof vest—flak-jacket, as you call it—and the weapons. I'm not sure about walkie-talkies but my men use them so I assume they should be easy to get. The explosives, the detonators, I know nothing about. Maybe my men do. I won't ask them . . . But I can ask someone on the Committee.'

'Who?'

'I don't know. I can ask the lot.'

'Won't they want to know what for?'

'They will. I'll tell them I'm curious. They won't ask me anything else.'

'All right,' I said, looking at my watch, 'time to move on. I've been talking here for too long. I'll call again in fifteen minutes.' I'd hang up and move on to another booth. One advantage of the light traffic at this time was that pursuit would be easy to spot.

I retrieved Gopi from the restaurant, where he was just finishing off the last of his tea with a distinctly beatific look on his face, and we took a taxi to Churchgate station, where I found another public telephone tucked away in a narrow street. 'I don't know why I take this from you,' Mankekar grumbled when I called him. 'You try an old man too far. I tire of it . . . But I spoke to my people. They can get you everything but the explosive. That I will try to get separately. I can have everything delivered in Bombay by this evening.

Now don't tell me you want it delivered to some impossible place at three in the morning because I won't.'

I laughed. 'Don't complain so much about old bones. You've got a lot of mileage left in you, enough for a campaign or two.'

There was a cautious silence, then an answering laugh. 'I like you, Colonel,' he said at last. 'Indeed I do. I wish we had met earlier. Forty years ago.'

'So do I . . . I'd like the weapons in a single large, rigid wheeled suitcase, with the body armour. Put a Lufthansa label right in the middle of the lid of the suitcase. The trickiest item to hide among those will be the rifle: none in that range is under thirty inches long, so get a case big enough.'

'I'll work something out, don't worry,' he said. 'Where?'

'The man carrying the suitcase should arrive at Churchgate station at a quarter past five, from the Nariman Point side, from the staircase across the road. He is to wait near the entrance for me to contact him. If I don't meet him by half past five, he is to call you for further instructions.'

'Right,' he said, repeating the instructions. 'Keep in touch, tell me what you're doing. And why don't you tell me what you intend to do with the arsenal? I don't like giving away dangerous things like this.'

I took a deep breath. He'd given me enough. Time for me to give him a little. 'There's a madman on my tail,' I explained, 'some crazy thickset guy in black who's been after me since I got out of hospital. I think he was one of the kidnappers as well. I suspect he's got contacts somewhere in government, and is part of a network that's been following me around.'

'What do you plan to do about this man?' he demanded.

'The next time I see him I'll take him,' I replied. 'So far it's always gone his way but now I'm recovering and he won't be able to take me so easily.'

'All right,' he said, 'all the best. Do you need money?'

'For once, no. I'd borrow from you if I did.'

'Who's financing you? You can't have got this far on your own.'

'Can't tell you.'

'Fine,' he sighed, 'I have something for you, young man. You might be on the right track. Our friend from Wesco, Saifuddin Ahmed: he's got a degree in business management from IIM Ahmedabad, he's rich, he shuttles between Cochin and Bombay . . . And has a cousin who's into organized crime. The cousin's certainly not big enough to engineer the kidnap, so we never thought of him, but there's a tenuous connection there that might hold.'

'Thanks,' I said, 'I'll chase it up.'

I walked back to the station entrance where Gopi was waiting. We had all morning and most of the afternoon in which to finish off the things we still had to do. I had clothes to buy, and bags in which to carry the weapons, a glass-cutter, and so on. We made our purchases in Chor Bazaar—Thieves' Market—about which people used to warn us, saying that shopkeepers were capable of stealing the hubcaps off your car and selling them back to you. We emerged intact at a quarter to one, with three large, empty bags besides the backpack and the bag we'd had before we went shopping. We went back to town by a quarter past one, better-dressed now, clean-shaven and respectable. We went this time to the Sea Lounge at the Taj where we had lunch, then parked ourselves in the low seats, enjoying the quiet and the relief from the drizzle outside.

We found no signs of a tail so Gopi sat back in his couch and dozed off until the waiters began to hover disapprovingly around us. We picked up our bags once again and left, this time for the Asiatic Society Library near the Reserve Bank, an old colonial building with high ceilings and comfortable sofas where we could drowse undisturbed until it was time to take the goods.

We left the Asiatic Library at a quarter to five, and made our way to Churchgate station, arriving by five, fifteen minutes ahead of time, in the thick of peak-hour traffic. The traffic would increase a little until it peaked between six and seven, and then drop off. By nine or so the trains would no longer be crowded. I found a vacant table in the Railways restaurant on the mezzanine, from where we could watch the concourse and the bottom of the staircase by which people crossed the road. Sure enough, at five forty-three, our man turned up, a tall, heavily-built youngster carrying a heavy black suitcase on wheels.

The commuter trains on the western line were running two to three minutes late, which was normal. I moved slowly down the staircase to the ground floor, walked past the man with the suitcase and onto the street to check if he was being followed. Gopi, who had followed me out of the restaurant, stopped at the end of the concourse by the row of ticket inspectors, facing the road, watching my back.

Minutes later I found the same public telephone from where I'd called Mankekar in the morning, and called him again. 'There's a change of plan,' I told him.

'What for?' he asked. 'Didn't my man turn up?'

'He did. He's waiting.'

'Then why the change?'

'Because I feel it's required. When your man calls, tell him to go to the north end of platform four. Tell him to get into the first carriage of the five fifty-four Virar fast. Since the train reverses direction here, this will be the last carriage when it comes. Is that clear?'

'Yes,' he said, 'he'll do it. The first carriage of the five fifty-four Virar fast.'

'Tell him not to sit. Tell him to stand in the doorway with his back facing the front of the train, and on the west side.'

'Okay. Facing the way the train is moving, on the west.' Some minutes later the man with the bag walked out of the station. He must have found another telephone, for he reappeared ten minutes later, sweating from the weight of the bag, struggling to force it through the crowd of commuters. He followed instructions to the letter, moving out onto platform four and going right to the edge, where the crowd was perhaps a fraction thinner. He stubbornly positioned himself where he thought the door of the carriage would halt, and stood his ground against all other commuters who tried to push him out of the way.

I moved in ahead of him and when the train arrived, three minutes late, I elbowed my way ahead with little difficulty and found myself a seat—one of the last, for most of them were already occupied when the train drew in—where I wouldn't have to turn around to keep an eye on the man with the suitcase. Gopi, who had entered the platform when the train drew in, was one of the last to enter the carriage. He found himself a place to squeeze in some three feet away from the man with the suitcase, half in and half out of the train. He could watch me from where he stood, which was what mattered: the moment I made my move, he'd make his. I'd grab the suitcase and run, while Gopi got in the way of the courier. He'd get off at the station after the one at which I got off, and wait for me at the western exit, where I'd pick him up in a taxi. It was a manoeuvre that put him at risk, but he insisted he didn't mind.

The train stopped at all the first four stations out of Churchgate: Marine Lines, Charni Road, Grant Road, and Bombay Central. I made my move as the train pulled into Grant Road. More commuters had climbed on at the two stations before it, and there was barely enough room to stand when I forced my way out near the door and positioned myself inches away from the suitcase. It was behind the man, between him and the wall against which he leant, the handle to a side. As the train stopped, I grabbed the handle and shoved my way out through the crowd of people surging their way in. I was pushed back in but after head-butting an incoming passenger. I shoved my way out. Gopi, who had moved in directly behind me, managed to block the courier.

When the train moved off after its half-minute halt the courier was still on it. I tugged the suitcase to the exit and walked out looking for a taxi, and found one as it pulled up to deposit a passenger at the exit. I told the driver to head for Bombay Central, and while he dealt with the rush-hour traffic, I shifted the weapons from the suitcase to two of the bags we'd bought from Chor Bazaar. They were heavy but manageable when I tested them. By the time the cab was pulling up outside Bombay Central I'd finished the transfer and stuck the suitcase between the rear seat and the driver's seat, where he wouldn't get to see it unless he stretched backwards. I tipped the driver ten rupees and in the rain walked into the shelter of the concourse, slowed down a little by the weight of the bags.

Gopi was right there, and we boarded a train back to Churchgate, carrying the heavy bags, the suitcase now in the back of an anonymous taxi. By a quarter to seven we were in a taxi heading for VT, where we intended to hang around until the next southbound train, a summer special bound for Madras. We had no reservations but I'd never intended to get any: it's far easier to submerge oneself travelling without a reservation in second class, in the general compartment, especially at this time of the year when people were willing to travel two days standing on their toes to get to wherever they planned to spend their vacations.

The train would be at the platform by half past seven, the man at the counter told us, and we had just enough time to buy a ticket to Madras before it came in. We waited where we thought the general coach would stop, amidst a knot of people who all intended to push their way in ahead of everyone else. When the train arrived the door of the coach was only six feet away from where I stood but I almost missed my chance in the rush. I pushed my way through anyway, using the heavy bag in my hand as a battering ram. With a massive effort I made it to a coveted window seat not far from the exit, having to push the bag into a short, squat man's stomach to get him out of the way. I put the bag on the seat next to mine to reserve it for Gopi, who had agreed to wait while I got in.

Less than two minutes after the train arrived the coach was full, all seats occupied, luggage overflowing into the aisle, and people sitting on the luggage racks overhead. In another couple of minutes, even standing room was short, with at least six people crammed on benches meant for four. A family of six, including three little children, had found their way into the coach and two of the children began to cry.

The man whom I'd poked in the tummy had found a seat opposite mine. He wiped his forehead with a kerchief and smiled at me. I was taken aback, for I'd probably done him serious bodily harm on the way in. I apologized to him in Hindi. His grin widened. 'It happens every day,' he replied, 'everybody does it. If I'd had a chance I'd have pushed you out of the way too. Don't worry about it.'

By a quarter to eight the rain began to come down hard. We could hear the drops falling on the metal roof. The glass shutters came down to keep the water out. Inside the coach, even with the little ceiling fans going, the temperature and the humidity rose to near unbearable levels. The coach was a sea of wilting humanity, too miserable even to protest. 'Is this how you normally travel?' Gopi asked, wedged into his seat between me on one side and a smelly old man on the other.

'We can fly,' I said, 'and take our chances with the bloke in black.'

He looked around and shook his head, grinning.

The train started half an hour late, moving slowly and painfully, stopping every now and again, often between stations. The rain persisted, and the shutters stayed shut, and the foul air worsened. By ten there was no water in the toilets and by half-past the smell of urine permeated the coach. Despite the raindrops hammering at the glass I lifted the shutter and let the rainwater pour in, but the others protested so much I had to shut it again minutes later. The night dragged purposelessly on and when the guilt became overwhelming I offered my seat to a woman standing, holding a baby in her arms. The train moved on through Kalyan and then on to Pune and when it pulled into Daund I decided we'd had enough. 'Let's split,' I told Gopi.

'Phew!' he said, wiping his forehead. 'If you hadn't said that, I'd have.'

We stepped out on the platform, got under a shelter from the rain, and considered our options. Daund has a fairly large Army establishment, which I wanted to avoid for fear of being recognized. We took a cycle rickshaw to the bus stand, where we found that the next bus to Pune was at five in the morning. We dozed then, in a ticket booth, on a sheet spread on the floor, thoroughly miserable but alone and confident now that we didn't have a tail.

By ten that morning, after an exhausting and painful bus ride, we were in a small hotel in Pune, with a ticket for the nine o'clock bus to Bangalore, and by six the following evening were getting off the bus near the Majestic Theatre hard by Bangalore Central station. We crossed the bridge to the railway station, found the day's train to Cochin full, and eventually found room on another bus to Cochin, leaving at half past seven.

My chest was aflame by seven. We checked into a hotel by the bus stand, and the moment the boy shut the door behind him I had the syringe out and the ampoule broken. Five minutes later the pain had begun to recede and to the bewilderment of the hotel staff we walked out to the bus stand. I boarded the bus in reasonable comfort, drooping with sleep. By ten next morning we were in the Abad Plaza hotel on MG Road, Cochin's main street. I'd slept through the entire journey and was feeling refreshed. But Gopi looked too tired for words.

'I've been patient so far,' he said edgily as we relaxed on the soft beds in the double room they had given us, 'now you've got to tell me why we're here.'

'Rawat's boss,' I replied, 'the managing director of Wesco Holdings. We've come to see him.'

'Why?' he asked. 'You're jumping steps.'

'Rawat was involved,' I said, 'that's why they killed him,

to stop him telling me anything that would point me at them. This guy Ahmed knew all about Rawat, and is by implication neck-deep in it. Ahmed, being the MD, could have engineered the cover-up: he could have told his men, either you cooperate or you look for another job some place.'

'So now what?'

'Now we wait for the man to turn up. He shuttles between here and Bombay, and is here at least three days a week. They say he spends every other day here. We find out where he lives and I go in one night and talk to him.'

'You're a bloody madman, Raja,' Gopi said. 'You've got nothing on the man, you're going purely on emotion.'

'Instinct,' I countered. 'The man was Rawat's boss, and he knew what Rawat had been up to. He's got a cousin who's a small-time smuggler. He's got gangland connections. What more do you want?'

'Bullshit,' he said, 'that's circumstantial.'

'Look, you make it sound as if I'm going to torture the man or something. I just want to talk to him.'

'And scare the daylights out of him.'

'Remember what people have said about omelettes and eggs?'

'Yeah. And what if this lead fails?'

'I get back to old man Mankekar. Ask him to use his influence with the police to get me information. If he's with the other side that could be disastrous, but I don't think he is.'

'I'll come with you when you go after this man Ahmed.'

'Nothing doing,' I said firmly. 'When I break the law I do it alone. If I'm caught, you get the hell out of here.'

'You're in bad shape. All that travel, and so on. You had to shoot yourself full of painkillers to get on your feet.'

'That's because of lugging that heavy bag around and that bus ride. It's over now.'

'Wait awhile.'

'I will,' I said. 'It's only tennish. I'll start on him only towards four in the evening or afterwards—check the directory to find out where he lives and if he's not listed, ring up his local office and tell them there's a parcel for him.'

'I meant rest for a couple of days.'

'That's the one thing we can't afford to do now. We've shaken off the pursuit but don't know when they'll catch up again. We haven't left any traces but god knows what kind of a network they have. We'll sleep now, and in the afternoon I go out. Reconnaissance.'

'What reconnaissance?'

'I'll do a recce. Look for points through which to get in or out. Look for weak spots in his armour. And I'm sure he has some armour, as much as Rawat had.'

At half past three that afternoon, much refreshed by a good, long nap and a light meal of seafood and rice, I went down to the lobby. The receptionist gave me the telephone directory with a smile and I sat in an overstuffed chair trying to trace Saifuddin Ahmed. He was easy to find: he hadn't tried to hide. He lived a kilometre from the hotel, off Marine Drive, in an independent bungalow. When I asked the receptionist about him, she said she knew of him. He was a well-known man in these parts, I gathered. A local boy made good, generous with his money when it came to the many Muslim charities in the erstwhile Malabar state. But the religion was restricted to his private life. In business he was totally professional, dealing equally bluntly with everyone. His senior executives included at least 50 per cent Hindus and quite a few Christians. Even the receptionist spoke well of him, of the business he had brought, and said there was talk that he should contest the Assembly elections when he retired from business. A solid citizen, and from all accounts an outstanding businessman.

It was all more or less in keeping with his education at one of the country's three best business schools. Then why was he associated with a low-life like Rawat? Why had he covered up for Rawat? Rawat's record with the Army was accessible to anyone who wanted to employ him. Hadn't he checked? Or had he taken the man on knowing his background?

Saifuddin Ahmed. There were half a dozen listings under his company's name, including a personal number and an after-hours number. I went out in the rain to a telephone booth and called the direct number. A female voice with a strong Malayali accent responded, 'Hello?'

I spoke in English. 'May I speak to Mr Saifuddin Ahmed, please?'

The voice replied haltingly in the same language. 'Saifuddin sar gone home, sar.'

'Is he in Cochin?' I asked. 'Or has he gone off to Bombay?'

'Here only, sar, here only,' came the enthusiastic reply, 'he go to Bombay only tomorrow. In the evening.'

'Thanks,' I said. 'And who are you?'

'I am typist, sar, sitting overtime. I also go now.'

'Can you confirm his address for me, then?' I asked. I read out the address.

The female shuffled papers, breathing heavily. 'Yes, sar, he is there only. He leave number with our security people for emergency.'

The man would be off to Bombay the next evening and I could talk to him only nights. I had to talk to him that same night, then, or lose a few days. A twinge in the chest said it would be wiser to wait but there was a growing urgency because I'd been on the run for weeks now and didn't want the police or the opposition catching up.

That left precious little time for preparation. A couple of hurried rounds, that was all I'd have time for. I went back to the hotel and told Gopi I was going out to have a look at Ahmed's house. 'I'll come along,' he said.

There wouldn't be any harm in that, I thought, because I was just going to walk around the man's house. He'd be able to talk to the watchman, or watch my back for a tail. 'All right,' I said, 'come on quick.'

As we stepped out of the hotel it began to rain again, rain heavily in thick grey sheets that filled the gutters in no time and then lay an inch deep on the road. Finding an auto was impossible. When we went back to the hotel to get a cab the receptionist apologized. 'Sorry, sir,' she said, 'all our taxis are gone. You can have one in an hour if you don't mind waiting, but that's the best I can do.' I shook my head and smiled at her and went back out to buy a sturdy raincoat at a department store.

Back in the hotel we changed out of our wet clothes and ventured out again, bundled this time in raincoats, into the threatening darkness.

As a reconnaissance mission that walk in the rain was a complete failure. All I found out was the exact location of the house, that it had an eight-foot stone wall around it, with large sheet-iron gates in front and a shelter inside for a watchman. About thirty feet from the wall stood a three-storey house with a balcony, but that was all I could see. In the light of a passing car, I saw atop the wall the glint of broken glass set into it: climbing the wall in the wet with that topping of glass wouldn't be easy but there was a tree by that wall with its lowest branches about twelve feet off the ground. And the surface of the wall was irregular, so it would be easy to get a good grip on it.

We returned to the hotel, where Gopi promptly went back to sleep. I went out and bought a pint of rum—I'd make an exception to my rules and have one small one before going out in that damned rain—and settled down to think. At nine, I ordered another seafood dinner for both of us, woke Gopi up, and ate with growing enjoyment. I set the wake-up call for half past one in the morning, then called the receptionist downstairs and asked for a taxi at two in the morning. 'Two o'clock, sir?' she asked, surprised.

'Yes,' I replied, 'we have to be at the temple at Guruvayoor by five. Earlier, if possible.' She accepted the explanation and told me the cab would be there.

When the alarm went off I came awake only partly rested; the remains of the rum still floating in my head, wishing I could sleep another twelve hours. The rain was pouring down outside, lashing the window panes, leaking in through cracks in the frames. I turned over and woke Gopi. When he mumbled in protest I told him to rise and shine. 'Get off your arse, you bum,' I yelled. 'You keep saying you want a part of the action but when the time comes you refuse to wake up on time.'

That fetched him out of bed. 'Wake up fully,' I told him. 'Shower, dress in dark clothes, and get ready to get the hell out of here.'

'Wh-what the hell for?' he asked, gaping.

'Change of plan,' I told him, 'you've been included.' 'Great!' he said, heading for the bathroom, 'I was getting bored watching you do all the heavy stuff.'

'Don't take it so lightly,' I told him, 'if our friend in black has got on our trail again and he finds you alone, he'll wrap that brown belt of yours around your neck and strangle you with it. And if he has a knife, he'll make chopped liver of you.'

'If he gets past my .45,' he reminded me. 'I'm taking it. And don't be a wet blanket. I'll be ready in fifteen minutes.'

He was. In another five minutes I'd briefed him, and handed him a walkie-talkie. 'You give me a boost up that tree by the wall,' I told him, 'it will be difficult making it up on my own. After that you get back to the cab and hang around, making circles in a holding pattern. Fifteen minutes, at most. If I yell, you get the hell out. If I need to bring the man out I'll call and you pick us up where I tell you to. And if I tell you to get out, you get right out of the country. Get to Madras and from there to the States as fast as you can. Right?'

'Right,' he acknowledged, hefting the Motorola walkie-talkie in his hands. 'Why is this thing so clunky? They could make it a quarter its size without making it costlier.'

'They've got to be rugged,' I said, 'to survive impacts from being thrown around, from having people land on them, and so on. You'll see before the night is out.'

The receptionist called at five to two to say that the taxi was waiting downstairs. Gopi and I went down to the lobby carrying a bag apiece—containing all the goodies Mankekar had sent us, so that we could take them with us just in case we were interrupted—leaving all the clothes and other inessentials behind. I told the driver to take us to Jos Junction on MG Road first, near the railway station and barely a hundred yards from Ahmed's house. The rain had decreased by then to a slight drizzle, enough to cut normal visibility but not enough to affect the NVGs, as Gopi and I walked from Jos Junction towards the sea.

With Gopi boosting me up the tree, the thick flak-jacket—fourteen-ply Kevlar, much thicker than body armour—keeping my torso off the glass on top of the wall, feet securely shod and hands gloved, I made it into the compound with no trouble. I dropped into a rose bed just inside the wall and stepped onto a lawn that through the NVGs looked like a black carpet.

This time, too, the attacker came with almost no warning. I heard a low growl behind me and whirled to see a dark shape, already in midair as I turned, flying straight at my throat. I ducked and stepped back, and the Rottweiler's teeth caught on my shoulder. As its powerful jaws closed, I could feel their crushing pressure right through the jacket. But for the jacket, my shoulder would have been a lump of mincemeat.

The rifle on my back was useless. I'd bought it for just such an eventuality but it was useless.

The dog was heavy. It must have weighed at least sixty pounds and it caught me off balance and I tumbled beneath it as it brought up its hind legs to disembowel me. I tried to roll over, and the dog, perhaps sensing that it wouldn't be able to bite through the jacket, shifted its position two inches to a spot where half its teeth were in the jacket and the rest in my shoulder. I rolled over, ignoring the pain, failing to dislodge or even loosen its grip on my shoulder. I got my hands on my knife, slashed at its throat between its forepaws.

In the drizzle my grip was slippery and the knife fell away into the grass, but for that moment its grip loosened and I turned onto my back and again all it had between its teeth was flak jacket. I heaved the animal up by its chest, got it on top of me, then got my hands on its throat, and squeezed for dear life, using my thumbs to try and break what seemed to be its windpipe. It loosened its grip a tiny bit and shifted. I scrabbled for the knife, got it in my hand, raised it, brought it down on the animal's back. I could feel its blood all over my arm but it didn't budge. I managed to get one of its forelegs off me and then its throat was exposed and I slashed at it, and this time made contact. Its blood gushed out onto my face and chest in a warm, thick stream, but its jaws refused to loosen up in the slightest. I let the rain wash the worst of the blood off me and lay quiet for a minute, getting my breath back.

It took me quite some effort to ease the dead jaws off my shoulder. The rain stung the bites on my shoulder as the dog fell off me, and the rainwater diluted the blood as it flowed all over my clothes. No time now to worry about the bites, I thought, there would be enough time for bandages and medication when I got back to the hotel.

Straight ahead was a balcony. No sunshades, no way to get up the wall. I jogged toward the balcony, to feel the surface of the wall. And in a moment of wavering concentration knocked over a flowerpot, because my eyes were on the railing and not where I was going.

A watchman emerged from the shelter just inside the gate, torch in hand, flashing it all around the lawn. I ducked behind the corner of the house, looked past it, saw the watchman notice the dog lying dead more or less in the centre of the lawn and stop. He took three steps towards the dead dog before he turned and yelled for help, presumably to a colleague in the sentrybox.

It was all over. I had to get out.

I charged the watchman as he straightened up from beside the dog, ran into him at full tilt, with my right shoulder—the one the dog hadn't managed to chew up—

butting his chest. He fell back on his bottom and hands, and I took three more running steps to the edge of the lawn, hopped over the flower-bed to the base of the compound wall and leapt up. My fingers hooked the edge of the wall, and with fresh pains surging through my side, I scrambled over, cutting my arms and legs on the glass but not enough to slow down my headlong flight. Before the watchman was up I was over the wall and running down the street towards TDM Hall, and then right towards Jos Junction. At the next right, I ducked into the lee of a building, took off jacket and shirt, and tossed the now bloodied shirt into a gutter. I put on the jacket, and over it the raincoat I was carrying in my pack. At least the blood wouldn't show.

Nothing stirred until a few minutes later, when a man emerged from the lane where Ahmed lived. He looked up and down the road, saw no one, and went back in. I jogged off towards MG Road, turning left when I reached it, away from the airport, a hundred yards away from Woodlands, outside which I'd told Gopi to check on every circuit he made.

I saw the car fifty yards off, forced myself not to run towards it and walked up to it swinging the pack. Gopi opened the door as the car drew up, and I climbed in with the raincoat still on. 'What happened?' Gopi asked, concerned.

'Nothing,' I said. 'No one's coming along.' I turned to the driver. 'Go ahead,' I told him, 'head for Guruvayoor.'

'What the hell happened?' Gopi repeated.

'Tell you when we get there,' I replied. In one of the bags we'd dumped in the car was a spare shirt. In the dark I took off the raincoat and jacket. There were sticking plaster and cotton wool and cream in the bag, and with Gopi's help I managed a makeshift dressing over the dogbites, taping up the deep gouges as best we could. I hoped that generous doses of antiseptic would ward off any infection resulting from not cleaning the muck out of the bites. I wiped myself clean, then changed shirts.

Guruvayoor was two hours away down NH 37. We drew up in front of a small rooming house right on the periphery of the temple, and Gopi got us a room without much trouble because this was the off-season at the temple. Gopi paid off the driver with a wad of hundred-rupee notes, telling him we wouldn't want to return to Kochi for a day or two.

Inside the room, I took off the shirt and the makeshift bandage I'd put on in the taxi. 'You screwed up,' Gopi said when he saw the bandage and the streaks of blood in the light. 'You screwed up badly.' He pushed me onto a bed and began to clean the bites out—there were two deep, jagged tooth marks and several shallower ones—before putting on more antiseptic and a secure bandage. 'You deserve to get hydrophobia,' he said when he was through, inspecting his handiwork with some satisfaction.

'No such luck,' I said, 'I've taken all the right shots. And you're right. I screwed up. It was a mess. First there was this bloody monster of a dog and after I got rid of it I stumbled into a bloody flowerpot.'

'Was there a watchman?' he asked.

'Yes. He heard me bumbling around in the garden and came running out with a torch. He saw the dog bleeding all over that manicured grass and yelled for help. I took off without waiting to see what the help would be like.'

'And now our friend in black knows where we are. I don't think they'll have any doubts as to who tried this one. All that bumming around on the train was a complete waste.'

'Not quite,' I said. 'It gave us breathing space. And I can still do the unexpected.'

'What do you mean?'

'We kiss our clothes goodbye, whatever we left at the hotel in Kochi.'

'Sure, but where do we go from here?'

'To Coimbatore. From there we take the afternoon flight to Bombay. This guy Ahmed is due to get there tomorrow—I mean, today—in any case, so we'll be there, waiting for him, goodies at the ready.'

'When do we move?'

'Eightish. We'll have time for a nap, a couple of hours or so. We can catch up with our sleep while travelling. We should be in Bombay by tea time.'

'When will you talk to this guy Ahmed, then?'

'As soon as possible. Maybe tonight. If he takes the last flight out of Kochi he should be in Bombay by about eight, home by about nine. I'd like to drop in straight away, before he gets his bearings.'

'Guards and such?'

'I don't care any more. The bloody diaries are getting further away with each passing day and with them go my chances of clearing up this mess. I can't prove my innocence without the diaries and without knowledge of who took them in the first place.'

'What about the fellow in black?'

'I'll be ready for him this time. I've fallen into a pattern without noticing it, and he's been using it.'

'What pattern?'

'I always start a raid between one and three in the morning. That's the safest time to go for it, and our man's got himself into position well in time to anticipate me. So now I change the timing and throw him off balance.'

'Can't you take the fellow out?'

'No way. He's stronger and faster than I am, and at least as experienced. Everything else being the same, he'll take me apart.'

The bites generated a dull pain that seemed to twitch all my other pains into wakefulness, and half an hour later I knew I wouldn't be able to sleep without help. I took out another ampoule of diclo, hoping that it wasn't addictive, and injected it into my thigh. Five minutes later the pain was gone and I fell back into a blessed darkness.

Gopi woke me at half past eight. I looked blearily at my watch and complained that we were late. 'Take it easy,' he said, 'I checked with the guy downstairs about the flight from Coimbatore. We'll make it. I've called a cab for nine. You have half-an-hour to get ready.'

I dozed most of the way to Coimbatore, drifting in and out of sleep. At Coimbatore we saw the news on TV: the attack on Ahmed's house hadn't made it to the headlines. It would have happened too late to get in the newspapers anyway. I felt a twinge of guilt at leaving a trail of such destruction behind me but Gopi, who saw what I was thinking, was on hand to buoy my flagging spirits. 'No time for remorse,' he said. 'Those damn diaries are worth a thousand lives. Go for it.'

chapter thirteen

The newspapers concentrated on the elections, in the heat of which Rawat's murder had been forgotten. There were posters and cutouts of leaders all over the place, and buntings and notices of impending campaign speeches. The PM's granddaughter had become a regular heroine, her once obscure face now smiling beguilingly at passersby from every other lamp-post as we drove from Bombay's Santa Cruz Airport to the Palm Grove hotel at Juhu, having selected it more or less at random from the yellow pages.

Ahmed, I discovered from the telephone directory, lived at the far end of town, in an apartment cooperative in Cuffe Parade. I tried his number, and got through to a manservant who told me that the master was expected in the evening. He didn't know what time, but he hadn't been told to cook dinner, so he expected Ahmed in only after ten. Yes, the master lived alone except for his servants. After yesterday's incident in Kochi he didn't want to put himself at risk, and was bringing a bodyguard down with him. What incident, I asked. Oh, said the servant, someone got into the master's garden last night, and killed a dog—an expensive dog—and knocked out a watchman before escaping over a high wall. And what do the police say? I asked. They're busy, came the reply, the master said they think it's that Colonel fellow, the one who did in Major Rawat. It seems the Colonel left a knife behind, with his fingerprints and the dog's blood all over it.

I should have remembered that knife . . .

The apartment building in which Ahmed's flat was turned out to be a snowy white seven-storey block with two watchmen at the gate round the clock and another in the large basement carpark. The windows were all barred up to the third floor, and there was no way an ordinary burglar could get beyond that floor from the outside. Ahmed's flat was on the fifth floor, facing the rear. I scouted around, found the names of two or three other tenants, and at seven in the evening, in the pouring rain, sent Gopi to the building with gift-wrapped parcels in his hand. On the parcels were the names and addresses of two tenants, both on the fifth floor.

The watchman let him into the building, and he took the lift to the top floor and then the stairs to the terrace. There he opened the parcels, in which I'd coiled rope and a hook. He found a place to anchor the hook, tied a rope to it, and lowered the end of the rope off the terrace onto the concrete eighty-five feet below, making sure the rope didn't pass in front of any of the windows. With the darkness and the rain no one would spot it for a few hours, or at least so I hoped.

Gopi returned at half past eight, with the rope in position. I got to the building at half past eleven, looked up, found the lights on in one of the bedrooms in Ahmed's flat. I hoped it wasn't his servant's. Gopi, meanwhile, was at the gate of the building, to distract the watchmen, and while they were busy with him I hopped over the wall from the rear. I found the end of the rope dangling some three feet off the ground. In my pack was another forty-foot section of rope that I planned to hitch onto the balcony, just in case someone found this rope and cut it off.

The rain had died down almost completely but the sky was dark and in the rear of the building there was some illumination from the lights of passing vehicles. I went quickly up the rope, counting off floors as I went, and in a couple of minutes, was two feet away from the large window of one of Ahmed's bedrooms. Four feet away to my left was a balcony.

I swung in increasing arcs forty feet above, getting closer to the balcony each time. When I judged it right, I hooked a foot on the railing and dropped softly into the balcony. I drew in the rest of the rope and left the roll on the balcony floor: to make a quick escape, all I had to do was toss it over the railing and rappel down. And I hitched on to the balcony the second rope I was carrying as a precaution.

The balcony door was closed. So were the two windows, but they weren't barred. From my pack I took out a glass-cutter—part of the hardware I'd bought earlier—and a sheet of greased paper. I cut a circle in the glass some eight inches wide, stuck the paper over it, making sure that the edges of the circle were covered by the paper, and tapped hard on the glass. When I peeled the paper off after that, the glass in the circle came away in my hands, leaving a slightly jagged-edged hole behind. I reached in, unlatched the window, and pushed it open.

The window came open with only a slight squeak of the hinges. I pushed the curtain aside, and saw in the NVGs the man sleeping restlessly on the bed. I clambered in and took a closer look at him. Clean-shaven, young-looking, a well-muscled shoulder showing over the sheet. It couldn't be Ahmed, I knew, it had to be a bodyguard. I tapped him on the shoulder and he came awake instantly, sitting up, hand sliding under his pillow. I slugged him hard on the point of the jaw with the butt of the Llama. There was a dull thud, a dark spot appeared on his chin, and he went down without a sound.

I poked him once again in the solar plexus to make sure he was out and not faking it, then tied him down to the bed with some of the spare nylon line that I always carried in my pack. I gagged him with a kerchief I found in the pockets of a pair of trousers lying on a chair, and crept out into the passage to look for Ahmed.

There was a light on in the living room and a man sat there dozing on a sofa, the TV set in front of him tuned to Zee Movies. I stepped up behind him and saw that his hand was on his sidearm, his finger hooked through the trigger guard. Anyone trying to take that pistol off him would set it off.

I didn't try. I hit him on the base of the skull with the Llama's butt with as much force as I could muster through the clouds of pain now building up in my side. He fell sideways on the sofa, twitched, and lay still. With what was left of the rope I tied and gagged him, put his pistol's safety on, dropped it in my pack, and went into the other bedroom, where Ahmed was almost sure to be.

He was curled up in bed when I opened the door, lying like a baby on his right side. I eased the door wide open, and two long steps brought me to the foot of his bed. I moved to the head of the bed, by the bedside table, and he snuffled in his sleep like a pig at the trough, then turned over onto his back, his face half hidden in the crook of his left arm. I slid my hand over his mouth and pinched his nostrils shut with thumb and forefinger.

He came awake struggling for breath and I upper-cut him on the jaw. He didn't go out, but I clamped my hands on his neck and put my knee on his chest. 'No noise,' I said, 'no movement. Or you die.' When he lay still, I continued, 'I'm going to ask you some questions and you'll answer me. I'll take my hand off your neck for you to answer me but my knife will be at your throat and if you fool around I will kill you. Your bodyguards are bound and gagged. There is no one to help you here, and if you call for help you'll be dead and I'll be away before anyone gets here. Clear?'

He nodded, terrified. I could feel the sweat breaking out all over his face and upper body even in the air-conditioned coolness of the bedroom. I turned on the reading lamp at his side. 'Did you have Rawat killed?' I asked.

He shook his head when I let go his throat. His voice, when he spoke, was hoarse and uneven. 'No,' he said, 'I had nothing to do with it. I swear I didn't. I just fired him.'

'Why did you fire him?'

'He . . . He lost the diaries. I swear he lost the diaries.'

'So where are the diaries now?' I asked.

'I don't know. They disappeared. Nobody knows where.'

'What's your part in all this?'

In the light of the reading lamp I saw his eyes shift to my side, go momentarily opaque. I turned and dropped off the bed and onto the floor in one movement as the man at the door fired his silenced pistol. The bullet passed over me and then I had both hands on my Llama. I fired as the instructor had taught me, twice through the heart. Always do that, the instructor had said, so that you don't have to waste time making sure he's dead, and I'd never forgotten his words.

I had the Llama trained on Ahmed before the bodyguard's corpse hit the floor. He was scrabbling under his pillow for a pistol. I hit him on the cheek with the barrel of the Llama and he sat back, stunned. I slapped him into some form of wakefulness. 'What's your part in this?' I asked again.

'I financed some of it, got the rest of the money together,' he said, 'about forty lakh rupees.'

'Where did you get the money?' I asked. 'Your legitimate business is profitable but not profitable enough for you to skim that much off it.'

'My business is only a cover. It's a laundry.' The man was gaining confidence as he saw that I wasn't about to kill him immediately. 'I arrange for things to be brought into the country. In the south . . . Mostly in north Kerala, north of Kasargod.'

'And the travel agency and the airline?'

'I use that to distribute whatever I bring in. Also to show losses.'

'Do you own the business?'

'No . . . I don't even run it. My cousin owns it. I'm . . . I'm only a figurehead. I have a good education, even a degree in business management. My cousin is barely literate and you can see that when he speaks. I front for him and he does the work.'

'What about Rawat?' I asked, 'why did you take him on and then fire him?'

'Abdul Karim—my cousin—told me to take him on a couple of years ago. He told me that Rawat had been kicked out of the Army, that we could use him as a security man, and that he would be useful if we wanted to get hold of more people in case of a gang-war or anything of the kind. Rawat . . . he was Abdul's man, not mine.'

'What did he do for Abdul?'

'I don't know all of it. But when Abdul needed it . . . he would set fire to other peoples' warehouses, have people beaten up. He was very good at organizing accidents. None of our people could go on strike. He got the police to look the other way when he wanted them to. Abdul gave him a free hand.'

'And how is all this connected with the diaries, with the kidnap?'

'It began more than four months ago. I don't know the details but Abdul took Rawat away four months ago. Later—about six weeks ago, I think—he got in touch with me again and told me that he needed Rawat to organize something, to build up a team to do something, and he took some more of my men. You see, he would make me employ some people and take them whenever he wanted.'

I listened, stunned. Four months ago! The Princess's trip had been planned long after that . . . The diaries! Someone had been after the diaries long before we'd even known they existed! I wrenched my mind off the diaries and came back to Rawat and Abdul Karim.

'Did he tell you what the people were for?'

'No. But after the kidnap I knew he must have taken them for it. And before that I heard something about the diaries. It didn't make sense until I read about them.'

'How many men did Abdul take from you for the kidnap?'

'One . . . He took two but he sent one back.'

'And why was Rawat killed?'

'I don't know. I swear I don't know. I haven't met Abdul lately. All I know is what I read in the papers, that Menon killed him and his wife. I didn't think that was right, because Menon wouldn't kill his wife, but I had nothing to do with it.'

'How was Rawat involved in the kidnap? How did he build his team? Do you know?'

'In the first place, Rawat organized it for Abdul, but there was someone with him all the time. A foreigner. He spoke Arabic.'

'Do you speak Arabic?'

'Yes. I learnt it in Kerala. But Abdul doesn't know that, and neither did this man.'

'So what did you hear?'

'This man was here to work with Rawat. He and Rawat planned it together. Rawat found the men to do it. That was all. Rawat had the contacts to get the men he needed.'

'What kind of contacts?'

'He got hold of ex-Army men from somewhere. I heard him talk about some rifles. Kashmir rifles, something like that.'

'J & K Rifles?' I asked. There were enough ex-servicemen who had put in fifteen years and retired to an insufficient pension. Most found jobs in some security function or other, but a few, especially the infantrymen who learnt skills useless in civilian life, turned to more lucrative professions: smuggling, drugs, protection rackets, and so on. Rawat could have got hold of men like those, he would have known how to get in touch with them.

Ahmed nodded. 'Yes,' he said, 'that's it. And that foreigner taught them. He spoke bad Urdu as well.'

'Who thought up the ultralights?'

'The foreigner. I think he's Libyan . . . from the kind of Arabic he speaks.'

'How did they bring the ultralights in?'

'I brought them in . . . imported them legitimately as spare parts for my aircraft.'

'Did Rawat do the groundwork for the kidnap?'

'Yes . . . he spoke to that man in Kabini, Basappa. It was

just our luck that Menon interrogated Basappa, no one else would have recognized Rawat. But I covered up for him. I organized his alibi because Abdul told me to.'

Regret twinged in my chest. Rawat had been good and capable. He'd done an excellent job of working out the kidnap and the campaign to get the diaries out of the CBI and putting pressure on the judiciary by taking the CJ's son. If only he'd kept on the right side of the law. 'Do you know where Rawat got his men from?' I asked.

'I told you, there was one in my company. He got some others, but I remember him saying that there were two more he couldn't get . . . He needed an electronics expert, and another who knew explosives well . . . Someone who could sit down with the electronics man and make bombs to order. Rawat got them through Abdul.'

'So Abdul is behind all this. He's looking for the diaries.'

'No, not Abdul. Abdul is a smuggler. He can't plan something this size.'

'Who was it then?'

'Someone else . . . someone who put the Libyan on to Abdul. I've never seen him, but the Libyan and Abdul talked about him sometimes. He's in India, and he seems a powerful man . . . a politician or a bureaucrat. That's all I know.'

'Why did they kill Basappa?'

'To prevent Menon from getting to Rawat.'

'You said Abdul began work on the diaries four months ago. The CBI got to know of them after that. How did Abdul know?'

'I don't know. I don't know anything about the bloody diaries. I don't know anything about anything but now everyone is after me. First someone tries to get me in Kochi. Now you come here and kill my people and interrogate me. I never wanted all this. I just wanted a quiet life.'

I put the knife to his throat. 'Shut up. Answer my questions. Say nothing else. Otherwise you're dead.'

He subsided. Back to the kidnap. Rawat had been two men short. 'Where did Rawat get his men from, the ones he said he couldn't provide?'

'I don't know. He spoke to Abdul about wanting two men and Abdul said he'd try to arrange it through someone he knew, some gangland type in Bombay.'

'Do you know who?'

'Not for sure. It's probably someone called Youssuf . . . A gang leader from Gujarat. Another smuggler, but he operates on a much bigger scale than Abdul. He's got a protection racket going, and several thousand prostitutes. He has pimps working for him all over Maharashtra. And he brings in drugs and weapons.'

'What are the weapons for?'

'For anyone who's willing to pay.'

'Where does Youssuf hang out?'

'I don't know. He is into drugs and prostitution and protection all over the country. But he runs things from Bombay.'

'How long has he been around?'

'Thirty years. He must be sixty now, if not more.'

It was falling into place now. Rawat, lacking men in his own outfit with the required expertise, had had to bring in outsiders, specialists. Maybe one of them had stolen the diaries. We never got to know how many people were inside that farmhouse, or whether anyone got away. I should have waited in the pond, waited for the searchlights and the cordon to come up.

And who was behind it all? Abdul had known about the diaries for four months!

Had Mehta been a plant?

Whoever was behind this had actually created those diaries. They would have financed all the bribes that Mehta had paid sundry people in positions of power, for licences, permissions, and other favours. With the diaries in their hands, they could rule the country regardless of who was in power.

This smelt of Hamid Gul. He must have worked this out in the course of one long evening at his bungalow not far from Benazir Bhutto's Bilawal House in Karachi, with a couple of jiggers of Johnnie Walker to help his thought processes along.

There was nothing further to be gained from this terrified man. I got the feeling he was speaking the truth, and he was only a front anyway. Besides, he was afraid of something bigger than me. But maybe he'd be able to help me catch Abdul. One of the specialists must have taken the diaries . . . they must have set it up for the Libyan to kill the hostages and leave with the diaries, and one of the members of the team must have scooted with the diaries instead.

'I need to get in touch with Abdul,' I asked, 'how do I do that?'

'He lives in Bombay . . . I can tell you where he lives.' He reached out for a diary on his table and read out an address from it, somewhere in Bandra.

I rose. 'What are you going to do?' Abdul asked.

'I'm leaving,' I said, 'I'm going to tie you up, a little loosely so that I have five minutes in which to get away. After that you can do what you dam' well like.'

'You can't do that!' he almost screamed. 'You can't leave me here just like that!'

'Why not?'

He quietened down. 'Look, it's obvious. You're Menon. You can't be anyone else.' I nodded, and he continued, 'That Libyan's been after you ever since you got out of hospital. He found Basappa before you did, and he got to Rawat before you did. You must have tried to get to me in Kochi yesterday?' I nodded again. 'Yes,' he said, 'it could only have been you. So now the Libyan knows you're after me. He'll be here then, to do to me what he did to Basappa and Rawat . . . Don't you see that?'

'I see it,' I said. I didn't tell him that was why I'd dropped in before midnight. 'But I don't see what I can do about it. I can't protect you.'

'You're looking for the diaries. I can help you get to them.'

'How?'

'I'll put you on to Abdul. I can use my contacts to find out about Youssuf, or whoever it was that provided the specialists . . . I can clear your name. I can tell the police you weren't involved. I can raise money for you . . .'

'And what do you want in return?'

'Keep me safe,' he said in a small voice, and then, to my surprise, he broke down and wept. It was as if the tension of the past few weeks had broken him. 'Just get me out of this,' he whispered softly when he got his voice back, 'just get me out of this mess. I didn't want to get into it but Abdul forced me and now Abdul will have me killed.'

'I'm myself on the run,' I told him, 'you know that. Why don't you go to the police? Or to the CBI?'

'Do you think I'd be safe with the police anywhere, or the CBI? Don't you know what happened to Mehta? He was killed in custody. Do you think these guys can't kill people in custody? And then, what evidence do I have? None. And these men here, they aren't bodyguards. They're minders. They're Abdul's men, kept here to make sure I don't make a move towards you.'

'If you come with me it'll get rough,' I said. 'You'll be in a great deal of physical trouble, and you might get hurt. And they might kill you anyway. Or the police might. Do you want to risk it?'

'I have to,' he cried. 'What choice do I have? Now that you've come and knocked out the bodyguards, Abdul will know for sure you've been here. They'll know I've talked . . . they won't leave me alive. But if I come with you, and the watchmen downstairs don't see me going out in good shape, they might think you've carried me off somewhere . . . they won't be sure I've joined you.'

'But you said Abdul is your cousin,' I said, 'won't he help?'

'You don't understand, Menon,' he hissed. 'These guys aren't like you and me. They have no qualms about killing. They don't give a damn about family. Abdul would quite happily kill his own mother for a profit, or if she talked about him. He demands absolute loyalty. And the Libyan is with him.'

'Okay,' I said, 'come along, then. Bring all the money you can find, we might need it when we go up against Abdul and Youssuf. Also anything you can sell, to raise quick money. Whatever you have in the house.'

He climbed out of bed, hitching up his lungi as he did so. I turned on a brighter lamp, took his pistol—an American Hi-Standard .22—and stuck it in my pack before turning to watch him. He was a short fat man, sharp-nosed, beginning to go bald, beetle-browed and hairy. He washed up in the bathroom, then changed quickly into trousers and a shirt. Then he opened a safe concealed in the wall right behind the bedstead. It had a seven-digit combination lock and he juggled it open without me getting the slightest idea what the combination was. And when at last he threw the door open I felt my jaw hang slack in astonishment.

The safe was a cavity about a foot to each side. Inside were thick bundles of cash, one of five-hundred-rupee notes at least six inches thick, and another six-inch bundle of hundred-rupee notes. Beside the money were several fat A4-size envelopes, and on the envelopes were several biscuit-sized bars of what even I could recognize as gold.

There must have been at least five cubic inches of it in there. Beside the gold was a leather jewel case that seemed ridiculously large, and by that a chamois leather bag. 'Don't take the jewellery,' I told him as soon as I got my jaw hitched up again.

'Why not?' he asked, 'there's at least five lakh rupees worth lying around here.'

'It's also easily identifiable,' I said. 'If you sell any of it to a fence or a jeweller, Abdul and Co. will find out about it fast enough. There can't be too many people around who own that kind of jewellery.'

'All right, then,' he said, 'I'll take the cash.'

'Not all of it,' I said, 'take the five hundreds.'

'Why?'

'To encourage them to think that I dragged you off.'

'Yes,' he said, picking up the notes and the leather bag.

'What's in the bag?' I asked.

'Hold out your hand,' he said. When I did, he poured out of the bag a small stream of white stones that sparkled in the lamplight. 'Diamonds,' he grinned, 'one to two carats. A hundred and twenty of them. No one knows about them. They come to Gujarat to be cut. These are all small ones, cut to standard specifications, each a carat or so. I got them from a friend who cuts them for a living.'

'Where can you exchange them for money?' I asked.

'Not on the bourse,' he said, 'but there are enough shady jewellers who'll buy this lot at half the market rate. That's very good, because they pay only a fifth to a tenth for jewellery.'

He threw some clothes in a soft bag, put the cash and diamonds in a lizardskin briefcase and stood waiting for orders. 'Could you go down a rope?' I asked.

He never got a chance to answer that question because the front door blew in with a bang. The Libyan.

I didn't hesitate. I dragged Ahmed off to the balcony and tossed down the rope coming down from the terrace. 'Slide down this,' I told him. I took his bag, stuck a hand through the handle of the briefcase, gripped the second rope, and jumped over the railing. Some three seconds later I was on the concrete below—you can travel upto ten feet in the first second of rappelling, and at peak speed over a hundred feet a second. Ahmed arrived a minute later, after a bumpier ride, having scraped himself on the wall several times. I pushed him along to the compound wall, forced him over it, and called Gopi on the walkie-talkie.

chapter fourteen

We met Gopi half a kilometre away five minutes later, and drove straight along to the Palm Grove, where I collected the key from the counter while Gopi sneaked our new friend into our room. 'What's all this?' Gopi asked when we had settled down. 'And who's your friend?'

'There've been defectors in the ranks on the other side,' I said. 'Meet Mr Saifuddin Ahmed, in whose company I got away seconds ahead of the man in black.'

Gopi's eyes widened. 'Did you run into him, then?'

'I did. He turned up a little after midnight. He must have thought I'd arrive at one or so. He must have heard us talking, because he blew in the door and that gave us time to get away.' I turned to Ahmed. 'This is my brother Gopi, who lives in America and came down here at my request to help me out of this mess. He's saved my skin a couple of times already.'

They eyed each other warily. 'Ahmed wants to go straight,' I explained to Gopi. 'Today he told me quite a bit at knife-point. Then he decided to come with me because he thinks the man in black—who's probably a Libyan—is a lot more dangerous than I am.'

'What's in it for you?' Gopi asked Ahmed.

Ahmed examined his hands and instead of answering asked for a drink. The bar was closed but Gopi had a bottle of scotch in his baggage—he'd got hold of it while I was chasing Ahmed—and he poured out a large slug for Ahmed, and then one for himself. Ahmed cleared his throat, then explained, 'They killed Basappa just before the Colonel got to him. They did the same to Rawat. And they tried to do the same to me. That's one reason. The other is, I'm a kind of small criminal. I smuggle stuff into the country, I make my money, and I'm more or less content with that. But now I've been forced into a bigger game, where the stakes are far higher, and I can't handle it. In the smuggling business I've had to deal mostly with competition and the police, but the violence here is of a far greater magnitude. I wanted out but couldn't leave . . . I was trapped. So when the Colonel came along I thought I'd take my chances with him.'

'And how can you help us?'

'My cousin Abdul is involved. I can tell you how to get him.' He gave Gopi a brief summary of what he'd told me in his flat.

At the end of it Gopi whistled. 'Those diaries, man,' he said, 'they've got to be plants. Someone did this on purpose!'

'Exactly,' I said, 'the local controller. That's the guy we want. The rest are just pawns like you and me.'

'I think I saw the man once, at a distance, with Abdul,' offered Ahmed. 'His face was covered. He had dark glasses and he stood in the shadows. He was north Indian. He wore a sherwani and churidar . . . and he had a talisman about his neck. I remember that talisman gleaming on his chest. I remember because they were speaking Arabic and no devout Muslim would wear a talisman. The religion doesn't permit icons.'

It could have been anyone, and the talisman could have been dust in our eyes. 'And our friend in black,' I said, 'met Abdul through him, and is looking for the diaries, which have ended up in the wrong hands. We will find out from Abdul whose hands those might be.'

It was past four in the morning before we slept. Gopi called reception and arranged for another room for himself, telling them that we had a guest who would be sharing my room. Ahmed didn't want to run the risk of being recognized—he said he came to this hotel once in a while—so he ducked into the bathroom whenever room service delivered.

Only I slept well that night, because of the painkiller I had. I came awake to find bright sunlight streaming in through the window and Ahmed sitting in a chair by the coffee table. My watch said half past nine. I lurched into a more or less vertical position and groaned when my chest protested. 'Where's Gopi?' I asked.

'Gone for a swim. I thought I'd wait.' Ahmed had changed and groomed himself and there was some brightness in his eyes, too. A fat, jolly man, one would have thought to look at him. He smiled wryly. 'I was getting impatient sitting here doing nothing.'

'Fill in the time by telling me about Abdul. Everything you know about him.'

Abdul, it turned out, was a self-made man. He was about fifty-five now, and had come from his hometown near Kasargod to Bombay over forty years ago to make his fortune. He had tried his hand at various things, failed at all of them, and ended up a bagman for a goon, collecting money from hawkers in the goon's neighbourhood. Starting there, he had worked his way up through the ranks, driven away his employer and enforced his own rule in the neighbourhood.

There were several years in between about which Ahmed knew nothing, during which Abdul had been out of contact with his family. When he resurfaced, he had made his fortune and offered to buy out his entire clan. Now he lived alone in a posh flat in Bandra, maintained an office of sorts on Mohammed Ali Road from where he operated as a loan shark, and another near the docks from where he ran his other businesses. He had two wives, each of whom he had gifted a flat in the same building where he lived, but on different floors. He usually drank Glen Livet, but when he got sentimental about the old days in Bombay he sent his servant out for a bottle of local rotgut.

'And how did you fall in with him?' I asked.

'After his parents died—they died when he was eight—my mother took him in. His mother and she were sisters. But after my father died there wasn't enough money. He ran away from home soon after that, when I was five. When he came back we heard a lot of rumours, that he was a thug, that he had killed a man, and so on, but he was kind to my mother. He told her that since she had taken him in when he was too young to look after himself, he'd take care of her children.

'She was a godfearing woman. She told him she didn't want money earned from crime, even though we were just surviving then. But she died months later, and I had no choice but to go to Abdul . . . There were three brothers to be taken care of. We sold the house but got cheated and then we were in real trouble. Abdul heard about us and took us under his wing. He had us educated. I made sure the others got out of the way . . . I made sure they left the country. One's a doctor, working in the US. Another is an engineer, in Saudi Arabia. The third . . . The third turned out to be a wastrel but the brother in America understood why I wanted them out of the country so he arranged a tourist visa for the boy and made sure that he disappeared when he got to the US. I stayed with Abdul, to pay him off.'

'And now he's asking too much, isn't he?'

'Look, Colonel, the man's ruthless. You killed one man in my flat but if you read the papers you'll see that all three are dead. He executed them for slackness, for letting you in and me out. If I'd stayed back, he'd have had me killed as well.'

'What about your family?' I asked. 'Wife, children?'

'I have no children. My wife I divorced three years ago. I have no hostages to fortune, if that's what you mean. I called my brothers this morning to tell them what's happening. They'll take care of themselves. When Abdul sees I've gone, he'll think I've gone with you but his next thought will be that I've fled to one of my brothers.'

'What about your passport?' I asked. 'You didn't take it.' He looked at me unblinkingly for a while, then laughed. 'Passports?' he said. 'No problem. How many do you want? There are half a dozen sources here where you can buy a false Indian passport, in any name you choose, for fifty thousand rupees. You can get an American passport for two lakhs . . . but you won't be able to go the US with it, that's all. The trouble is that Abdul knows all those sources. If I get a passport from one of them Abdul will get to know.'

'As a matter of interest, how do these guys get passports?'

'The foreign ones, the ones from the west, are all stolen. There's a ring of thieves around here looking for careless foreigners. I've also got men doing the same thing in Karachi and Lahore and Islamabad. We put new pictures on the passports, and fudge the signatures. They can't be used in the countries where they were issued, but if you want to go somewhere in Europe on an American passport it's no problem. Or an EC passport: take one and wander all over Europe.'

'What about Indian ones?'

'There's a man in the Passport Office who rejects usable blanks. The blanks are delivered to us. We pay him about ten times his salary but he's worth it. He also runs a business forging visas. You see, we can send a man out on one passport and bring him in on another. Send him out again and bring him back in on the passport on which he went out first. So it's easy to prove that someone who was actually in India on a particular date was travelling abroad at the time. We should have done that for Rawat but too many people had seen him here so we dropped the idea of covering him that way.'

'Have you been covering the Libyan this way?'

'No. He does his own documentation. Or maybe his employer, the one with the talisman . . . But that man is frightening. I haven't slept well since this thing started, for fear of the man.'

'Why did you cross over, then?'

'It's just that I understood for the first time that I'm a small-timer. I've been in this business for a long while now but it's all small stuff, bringing in gold and liquor and cigarettes and electronic goods. But killing the Prime Minister's granddaughter . . . That's a different order of magnitude altogether . . . And you know, I've lived in this country all my life, except for a few trips overseas, and I like it. I might smuggle in booze but I wouldn't get into outright treason. You might think it funny but it's true. My roots are here.'

'I don't know how much I can help you,' I said. 'Even if you help me out you might end up doing a few years in prison. You know that.'

'Yes. I have enough money. Enough to last the rest of my life. With the kind of cooperation I've given you I might serve two or three years in prison, no more, and after that I'll retire.

'I'll live on a quiet beach somewhere and enjoy myself and be free. Unless they have me killed in prison.'

It was a pipe dream and he knew it but I didn't want to take his dreams away from him because at the moment they were all he had. He'd changed overnight and he knew it. He knew there was almost no chance of his getting away alive but he'd made up his mind to meet his death in peace and I could see it in his face. He smiled suddenly. 'I'd have liked to go to Mecca,' he said. 'In the old days the Hajj used to be something you tried to do in your final years. Before you left you wound up your businesses and paid off your debts because it was such a dangerous, difficult journey that few came back alive. Now you charter an aircraft and go there and return in a few days. You know, Indians have been complaining that the government doesn't do enough for people going on Hajj.

'Actually you're not supposed to accept help from anyone. It's remarkably like your sanyas. You should be totally free from obligation when you go and if you take help from the government you are obliged to the government. I wish I could go now. I have no debts, no obligations. Not even to you.'

I smiled back at him although I didn't feel like smiling. 'Tell me more about Abdul,' I said. 'What he loves, and the patterns in his life. I'll catch him on one of the two.'

'He sleeps late,' Ahmed said. 'His day begins at noon. In all the adult years I've known him he's got up before noon only half a dozen times. By noon, the collections from his red light areas begin to come in. He checks the receipts, decides whether everything is as it should be—sometimes a pimp and few girls get together and decide to keep part of the take—and then decides what is to be done with the money, who is to be paid off, and so on. In the evenings it's satta, the gambling dens he runs. Early in the evening he gets his pushers on the road, because their business peaks between nine and eleven. The drug collections are in by early morning. Every other day he goes to a hotel on Linking Road, Caesar's Palace. That's where the police hang out, the middle level types. He pays them off, buys them drinks, chats with them for a while to make them happy, then returns home. People keep visiting him until two or even later if a shipment is coming in. If it's a big shipment he waits until someone reports that it's in. Most of the time we like to bring our stuff in between three and four—that's when people pay the least attention—so he usually gets to bed very late.'

'How many people live with him?' I asked.

'One of his wives stays with him each night. When one of his sons comes visiting, he might stay over. There are always at least two goons hanging around, and usually at least half a dozen. You won't get him to talk there, he's tough. And there's no way you'll get into that flat and smuggle him out of it, Colonel, no way.'

'Call me Raja,' I said.

'I can't do that. I've got used to addressing officials by their titles. It makes them feel good most of the time, you know, especially policemen and so on . . .'

'Right,' I said, 'if I can't take him in his flat I'll take him in transit. You said something about Caesar's Palace, what time does he usually return home from there?'

'He gets there about eleven and stays there until half past one or thereabouts. After that the policemen begin to disperse, and he gets out ahead of them. He's got a Mercedes, a five-year-old Mercedes 600 . . . it's the only one in Bombay, I think. He has a chauffeur who's armed with a knife and a pistol, and there's a bodyguard who sits up in front. These days I think the bodyguard carries an AK-47.'

'Single car?'

'No. There's one more car following his, with two men in it. He thinks that's enough. Besides, no one in Bombay would dare touch that Mercedes.'

'What's this bodyguard like?'

'Dangerous. He was a rebel in Afghanistan. He smashed a leg some years ago and after that he couldn't run any more and Abdul took him on as a bodyguard . . . But don't think that damaged leg makes him any less effective.'

'Where did Abdul find him?'

'Somewhere in Kashmir. There are lots of Afghans there, men who used to fight the Russians. Now they've nowhere to go so they go wherever they can make some money. Many of them have been trained in Libya or Iran . . . It's expensive, it takes about thirty thousand US dollars to put one man through a four-week course but the Pakis have money from their drug smuggling so they can afford it.'

'Is this bodyguard Libyan-trained?' I asked.

'I don't know . . . The man's a psychopath. He kills without feeling.'

'How would you like to be a bait?' I asked.

'What?' he said, frowning. 'Are you serious?'

'I need to get hold of Abdul, to talk to him. About where the diaries are, about this shadowy man who's behind him, and about Youssuf or whoever gave him the specialists. I'll have to take his bodyguards completely by surprise, otherwise I have no chance of getting through to him. I have to hit him while he's on the move. So if you can get him to stop his car and open any door I'll take him. I'll take the bodyguard and the driver and you can get into that car and drive away wherever you like.'

He looked at me for a while, without speaking. Then he looked away, to his left, out of the glass window at something distant. He spoke slowly. 'All my life I've lived in terror of the man,' he said. 'He was soft-spoken in my mother's presence but you could sense the violence in him. Like a leopard. He used to thrash us when we were children . . . He had a hard streak in him even then. He is hard on his children now, and his wives. They don't even look him in the face. I've always wanted to defy him . . . I think I'll do this for you. In fact, it will be a pleasure.'

'When is the best time?'

'As you said, when he's returning from Caesar's Palace. He has to drive up three kilometres from Linking Road, along lonely roads, to get home. You can't take him at the hotel, there'll be too many people around, and you can't take him near his house, because there'll be a couple of bagmen around. So it has to be somewhere in the middle.'

'Today's Saturday. Do you think he'll visit the hotel tonight?'

'Tonight or tomorrow night. He always goes on Friday nights, and again either on Saturday or Sunday.'

'He's become complacent. Regularity is a mistake. We'll use that to take him. We'll wait for him.'

'Yes. I'll show you the route, and you can decide where. I know his car, I'll stop it one way or another, and you can move in.'

We collected Gopi from the pool and went out in a taxi to have a look at the route Abdul took on his way home from Caesar's Palace and I found a good position for an ambush at a bus stop close to a small roundabout. It wasn't far from the seashore, on a winding road that ran through some of the most expensive residential areas in Bombay. This was where the rich creative crowd hung out. The roundabout was a hundred yards from the bus stop, at a T: one road led 180 degrees away from the stop while the other was more or less perpendicular. By the bus stop was a small sapling with a sort of brick fence around it to keep the cattle off, and across the road was another.

Back in the hotel I looked at the materials available and worked up an improvised grenade. I took the top off an empty can of Coke, lined it with one-rupee coins, stuffed a handful of plastic into the can, rigged it up with a primer and a three-second time pencil.

We were in position at the bus stop by a quarter to one. Ahmed and I hunkered down behind the bus stop itself while Gopi waited behind the brick shelter of the sapling. In the dim light from a street lamp twenty yards away, I could see Ahmed's face, set in hard lines of determination and right at that moment I couldn't help admiring his resolve and sympathizing with him, regardless of his history.

Abdul's gigantic car arrived at the roundabout at eighteen minutes to two. We saw it sweeping up the slope and past the roundabout at thirty kilometres an hour, followed by a white Ambassador with two men in it. Ahmed stepped out on the road in front of the limousine, his arms outstretched, when it was just twenty yards away. It was accelerating away from the curve but was still going slow because the chauffeur stopped it with only mild protest from the tyres and five yards to spare. The driver's door opened and a tall man in a white uniform with a peaked cap stepped out, his hand at his side. Ahmed let his arms drop and walked to the car.

He didn't hurry. He took his own time walking up to the rear passenger door on the left, ignoring the front door which also opened, ignoring the giant of a man who stepped out of that door. He reached down for the handle of the rear door, found it locked, and gestured to the bodyguard to open it. The driver stood on the far side, watching Ahmed over the top of the car, and the bodyguard himself was reaching in to talk to the passenger in the rear when Gopi decided to move.

He ran at the chauffeur from behind, covering the fifteen metres between them in a dozen quick steps, soundless on rubber-soled shoes. The bodyguard, who was bent down, saw the movement and began to straighten up and draw, and I shot him twice in the head with the rifle from a distance of twenty metres.

The white Ambassador had dropped behind as the Mercedes swept out of the curve. It came to a halt thirty yards behind the Mercedes and I tossed the jury-rigged grenade at it as two men erupted from its front doors. The Coke-can grenade exploded on the Ambassador's bonnet and the blast threw the two men off in a tangle of limbs: unless I was mistaken, they were as drunk as their master. The blast rocked the Mercedes, and I shrank involuntarily from the sound and the flash. The chauffeur, confused by the poor light, taken aback by the blast and the strange combination of signals—Gopi coming up behind him, Ahmed standing across the car with the bodyguard falling on him, and me coming from behind the bus stop with the bomb—stood irresolute for a moment and by then I had the rifle swung around and lined up on him. He did get off a shot at me that boomed through the night—his pistol, unlike my rifle, was unsilenced—and then I shot him. My shot, taken off true by the movement, hit him in the shoulder and not the head: not a serious wound, but enough to disarm him.

The chauffeur was tough. Even though the 7.62 mm rifle bullet knocked him down he straightened and reached for the pistol that he had dropped, but by then Gopi was on him. Gopi, too, had a pistol—the Llama—but that night he didn't use it. He'd been dragged out of the States to the side of a brother who'd been framed, beaten, chased through the forest, and driven into hiding, and all the pent up anger of those weeks exploded in the one high kick he delivered to the chauffeur's head as he straightened up. There was the thud of Gopi's foot making contact with the man's skull, and the sharper crack of the chauffeur's head hitting the metal doorframe, and then he slid out of sight.

My second shot at the bodyguard had only scraped him as he fell. It had gone on past him and shattered the partition between the front seat and the passenger seat, and in the dark behind I could see the man inside scrabbling for something in his coat. I fired into the side of the passenger compartment and the man sat still. I went in close, stuck my hand in through the space where the partition had been, fumbled for the catch, and opened the door. Gopi came around, past Ahmed, reached inside, and dragged Abdul out. He frisked him, and found in a pocket a small Beretta. While I watched Abdul in silence—silence is a weapon—Gopi and Ahmed dragged the chauffeur around to the back of the car, dumped him in the boot, and locked the lid. The dead bodyguard went into the passenger area, leaving just enough room for Abdul and me in the back. Gopi collected the firearms lying around and climbed into the front passenger seat while Ahmed took the wheel.

Abdul smelt powerfully of whisky but while it might have slowed his body down he was by no means senseless. He turned to face me. 'You will die for this,' he said, in Hindi.

I wasn't watching Gopi so he took me by surprise. He reached over the back of his seat and punched Abdul in the mouth. We had decided earlier that we wouldn't speak to Abdul for the first hour or so: we'd let him rave and rant and when his bluster collapsed move in for the kill. Abdul gasped in pain when Gopi hit him but he recovered soon enough. 'You've come from Salim,' he ground out. 'Tell him I'll pay him back.'

This time I hit him, with the knuckles of my right hand, across his face. He subsided in his seat, bleeding from his nose and mouth. He reached into a pocket for something and I hit him again in the same way, in the same place. I reached into his pocket and found a packet of cigarettes. Benson and Hedges. I threw them out of the window, along with a Dunhill lighter that I'd found in the same pocket. Abdul sat still, watching Gopi and me alternately, his hands in his lap. Not particularly disturbed. But for the blood trickling down his face onto his shirt he could have been out for a late-night drive with friends.

A kind of respect for the man arose in my mind but with it came the thought of the two dead girls and Basappa and Mrs Rawat, all with their throats cut, the work of this man and others like him. I had to destroy his enormous composure first: only then would he open up. I caught his left hand and twisted his arm all the way up between his shoulder-blades until he gasped in pain, then bumped his head against the toughened glass of the partition. I held him firmly and thumped his head against the partition once again, this time making sure his face hit the flat surface, and felt the impact of his nose and teeth on the glass. There was a small stain on the glass now, a smear of blood from his teeth and his broken nose.

A tinge of fear entered his eyes for the first time but his back remained as straight as ever. We were past Chembur now, headed towards Deonar. Further up, past the BARC, we could turn off this road towards New Bombay, or keep going on to Nerul and further beyond. I'd told Ahmed to drive past the BARC towards Nerul—there was always traffic on the way to Vashi—and keep going until we hit a lonely stretch of road, with no houses or apartment blocks in the vicinity, and no street lamps. We hit one some fifteen minutes later, near Karjat, and Ahmed stopped the car and cut off the engine.

I flung the rear door open and climbed out, then dragged the cringing Abdul out onto the grass by the road, wet in the drizzle. In the silence I asked Abdul, 'Do you know who I am?' He shook his head. 'Colonel Menon,' I continued. 'They blamed me for the diaries you stole. I want them back.'

The fear in his eyes receded when he heard who I was. 'I don't know what you're talking about,' he said in Hindi, 'if you've been listening to the stories that bastard Ahmed has been telling you, you're a fool.'

'I don't have time to argue with you,' I said, 'so I'm not going to try. I've been on the run for weeks now and unless I get the diaries back I've got no future and everything to lose. I wouldn't hesitate to kill you, or to maim you so badly you won't be able to do a thing for yourself ever again. Do you understand?'

'Say what you like,' he said, gaining confidence, 'I don't know anything about the diaries.'

'Get some petrol out of the tank,' I said to Ahmed and Gopi. 'And some cotton waste, if there's any.'

Ahmed opened the boot and beside the chauffeur found a jerrycan and a tube. He opened the tank and siphoned out half a litre of petrol into the jerrycan and brought it to me. I took a length of rope out of my pack and tied Abdul's wrists behind his back, then his ankles. I jabbed him in the solar plexus and when he opened his mouth I stuffed a rag into it. His shirt was fine cotton, damp with sweat. I sprinkled a little petrol on his shirtfront from the can, and his eyes opened wide in terror. I lit a matchstick from a box Ahmed gave me and tossed it at Abdul's chest. The petrol in his shirt caught and flared and he writhed in pain on the ground. The fine drizzle put the fire out quickly, but it stayed live long enough to sear spots on his chest. Nothing serious.

I found Abdul's kerchief in his trouser pocket and soaked it in petrol. 'This goes just under your eyes,' I told him flatly, 'I'm going to take the gag out of your mouth and ask you questions. If you don't answer satisfactorily I'll set it on fire . . . Do you know that your eyeballs will melt in the fire, and the rain will only stretch the pain?' I forced him into a prone position, arms underneath his body, and used more rope to tie the kerchief on over his nose. He blinked and shut his eyes as a drop of petrol went into one. 'Open your eyes,' I continued, 'or I light the fire anyway.'

The eyes opened. The rock-like composure was gone now, under the threat of fire. I sat on his stomach and tugged the gag out of his mouth. 'The diaries,' I said.

'I don't have them,' he cried, almost gibbering in his haste to speak, 'I don't know where they are. I swear on my dead mother I don't know.'

'Tell me what you do know,' I said. 'Starting with the diaries. Who was Mehta? Who was behind him?'

'Mehta . . . Mehta wasn't Mehta. His father was a follower of Gandhi . . . Mehta's father adopted him when he was a boy of ten . . . His real parents had been killed by a mob in '47. His real name was Liaquat. Liaquat Hussain.'

'How's that relevant?' I asked.

'It is. Among the thousands of orphaned children adopted after '47 there are a few—less than twenty—who were planted here by Jinnah's men . . . Young boys, already indoctrinated, real orphans, brought to Gandhi's supporters by Jinnah's agents in the chaos after Partition. The idea was to have them in positions of power by this time, by the nineties . . . But it failed.' He stopped, gasping for air. I allowed him a few seconds, then commanded threateningly, 'Talk.'

'It failed . . . Only two of the Orphans—that was what they were named, the Orphans—only two went back to the Pakistanis. One was Liaquat . . . that Mehta. The other . . . The other is the man behind this.'

'Who is he?'

'I don't know. I have met him once, in the dark. I couldn't see his features . . . All I know is that he has a locket. He has a locket with Shiva on it.'

The talisman again. I prodded Abdul with my pistol. 'Go on.'

'He planned it long ago but told me only a few months back. He told me there was something afoot . . . Mehta had bribed several dozen senior politicians and bureaucrats . . . Even police and Army officers . . . He paid out three hundred crores over five years, and he kept records of all payments in his diaries. There were more than a thousand entries in those diaries, and wherever possible he wrote down the purpose of the bribe, and in what form it was paid. Some people wanted gold, some wanted cash—that was mostly for the party—and one politician took a kilo of opium.'

'Was Mehta's arrest part of the plan?'

'No. But Mehta was playing on the stock market and he ran up huge losses. He was a fool . . . he forged shares and took loans using the forged certificates as security. And someone complained to the police. They came for him before he could send us the diaries.'

'Why did you have him killed?'

'We didn't. It must have been done by one of his enemies . . . Someone whom he had bribed must have thought that if he had Mehta killed he'd be safe . . . Mehta died before telling us where the diaries were hidden and then the CBI got to them.'

'And whose idea was the kidnap?'

'The same man's. The other Orphan's.'

'Tell me what you know about it. How many people were involved in it, where you got your background information, how many men were in the team, who they were, what your communication systems were, everything.'

'Rawat,' came the reply, 'Rawat and the Libyan, Mahmoud. They planned everything. Rawat selected all the sites, he visited all of them, bribed people left and right for information. He had a budget of a crore just for information, and the total budget was over five crore . . . We raised it from three or four sources, to avoid anyone getting suspicious. And there was the Orphan—he paid us whenever we needed money.

'We smuggled in whatever we needed; Ahmed took care of that for us. Rawat got people . . . He was in touch with the Orphan, through Mahmoud. He often did things without telling me. But I was paid to take it all.'

'How did you get in touch with the Orphan or his men?'

'They would call me every day. There was a password that I had to give. They changed it every two or three days. Sometimes every day. I gave the caller the password and when he was sure it was really me I told him what I wanted, or what the situation was. That was the only contact we had.'

'And Rawat?'

'I don't know. They must have been in touch the same way. Or through Mahmoud. Sometimes Mahmoud used to get in touch with him and I'd give Mahmoud messages to be passed on.'

'What's the password now?'

'I don't know. He hasn't called for more than a week. I am a little nervous . . . And there are others in Bombay who are out for my blood.'

'What was in it for you?'

'Money. More money than you can imagine. And a promise that I could expand my business here . . . That no one would touch me after my friends got the diaries. They could make sure of that, I knew.'

'So you have no idea what really went on in that farmhouse where the hostages were kept?'

'No. But the plan was for Mahmoud to kill everyone, the hostages and the kidnappers, everyone, and get away with the diaries . . . But you changed your plan, and attacked early. Mahmoud did his best to get the diaries. He even knocked you out, but someone else got them. Someone else got them and escaped. Mahmoud said that the cordon around the farmhouse wasn't complete so he couldn't be sure who else got out. . . He killed only two of them, besides the hostages.'

'Who could have taken the diaries?'

'From the body count, we know that one man besides Mahmoud got away. He could have been anyone . . . The police have no idea who was killed.'

'Rawat got all the men in the team, didn't he?'

'Yes, except for two. He needed two specialists . . . One electronics man, and one who knew explosives well. I got them from a friend, both very good men . . . Both must be dead now.'

'Why do you say that?'

'The explosives man had a wooden leg. He can barely walk. The other man, the electronics man, he was a true engineer. He was the laziest man I ever knew. He couldn't walk a hundred metres without beginning to pant. But he knew his electronics.'

'Where did you get these men?' I asked.

'From a friend. Youssuf.'

'Who is he?'

'Youssuf is my godfather. He has a gang here. He's a smuggler like me, but much bigger.'

'How long have you known him?'

'Thirty-eight years. When I came to Bombay I worked for a cheap thug who once refused to pay Youssuf his tax. I killed the man though he was my boss. Then I worked for Youssuf. I joined him as a common labourer, working on the beaches bringing in the crates when the fishing boats arrived off the coast. I used to be one of the men who would row out to the boats in dinghies and bring the goods to the beach. Youssuf thought I was good. He encouraged me. He trusted me.'

'And why did you split from him?'

'I was ambitious, and he owed me . . . I spent time in jail for him. I spent a year in your stinking jail to protect Youssuf's son and after I came out I told him I wanted my own business. He gave it to me. Youssuf agreed, though no *dada* ever agrees to such a thing. He agreed because he knew that he had to agree or kill me right there because otherwise I would kill him. He gave me a territory and some men . . . I have never let him down. We have an arrangement now, and he deals with me as an equal, though he's much bigger.'

'I need to talk to Youssuf about those two men,' I said. 'How do I reach him.'

'I went to jail to save Youssuf's son. Do you think I'll tell you about him?'

'Abdul,' I said, 'we're alone here. I can do whatever I

like to you, and no one will know. You will lie here in the rain, Abdul, in the rain, hurting more than you ever thought possible. I'll burn you millimetre by millimetre and break your bones one by one. You'll smell your own flesh frying, Abdul.' I doubted I could bring myself to do that but there was no harm threatening the man. 'You'll lie here and you won't be able to talk or do anything. If you tell me straight, I'll leave you. Someone will find you in the morning and you will be all right. And I'll find Youssuf anyway: you can't save him. So tell me now, Abdul. For your sake.' I picked up the jerrycan and began to pour petrol on the kerchief tied over his nose. He looked in my eyes and I caught a glimpse at the depth of his despair and shame. For a moment the shame touched me as well. Abdul would have done the kind of thing I was doing to him now. What was the difference, then, between him and me? I pushed these troublesome thoughts aside and pressed on.

'All right,' he said wearily. 'What do you want to know about Youssuf?'

'I need to talk to him alone. From what you've told me it looks like the Orphan was running an operation where the left hand didn't know what the right hand did. Youssuf might know more about the kidnap than you think.'

'You'll never talk to him alone. He'll have you killed before you get within a hundred yards of him.'

'How does he travel? Like you, in a car?'

'Yes, but he has a convoy. Not like mine. He has two cars ahead and another two behind. And his men all carry machine guns, and they are willing to die for him. You won't get him like you got me.'

There was a perverse pleasure in his voice when he said this but I ignored it. 'Where does he live?' I asked.

'In a bungalow in Juhu. It has sixteen rooms, and he uses just ten of them. The rest are full of his men. You won't be able to get into that bungalow alone, not without some heavy equipment.'

'Why not?'

'He has burglar alarms, guard dogs, watchmen and bodyguards. The neighbourhood shits when he glares. He's very careful. His wives live in the bungalow and so do his children. They don't stir from there without a bodyguard . . .' He paused, and looked at me consideringly. 'Despite your threats you're not someone who will take his children and try to force him to meet you. You know you won't survive that because he'll take your family.'

'He won't survive that,' I said. 'Tell me about Youssuf. About his weaknesses.'

'No,' he said, lying back. 'He'll kill me if he gets to know I've told you about him.'

'I'll burn you slowly to death if you don't tell me,' I said, lighting a match and moving it towards his face.

'All right,' he cried, 'enough! Take that matchstick away! I'll tell you.' I threw the stick away and he paused, gasping for breath again. 'Youssuf has a mistress. He has four wives and he can't take one more. He can't divorce his wives because his fathers-in-law are all in his gang, all senior members with their own armies, and if he divorces one of his wives his position will be threatened. And while his in-laws are family, they're also fanatics about religion: if he takes a mistress besides his wives, they won't like it. But he has a mistress. A young one.' He paused to gulp air. 'Please give me some water. There's a bottle in the car.'

Ahmed found a bottle of mineral water in the car and brought it out to me. I poured some into Abdul's mouth and he swallowed. 'Tell me about this mistress,' I said.

'She's seventeen years old, nearly fifty years younger than him. He is a fool to take up with her but there is no fool like an old fool. He picked her up last year and bought her a flat in Deonar, far away from Juhu.'

'How does she live? And when does he see her?'

'He provides her everything. He arranged for three people to live with her in her flat, a minder—like a chaperon—and a maid, and a bodyguard. He must have had enough trouble making sure that no word of this gets back to his in-laws . . . He makes sure that the minder has all the cash that the girl needs. The girl herself has nothing: it's all with the minder. He visits her on Thursdays and Saturdays, but only if he has no other engagements. He never tells her in advance when he is coming. She has to be around all the time, waiting for him: if he visits her and finds that she's gone out he might kill her. He's insanely jealous of her. He can't live with her and he can't live without her . . . Fool!'

'What about her family?'

'They don't care about her . . . They're dirt poor, from Lucknow. Her father was a labourer on a farm. Then Youssuf gave him enough money for a farm and fifty buffaloes and he took his family back to Lucknow. They don't get in touch with her now . . . They're all illiterate, and they don't have a telephone.'

'When can I go there with the certainty of having him come in afterwards?' I asked.

He cringed again, and I lit a matchstick, moving it dangerously close to his face. I could smell the petrol vapour in the air. He relented. 'Her birthday. Her birthday is three days from now. He'll visit her for sure, with presents . . . His bodyguards will have their arms full of presents.'

'When does he visit her?' I asked. 'What time of the day?'

'In the afternoon and early evening. He's busy late in the evening and at night, and he sleeps until eleven or twelve. He visits her after lunch, and stays with her until six or so in the evening. He has to get back by dusk . . . that's when the money begins to come in.'

'All right, Abdul,' I said, 'you're coming for a little drive. You're going to show us exactly where this little love nest is.' I picked him up, took the kerchief off his face and gagged him with a handful of dirty cotton waste. I hauled him to the car, pushed him in, and Ahmed drove off.

The girl, Nasreen, lived in a block of middle-class flats two kilometres from the BARC. After her childhood in the slums of Lucknow it would have been heaven, and she hadn't been around long enough to acquire expensive tastes. For the time being she must be happy with her minder and the chauffeur–bodyguard and maid because she could buy whatever clothes or baubles she wanted, and she didn't have to worry about going to school or college. The watchman wouldn't stop any respectably dressed person from going into the building, and it struck me that the minder and bodyguard might not be top-grade: Youssuf had had to get them on the sly. We stopped at the gate, on the opposite side of the road. 'Is the bodyguard armed?' I asked Abdul. 'Nod for yes, shake your head for no.'

He nodded. 'Pistol?' I asked. Another nod. 'Is that all?' A shake. 'A knife, besides?' A nod. 'That's it?' Nod.

'More questions,' I said, 'the last round. I'm going to take the gag out of your mouth and you'd better answer me straight.'

He nodded and I took the gag out of his mouth. 'What's Youssuf's visit like? Where does the convoy park, and who is with him at the time?'

'The lead car stops there.' He pointed with his chin at a spot just ahead of the gate. 'One man with a pistol goes into the building to check it out. He checks the landings and the corridors and then rings the doorbell of the flat where the girl lives. When the bodyguard opens the door, the man goes in and checks out every room in the house, and the balcony behind. Then he waves from the window, and Youssuf comes in. The man who checked out the flat stays inside—there is a spare room—while Youssuf is around, and another comes with Youssuf and waits at the door. They all leave together when Youssuf is done.'

'What about the other people on that floor?'

Abdul smiled. 'A bunch of mice. They know who Youssuf is. They don't interfere with anything he does. Nobody goes near that flat, no matter what. Youssuf once had a quarrel with one of his suppliers in the building. The man came up to talk to him and the bodyguards let him in because they all knew him. He insulted Youssuf in front of the girl and Youssuf tortured him there. They say they could hear his screams two buildings away, but no one interfered. The police couldn't find a witness to say that Youssuf shot the man, though he did it out here, in the open, because he didn't want to dirty the girl's flat.'

I could see what he meant. I'd have to get into the flat, looking like an innocent visitor, neutralize the minder and the bodyguard, and wait for the advance man to come in. Then I'd have to get him out of the way, and impersonate him from the window. And after all that I'd have to take Youssuf when he entered the flat . . . After silencing the man with him, the one with the presents.

I'd have to keep Youssuf inside the flat. I'd talk to him here. I couldn't take him for a drive the way I'd taken Abdul. I'd have to talk to him for some time, to find out whether one of his specialists had got away with the diaries. From what Abdul had told me it was unlikely but it had to be confirmed . . . And I wanted the Orphan. I'd make Youssuf tell me whatever he knew about the Orphan. I'd break his mistress first if necessary, but in the end I'd make him talk . . . A fresh wave of shame flowed over me. I remembered how Ismail had taken Sandhya captive and retched at the memory.

'What angers him most?' I asked Abdul. 'What scares him most? You should know well enough.'

'After all these years as a gangland don he's unused to physical effort, and there's been no violence in his presence for twenty years except for what he himself has done. I heard he executed a man last year but that doesn't mean anything. One of his men would have held the victim and Youssuf would have shot him. He's old now, and fat, and he wheezes when he has to walk fast. But his men all suck up to him. They tell him that he's fit and strong and he believes them. The truth is that his organization is strong because people are loyal to him, and his mind . . . that's what keeps him in power now. But he is gone. Get him alone and you will find that he breaks easily.'

'All these wives, and this mistress: do you think he's covering up his impotence, or homosexuality, or something?'

'I don't think he's homosexual. I'd have known if he were. But maybe you're right about his impotence. In his youth he was a bull of a man but now I think he keeps this girl more to prop up his image than for pleasure.'

A fat, impotent old man was ripe for a heart attack under pressure and I didn't want Youssuf dying on my hands. But there was no choice . . . I didn't care if he died after talking to me.

A new problem arose, one that I'd been avoiding thinking about all this while. Now that Abdul had told me what I needed to know, what was I to do with him? If I let him loose the best thing for him to do would be to tell Youssuf, in which case they'd blow me out of the water. There was no way I could trust Abdul. I couldn't hold on to him for three days, either. I had neither the people for it, nor the inclination.

That left one alternative. Kill him.

I'd never killed a man in cold blood and now on the razor's edge, I found I couldn't bring myself to do it. I looked up to find Ahmed staring at my face, and in a moment of insight I knew he'd been thinking of exactly the same thing and he knew I wouldn't be able to bring it off. 'Well, Colonel,' he said, 'you got what you wanted. Where do we go from here?'

'I don't know,' I said. 'What I do on the battlefield is not what I can do in cold blood.'

Abdul looked from me to Ahmed, then back again. Comprehension dawned slowly, and then a faint ray of hope that died quickly when he took a closer look at Ahmed's face. He must have executed men himself, and watched many more, but faced with his own death he turned out to be a man of straw. 'Let me go,' he pleaded with Ahmed, 'I won't talk to Youssuf . . . I promise I won't come after you . . . Look, I'm your family. I brought you up.'

In answer Ahmed raised the pistol he'd taken from Abdul's bodyguard and shot him in his open mouth, smoothly and unhesitatingly. Abdul's body slumped back in the seat next to me and I felt a great coldness welling up in my chest. Ahmed might have pulled the trigger but I was as responsible for it as he was. Gopi sat in the front passenger seat, his eyes shut tight in shock. Then Ahmed started the engine, put the car in gear, and we moved smoothly forward.

chapter fifteen

The killing of Abdul and his men made the front pages of Bombay's afternoon papers and eveningers, ahead of the election news. My fingerprints, on record with Army Headquarters, were found to match one set lifted off the Mercedes, and the CBI, who had taken over the case because of the possibility that it had something to do with the kidnap, jumped to the obvious conclusion with the easy joy of a mountain goat leaping for a succulent bush. More photographs were printed, all old ones, and in the text beside them was the speculation that I'd joined up with a gang and killed Abdul as an initiation. Only one of the newspapers made the connections from Basappa to Rawat, from Rawat to Ahmed, and from Ahmed to Abdul, and proceeded to roughly the right conclusion, that I was after the diaries. But even that one went on to say that I'd had a hand in their loss. I threw the papers down in disgust and reached for my coffee.

With three days to go, Ahmed, Gopi and I checked out of the Palm Grove and took the next flight to Delhi, where—thanks to Ahmed's reserves of cash—we had the money to check into the Hyatt. I'd asked Gopi to call Deepak from a public telephone to ask Sandhya to come to the hotel with Kiran at half past three that afternoon. While waiting for Gopi to get back I'd picked up the papers and read about my own duplicity.

Sandhya arrived on the dot of half past three, practically bursting into the room with Kiran trailing behind her. 'What have you been up to?' she asked, her composure shattering as the door shut behind her. 'I see your name in the papers every day and each time they say you've gone and killed someone or the other.'

'All that's bullshit,' I said, 'and you know it.'

'Yes,' she replied, 'but the police don't.'

'They know some of it,' I said, 'the papers never follow up properly. They know by now that the pistol with which Rawat was killed had a fake number etched onto it. And I'll get those diaries one way or another and then we'll get down to deciding what I'm going to do for a living . . . How've you been? Anyone troubling you?'

She shook her head. 'I've been fine, and there's been trouble. There've been lots of government-type letters saying you should report for duty on or before such-and-such otherwise they'll serve more notices on you. And people have been avoiding me. They cross the road when they see me. I want to get out of there . . . But I don't know where to go. You told me to stay because it's safe and I don't want anyone coming after Kiran. He hasn't been going to school. It's like we're lepers . . . I didn't know it would be so bad.'

She began to cry again and I put my arms around her. 'What about your parents?' I asked. 'They seemed pretty open the last time I spoke to your father.'

'That was a long time ago,' she sniffed. 'They've begun to believe some of the stuff they've seen on the news. No smoke without a fire, that's what they say.'

'That shouldn't stop you going and staying with them for a few days.'

'I stayed because I thought you'd get in touch . . . And there's Harkishen, and Venkat, the driver. They're around whenever they have the time off. And that old man Mankekar, he called up to say that if there was any talk of my having to get out of the quarters before you turned up, he'd take care of it. And there are a few who stay in touch . . . There's Prabha and Shanti, and Ramu and Hari come once in a while . . . But thats it.'

'What have they been saying, Ramu and Hari?'

'Comforting things. You'll be all right, you can take care of yourself, you've gone undercover, things like that. But they've also been isolated. The SOF is on hold. General Kelkar came once, to say they're planning to disband it but they won't do anything until after the elections, and after they get the diaries.'

'What else did Kelkar have to say?'

'He's in trouble himself . . . It's different for a man in his position. I heard he's got nothing to do. He asked if you'd been in touch and I said no and he smiled and didn't ask any further.'

'If you still want to get out I can fix it. Go home. Take Harkishen along. And Venkat, if he has the leave.'

'I can't do that, that'd be even worse. Here . . . here I can call on Ramu or Hari or General Kelkar for help,' she said, wiping her tears. 'I'm staying put. But first I want to know what you're up to.'

'All right,' I said, 'but send Kiran off to your folks.'

'Alone?' she asked.

'Yes. We'll put him on a plane to Calcutta. The stewardesses can take care of him on the flight and his grandparents can take him off the plane.'

'Okay,' she said. 'And what do I do?'

'Come with me.'

Her face lit up. 'Anything would be better than what I've been up to these past few weeks. Give me a minute to go home and pack the essentials. Then we'll see Kiran off, and I'm ready.'

'No,' I said, 'we don't go back home. Gopi goes out to tell your folks to collect Kiran at the airport. We buy whatever he needs before we send him off. And we buy whatever we need to keep going.'

'My, my,' she grinned, 'aren't we rich!'

I grinned back at her in relief. 'Gopi's money, and Ahmed's . . . He's a new friend. We can't afford to have anyone guess where I'm headed.'

There was a knock on the door and Gopi walked in, with Ahmed behind. I introduced the two of them to Sandhya, and Gopi greeted her with the fake shy smile of a ladies' man. 'I'd expected someone a great deal fiercer,' he said, 'someone with long teeth and a bullwhip to keep this fellow in order.'

'I dropped all that long back,' she replied, falling in with him, 'I've got him properly house-trained now.'

Kiran was enchanted with his new uncle—Gopi showed him breathtaking tricks, pulling a coin out of his ear, twisting and breaking his thumb off, then making it reappear magically—and in the end Gopi took him out to speak to Sandhya's parents while Ahmed went off to his room to catch up with his sleep. Sandhya went to the travel agent downstairs and bought Kiran's ticket, paying for it in cash from Ahmed's stock. When Gopi returned there were still three hours to the flight to Calcutta, and we spent the time buying Kiran clothes and toiletries and a book and a small remote-controlled car to while away the time.

We saw him off at the airport with carefully concealed apprehension, and when we returned to the hotel I brought up the idea that had been simmering in my mind since Sandhya turned up. I brought her up to date on the diaries, and explained why I was going after Youssuf. 'Youssuf's security is a little too good for me to risk on my own,' I told her. 'A little company would help.'

'What kind of company?' she asked.

'Feminine company,' I replied. 'His mistress, Nasreen, and her bodyguard won't be on guard when a well-dressed couple rings their doorbell. Especially when the woman is young and pretty, and perhaps a bit brassy.' Sandhya looked her age but with her extensive knowledge of makeup, gained from her training as an actress, could knock ten years off her thirty summers with no trouble. And she was undeniably beautiful.

She leapt at the chance to act. 'Yes,' she said, 'we'll do it that way. I'll even change your face so no one'll recognize you.'

'It could get rough,' I warned her. 'There'll be a young girl, and her chaperone, a maid, and a bodyguard. I'll have to knock off the whole lot of them. So you get us in, and then get out of the way. Otherwise you'll be a liability.'

She turned on me, eyes blazing. I'd seen her that angry just once before, and on that occasion had myself been the object of her anger. 'Listen, Raja,' she said, 'these people have hounded you for weeks, besides killing those kids and god knows how many people. I'm not even involved but I've been living like a leper ever since you left . . . I've had it with them. Give me a gun and I'll shoot the man behind it. I'd be thrilled to get a chance to give them a dose of their own medicine. So cut out the chivalrous crap, okay?'

This from a person who had avoided violence in all its forms until she married me. Our lives had changed, and our minds, permanently. I shrugged and left it at that.

Sandhya's parents called in the evening to say that Kiran had arrived safely, and what the hell was going on. Sandhya fobbed them off with a story to the effect that it would be all over in a week. Gopi went out to have a tourist's look at Delhi since this was his first visit there. Ahmed spent his time on the telephone calling his brothers and their children and seemed in a strange way to be saying his goodbyes to his friends.

We arrived together in Bombay early on the morning of Nasreen's birthday, a Saturday, with return tickets to Delhi on the night flight. We didn't plan to stay in Bombay an hour longer than essential, and checked into one room at the Centaur outside the airport. By noon we were ready to move. Sandhya and I took a yellowback cab to Deonar, Sandhya empty-handed, me with a suitcase full of odds and ends. Gopi and Ahmed followed in more leisurely fashion, aiming to get to Youssuf's little love nest by three.

At the gate to the apartment building stood the watchman, huddled inside a huge old raincoat that flapped about him in the wind. My watch said one, about the time the girl and her chaperone would be sitting down to lunch, with the maid busy serving or in the kitchen. The watchman didn't look at me as we passed by: all his attention was concentrated on Sandhya, who swayed past him under a colourful umbrella, hardly deigning to notice him. We walked up the stairs to Nasreen's second-floor flat, not bothering to wait for the creaking old lift, and at the door Sandhya briefly gripped my hand before putting her forefinger firmly on the doorbell.

There was a click and the door opened three inches on a chain. 'Yes?' asked a man, obviously the bodyguard, whom I, standing a few feet away from Sandhya, could not see. Almost simultaneously there were the clicks of cutlery from behind, and a female voice called out in Hindi, 'Who is it?'

'Is Nasreen Begum here?' Sandhya asked the bodyguard haughtily, also in Hindi.

'Who are you?' asked the bodyguard, not in the least impressed.

'None of your business,' snapped Sandhya. 'If my business was with you would I ask for my cousin?'

The bodyguard didn't relent an inch. Through the gap in the door I saw his hand move and he said, 'Tell me who you are or go away, or I will come out and drive you away.' The door opened another two inches and I got a look at a five-inch-thick slice of him. Tall, lean, hawk-nosed, three or four days' stubble on his face, thick black hair falling over his forehead, pinched, narrow eyes, fair skin. A Pathan, from the looks of him.

'I don't mind going away,' Sandhya said, 'but I don't think Youssuf bhai will like it when I tell him you sent me away.'

The bodyguard hesitated at the sound of Youssuf's name. He stepped back, then undid the chain and held the door open. Sandhya swayed in and I followed. As I entered, the young Pathan turned to bolt the door behind us and I whirled and hit him on the neck, just below the ear, with an improvised cosh. His head bumped the doorjamb and he slipped down, unconscious, as I whirled again to face the women, all three of whom had frozen in position: the girl and her chaperone in their chairs at the table, and the cook–housemaid in the doorway of the kitchen. The cook was the least endangered and she knew it, while the chaperone was old enough to know when to keep shut, but the girl's shoulders lifted in a prelude to a shriek as I pointed a pistol at her. 'Shut up,' I said, 'make a noise and I'll kill the lot of you.'

The girl burst into tears. She looked about twenty, plump and healthy, bovinely pretty in her blue silk salwar-kameez but not in the least chic. I opened the suitcase, took out lengths of rope and bits of cloth to tie and gag the women. Sandhya tied them up one by one, first their wrists behind their backs, then their ankles, tightening their knots as I'd shown her earlier, and then gagged them with the strips of cloth. The bodyguard, a much tougher proposition than the women, I tied up myself, and one by one I dragged them off into a small pantry next to the kitchen. I checked the ropes once again, made sure no one's hands were within reach of a knot, and we settled down to wait.

It was a quarter past one, and we waited an hour and a half. In between I sawed off part of the grille covering the bedroom window, enough for me to slip out, and anchored a rope to the hook in the ceiling from which the fan hung. If I needed to get away quickly, I'd go through the window. I propped the sawn-off section of grille back in place, tying it firmly with a bit of wire that would break at the first hard tug. I checked the captives once, at two, and found that the girl had wet her clothes. She struggled when she saw me, and I took the gag off for a moment. 'Water,' she said, 'please!' I gave her some in a bottle and gagged her again, ignoring her frantic pleas to change her clothes. It would all help when Youssuf turned up.

The advance man arrived at a quarter to three. I hid behind curtains to the bedroom door and Sandhya opened the front door to him. He frowned when he saw her, asking where Nasreen was. 'In the bedroom,' she said, smiling and pouting at the man, teasing him. Perfect. Pride for her flared, mixed with more than a tinge of jealousy.

She held the door open, welcoming him on, and he stepped warily in, taking off his Ray-Bans as he did. He was a short, fair young man, unshaven and long-haired, dressed in a tight white T-shirt that displayed his powerful chest and shoulders, baggy cotton trousers and Nike shoes. He looked suspiciously at Sandhya as he swaggered in, hefting his pistol as he did so. He looked fit and strong and well-trained, and supremely confident.

His confidence was his undoing. He turned to examine the corner behind Sandhya and I charged him silently. He must have felt a breath of breeze behind for he turned as I closed in but I swerved and his pistol was out of line. Before he could get it lined up I shot him in the head with the silenced .22, knowing he was far too good for me to overpower him without the pistol.

His skull was very thick and the .22 bullet hit it obliquely, ricocheting off his head into the wall. He went down on his knees, putting his hands to the side of his head. I kicked him in his unprotected groin as hard as I could, and when he bent involuntarily forward, kicked him in the face as well.

He'd be out for some time now, there was no doubt about that, but having seen how thick his skull was I whipped the pistol across his head once again. I held his head back so the blood dripping from his head wound wouldn't drip onto his shirt, and lowered him onto the floor. With Sandhya holding a piece of cloth around his head I got the T-shirt off without getting any blood on it.

Forty seconds gone. He wouldn't take more than a minute to check the flat out. I put his T-shirt on over my own, put on my own dark glasses and went to the window. At a distance, seen from below, I wouldn't have looked too different from the advance man. I waved, hoping Youssuf and his men wouldn't smell a rat.

They should have, but Youssuf had been top dog too long and his men were sloppy. I ran back to the living room, where Sandhya was wiping the blood off the floor, and dragged the man by his ankles into the kitchen. Less than a minute later, the bell rang, and when Sandhya opened the door Youssuf walked in, smiling in anticipation, eyeing Sandhya with surprise that turned quickly into appreciation. The bodyguard was right behind, loaded with gift-wrapped parcels, and as he straightened up after putting the packages on the sofa I shot him twice in the chest with the .22, and had it lined up on Youssuf before he quite understood what was happening.

Sandhya, beginning to look a little bewildered and uneasy now, slammed the front door shut a bit too noisily, and I hit Youssuf on the side of the head, above the ear. For all his ailments this was a tough old man and I'd have to break his spirit as I'd done with Abdul. He went down on his knees and I caught his collar and pushed him forwards until he was flat on the floor on his stomach.

I clouted him again on the head with the pistol, and when he lay back, stunned, I tied his wrists together as tight as I could, the thin nylon digging into aged, sagging flesh. Then I tied his ankles as well, as tightly as his wrists, and rolled him over onto his back. Then I checked the man who had come in with him. He'd got one shot in the region of the heart and another higher up, in his throat. He was dead.

'Get a glass of water,' I told Sandhya, and she got one from the kitchen. She'd done as much as she could; I could now see that she was shaken. When I told her to leave she began to protest but then changed her mind and went, kissing me goodbye at the door. I went to the window and watched as she went down, past the goons standing around Youssuf's car, and round the corner where I knew Gopi was waiting to take her back to the hotel.

I came back into the living room and poured the water on Youssuf's face and he came awake, gasping and gulping, and I slapped him on the face. He looked at me silently when he got back to his senses. No threats, no violence, just a cold level look that had me wondering if I'd left anything out. 'Make no noise,' I said, 'I've got Nasreen tied up in the pantry. Try to do anything funny and she dies.'

He was lying as I'd left him when I dragged Nasreen out of the pantry for him to see. Her hair was dishevelled and her eyes were frantic and wet and her clothes stank of urine and when he saw her his composure snapped. 'What do you want?' he asked. 'Tell me. I'll give you anything if you'll let her go free.'

'Do you know who I am?' I asked.

He shook his head, the anger surfacing. 'I don't know

and I don't care, but whoever you are, if you hurt my girl you'll pay for it. My men will kill you if I don't.'

I knelt on his chest and he opened his mouth to exhale. I stuck a gag in, tied it securely around his head, then pinched his nostrils shut with my right thumb and forefinger. He couldn't breathe through his mouth and when he tried to get his head free I held him clamped down with a knee on his chest.

His face went red, and when it began to purple I released his nostrils. 'I will ask you some questions. If you don't answer, that's what I'll do again. But I won't do it to you. I'll do it to Nasreen, I'll do it again and again until you answer, and then I'll kill her anyway. Then I'll shoot in your kneecaps and wrists and cut your tongue out and leave. You'll live but you won't be able to tell anyone who did it to you. Not for weeks. Understand?'

He shut his eyes tight and nodded slowly. When he opened his eyes, I saw how completely I'd broken him, and how easily. I took the gag out of his mouth. 'Ask,' he said, 'I'll tell you.'

'The Mehta diaries,' I said, 'where are they?'

He swallowed before answering. 'I have them. Not with me, but in one of my houses.'

Several knots in my chest came undone and I sagged and almost fell to the floor in relief. 'Where?' I asked. 'How did you get them? You'd better tell me from the beginning.'

He lay back and spoke in a lifeless voice. 'It all began with a man I know only as the Orphan. The whole plan is his, and he distributed different parts of it to different people. Some of it he gave me five months ago. He told me that he was on the verge of getting the diaries, that he would need help in blackmailing the people named in the diaries. There were more than two hundred people named in those diaries, and he needed a network to handle them.

'Then Mehta was taken by the police and they also found his diaries. We tried to bribe someone in the CBI to release them to us but by then they had already passed into judicial custody and been admitted as evidence . . . meanwhile, someone had Mehta killed in prison, not the Orphan.

'We were stuck. Mahmoud—he is a Libyan working with the Orphan—came up with the idea of kidnapping someone in power . . . Then we came to know of the Prime Minister's granddaughter . . . We heard that her security was lax, so we decided to take her, and the Chief Justice's son.

'Mahmoud arranged it, and Abdul's man Rawat . . . You killed Abdul, didn't you?' His eyes glared straight at me. 'You had to torture him to make him tell you about me.'

I nodded. 'Like I'm torturing you for the diaries.'

'Colonel Menon,' he said, 'we should have killed you in the jungles.'

'Keep going with the story,' I said, 'you can curse me to your heart's content afterwards.'

'Where were we? Yes, Mahmoud. Mahmoud thought up the kidnap, and the Orphan found out about the girl's visit to Kabini . . . Mahmoud was supposed to get away with the diaries but as it happened you got there early and everything went wrong . . .'

'How did you get the diaries?'

'Abdul came to me for two men for the kidnap team. He wanted one electronics expert, to help him keep in touch with them, and an explosives man. I have many men who can deal with such things, and I told him so. But then he said he needed special men, very good men who could work under pressure, who would be able to take a siege, and who would be able to live cooped up in a house for more than a month.

'I said I'd try to get such men. I have friends in Karachi, near the port. I get a lot of material from there.'

'What kind of material?'

'In the beginning it was mainly gold. Then, in the eighties, I found that people wanted bombs, and drugs, so I diversified. In Karachi I found a man to supply me with plastic explosive. There is a lot of Czech Semtex available in Pakistan . . . And other kinds of weapons, diverted from American shipments to the Afghan border.'

'Did you also bring in military communications equipment? Radios, communication sets?'

'Only a little. I got some SYR-31s from Pakistan—it was meant to be used by the Afghan Mujahideen but we diverted it—but no one wants that stuff now.'

'Go on,' I prodded him, 'you were talking about your pals in Karachi.'

'Then I got into drugs. Opium, from Afghanistan, from Pakistan. Their governments look the other way if we pay them enough. I made most of my money there. And I asked my friends if they knew anyone who would be able to do what Abdul wanted them to. They sent me two men, and as it happened, the electronics man turned out to be a relative of mine. The fat one. He is my cousin's son.'

'How much did you pay?'

'They wanted one lakh down per man we selected. Besides that, we had to pay all expenses and three lakh per man per month. It was expensive, but Abdul had told me he had to get the men.'

'What did he say when you told him the prices?'

'Nothing. He paid. I sent those men on to Abdul. One of them, the bombs man, had only one leg, and the other man, my nephew, was fat and lazy. But what I didn't tell them was that the fat one was a black belt in judo, and he had been a gymnast in his childhood before he got too heavy for it. He found out that Mahmoud was supposed to kill everyone when you attacked, and he was prepared for it. He called me.'

'What did you do?'

'It was fairly clear that it was your group that would attack the farmhouse. I managed to have a uniform sent out to him, a uniform like yours, for him to sneak out in the confusion. He did that. He knew what the diaries looked like, and before Mahmoud could get to him he got the diaries and hid in a loft, and then he picked a quiet moment and got away.'

'Where did he go first?'

'He came straight to me, of course. He told me he had the diaries and I sent him into hiding.'

'Where?'

'To my plantation. In Coorg. I bought a coffee plantation there last year. I go there once in a while to rest, it is peaceful there. I don't talk to the locals and they don't trouble me. The owners of the other plantations treat me like an outcast but who cares?'

'All right,' I said, 'tell me about this plantation.'

'What can I tell you about it? It is near Virajpet. It is in my name. You can check the records. It is easy to find. Three hundred acres of Arabica coffee.'

'Who killed Rawat?' I asked.

The change of subject took him by surprise. He collected his wits and ploughed on. 'Mahmoud. They have been following you. The Orphan told me that you will find the diaries, and his men will be right behind you. Whenever they felt you would get evidence to go to the police, they did something to make sure you wouldn't go back to the police. They killed Rawat, they killed Basappa, they killed everyone . . . And they bugged you.'

'Bugged me? How?'

'My cousin . . . He is a genius. They got him to make a whole lot of small bugs. They followed you around, and whenever you checked into a hotel they stole in and planted a bug. They know everything you spoke about. In Kabini, in the forest, and later in Mysore. They lost you for a while in Bombay but they picked you up again in Kochi when you went to Ahmed's house.'

'Why didn't they come after you? They must have suspected that you had the diaries.'

'The bomb man had only one leg. My nephew was fat

and they thought he wouldn't be able to walk fifty yards. How could two such people escape from that farmhouse? No, they think it is one of their own men.'

'All right,' I said, 'what do you know about the Orphan?'

'Abdul must have told you . . . about the Orphans. About what was done after Partition.'

'He did.'

'The Orphan is possibly the last survivor of those children. The one that died last was Mehta . . . Liaquat. But this last man . . . I don't know who he is. He knows everything. He controls everything. See, you are heading for the diaries and he is right behind you. He even knew that you have weapons. He knew that you spoke to Mankekar, that you gave him a list of things you want.'

'If he's bugged me that's no surprise,' I said. But if he had bugged me, had he also bugged Mankekar? Or . . . had Mankekar told him? But Mankekar said that his telephone was checked regularly for bugs. And if Mankekar had told him, he was on the Committee.

One of those five men, ministers all.

'Tell me more about the bugs,' I said. 'What are they like?'

'Very small, very powerful. Some are the size of a shirt button. Others you can disguise in a zipper, or a watch bracelet. Tiny little things. He gave them two tiny bugs that would go into your baggage, so small you wouldn't find them. The others were also small, but not small enough to put in your baggage: they planted them in your hotel rooms.'

'Tell me about your estate,' I said.

He smiled. 'Do you think you can just walk in there, get

into the master bedroom, open my safe, take the diaries and walk out?' he asked. 'No, Colonel, you won't. You can't keep me here much longer. My men will come to investigate. And if you kill me you'll have to kill the women as well. They heard every word you've spoken, and by the time you get to my plantation, there'll be a hundred men guarding it. No, Colonel, you're the one in trouble now, all because you're too soft to kill an old man and three women. You didn't . . .'

The front door blew in before he completed the sentence and as I turned I saw a figure in black charge into the room. Mahmoud was back. I'd been expecting him.

I shot him twice, hitting him both times, but he must have been wearing a flak jacket because he went down and came back up very fast, spraying the room with an automatic rifle. Youssuf died first, and then Nasreen, and then I got him off balance again.

There was commotion below. I didn't have time to stay and mix it with Mahmoud so I dived out into the bedroom. I heard more automatic fire and then I had the grille off the window and was out in the rain, sliding down the rope to the concrete two floors below.

Rain, blessed rain, I thought. It drove people in, and it cut off the light. I vaulted the wall and took off, keeping as low as I could. From above came the sounds of more small-arms fire, and then an explosion. As I turned to look, the grille came off the window of the second bedroom and Mahmoud erupted out of it, also on a rope. He'd blown the frame right out of the window.

Under the cover of the rain I made it out of the building, across the street, and thence to a bus stop where several dozen people were sheltering from the rain. I gave it a minute, then stepped bravely out into the rain, like an office-goer returning home with a briefcase. Half a kilometre up the road I found a taxi wandering in search of a passenger, and flagged it down.

I had arranged to meet the others at the airport. I stopped off on the way to buy clothes for myself, and to change out of the soaked set I was wearing. With the wet clothes in a carrier bag I had to purchase a ticket to enter the airport complex because our travel tickets were with Sandhya. I found the three of them drinking dispiritedly in the bar, Gopi and Ahmed sipping beer while Sandhya drank black coffee.

Sandhya saw me first and came running. 'What happened?' she asked. 'You look like you've seen a ghost.'

I sat down at their table before answering. 'I did . . . The man in black. Mahmoud. He turned up at just the right time.'

'What do you mean?' asked Gopi.

'I got what I wanted out of friend Youssuf and was wondering what to do with him and his girlfriend when Mahmoud turned up. I saw him kill Youssuf, and I bet he got the others as well. He must have been carrying some fancy new explosive because when the bodyguards came up he blew the window frame out and hopped it.'

'What happened to the others?' Sandhya asked.

A waiter came up to take my order. I asked for a coffee,

and waited for him to get out of earshot before answering. 'I didn't wait to see. I left through the window: the section of grille that I sawed off with you. I didn't hang around below but I saw Mahmoud get away and I heard a whole lot of small-arms fire, like a small war.'

'Any trouble afterwards?' Gopi asked.

'None at all. But I'm not coming with you to Delhi.'

'Where are you going, then?' Sandhya asked, frowning.

'Coorg. Virajpet.'

'How about us?' asked Gopi.

'You all lie low. Look, our hotel rooms were bugged. Our baggage is probably bugged. They know most of what we plan to do. So now I'll separate and join you in a couple of days. Hopefully with the diaries in hand.'

'What will you do?' Sandhya asked.

'Get the diaries. Get to you after that. You head for Delhi, go back to Delhi with Gopi. Check into a hotel. Get Harkishen or Venkat. With one of them around you'll be safe.'

'Are you going to chase those diaries on your own?' Gopi asked. 'I don't know the specifics but I'm sure it'll be pretty well-guarded. Raja, you're a bloody madman. I'll come with you.'

'No. I'm going to take them completely by surprise.' I was pretty sure Mahmoud had finished off everyone in that flat in Deonar: no one knew that Youssuf had told me where the diaries were. We hadn't talked of it in any hotel room.

I saw them off on their flight and got myself a seat on

the last flight to Bangalore, and checked the bags with the goodies. Before boarding, I called Mankekar. 'Where have you been all this while?' he asked angrily when he heard my voice. 'You've been silent for days!'

'I was getting along fine on my own,' I said.

'Yes,' he said heavily, 'with the usual disastrous results. Your name came up some time ago. It seems you killed a gang of smugglers in Bombay. A don and his bodyguards.'

'That wasn't me,' I said. 'But now I know who did it.'

'I find that hard to believe, Raja,' he said. 'Everywhere you go people die . . . You say that there's someone following you around, committing murder and mayhem as he goes. You spoke to Abdul Karim before he died, didn't you? There were burns on his chest. Did you do that?'

'Yes,' I said, 'but I didn't kill the man. But I know where the diaries are.'

'Where?' he asked, all else forgotten, 'I'll have them retrieved.'

'No,' I answered, my voice sharp and firm. 'One thing I discovered was that I was bugged . . . The guy behind this knows that I'm in touch with you. He even knows the contents of the list I gave you. Are you sure this line is secure?'

'Of course it is! My friend tells the boys in RAW and the police to check it out every day.'

'Whom have you told about my calling you?'

'Only the Committee . . . The PM himself, the other ministers you saw there. I get rid of even the stenos when I tell them about your call . . . No records, nothing.'

'So it's one of them,' I said. 'That's why I'm not telling you where the diaries are. I'll go get them myself.'

'When?'

'I don't know. But I need more of what you gave me last time. The same list. A repeat order. And some extras. An RPG-7/D.'

'Let me write that down,' he said, adding, 'that sounds like one of the things they used at Kabini.'

'Yes,' I said.

There was a pause. 'All right,' he said, 'I'll try to get this, but no guarantees. When do you want it? And where?'

'I haven't decided yet. Have it all organized, and I'll call you tomorrow morning to tell you how it's to be delivered to me.'

'The same way as before? A crowded suburban train?'

'No, this time it'll be easier. And somewhere in Bangalore. I'll call you tomorrow morning.'

I hung up and boarded the flight, which arrived in Bangalore late. I took a taxi from the airport to the Taj Residency, and with a wad of Ahmed's notes paid a three-day deposit on rent at the reception counter. I went to bed early, the weariness taking hold bone-deep, and lay awake worrying about Sandhya and Gopi.

In the morning I went down to the health club and spent a vigorous twenty minutes on an exercycle, working up a good sweat. I was still a little stiff about the torso but the inflammation was more or less gone, and with it most of the pain, though the bones would take some more weeks to knit.

At eight I went out to call Mankekar. 'I got what you wanted,' he told me, 'but not the RPG-7. God knows what you want with such a thing . . . They told me it takes two men to operate.'

'Not if you know how,' I said. 'You need two men if you want to reload and fire quickly. For a one-off, or if there's no hurry to reload, a single man would do. And its barrel unscrews in the middle so one man can lug it around.'

'I won't argue with you,' he said. 'There's been fresh evidence that Rawat and his wife were knocked out in some other room in that house and dragged into the bedroom. Their throats were cut after that . . . Also the numbers on the pistol. Young man, I don't know whether to believe you but there is enough evidence so I don't dismiss your story out of hand.'

'Thanks,' I said. 'Do the CBI feel the same?'

'One of the men there, a man called Chauhan, has been pushing the forensic labs. He made them examine everything, fingerprints, splashes of blood, the positions of the bodies, everything . . . They're now sure that the evidence pointing at you was faked. But they think you're a devious man. They say you could have planted the trail yourself to create the impression that you're innocent.'

'Who's been saying that?'

'None other than the defence minister. Pravin Kumar.'

'The man doesn't know a thing.'

'I grant you that, but he is, after all, a minister, and ministers have advisers.'

Pravin Kumar was sixtyish. In 1947 he would have been

ten, perhaps a little more . . . About the right age to be the Orphan. Anyone past his late sixties was more or less eliminated, as was anyone under fifty. Everyone on the Committee qualified, I realized, except the PM and Mankekar. 'Have you heard of a person they refer to as the Orphan?' I asked Mankekar.

'The Orphan? No. Why?'

'I believe that's what they call the man behind this.'

'Strange name.'

'Tell you why,' and I explained.

'I'd heard rumours of some such thing many years ago, but at the time I thought they were wild rumours floated by the fanatics. It seems too far-fetched.'

'Listen for the Orphan, then, and let me know the next time I call.'

'All right,' he said, 'now where do you want your goods?'

'At the Bangalore airport. Ask your man to put it in a suitcase and hang around the big bookshop—near the IA check-in counters. He's got to leave it on the floor. I'll have it collected.'

'You ask a lot, young man. Maybe too much. Tell me what you're going to do.'

'I'll get the diaries. I know where they're hidden and I'll get them. Or destroy them.'

'You sound as if you know something about them that I don't.'

'Yes . . . They were created. Have Mehta's background investigated. His childhood. His roots. You'll find that he, too, was an Orphan. He was given the seed money with which to pay those bribes. He got caught because all that money made him too greedy for his own good.'

'I'll have it checked,' he said. 'And what do we do if you don't succeed in getting those diaries?'

'There'll be bloodshed. Have it followed.'

'I've been trying to get the Committee to understand you. I've told them that you've been in touch. A closed session, just the five of them and my friend. Despite Pravin Kumar, I think my point is getting through.'

'Thanks.'

'Young man . . . All the best.'

I went out to the City Market at ten and bought a few sets of blank number plates for cars, a pot each of black and white paint, and a set of brushes. Back in my room at the hotel I put the 'Do not disturb' sign on the door, opened up the windows, went out on the balcony, and set to work painting sets of ordinary-looking vehicle registration numbers on the plates. I made four sets of amateurish-looking plates—two sets to spare, just in case—and left them to dry in pale sunlight. They dried in an hour, and I wrapped them in sheets of opaque white plastic and put them in my bags. I slept in the afternoon, spent some more time warming up on the exercycle after that, and at six went out to the airport to collect the ticket.

At the airport I spotted Mankekar's man, the same man from whom I'd taken the suitcase in Bombay. I now sported shoes which added three inches to my height. With a new haircut and a golf cap on my head and stubble on my cheeks I was different enough for him not to recognize me instantly. I took a cup of coffee at the dispenser in the corridor, and waited for a crowd to build up inside the bookshop.

A family went in. Father, mother and three kids. There were two businessmen in there already, and I walked into the shop behind a well-dressed, snobbish lady who looked haughtily at Mankekar's man as she went in, telling him not to stand in the doorway. I relieved him of the suitcase, which he had left standing by the wall behind him, and was gone around the corner before he quite knew it was gone.

I went to the gents' on the ground floor, and finding it empty, transferred the contents of the suitcase into the bag I'd carried with me. Then I left the airport, struggling with the bag as I went. Outside, I took a prepaid taxi to Jayanagar, to the large shopping complex by the bus stand in Fourth Block.

At half past seven the complex was crowded, and people were still coming in to make their purchases before the shops closed at half past eight. I waited for the right kind of car to come into the unsupervised parking lot outside, an anonymous Maruti or Esteem without anti-theft devices. A blue Maruti drew up ten minutes later, disgorging a family of four. I waited for the family to disappear into the complex, and then went out to the car. A hacksaw blade inserted into the rubber lining between the door panel and the glass just outside of the door lock on the driver's side unlocked the door. I opened it and stepped inside. The plastic panel at the top of the steering column came off when I jerked it back with my fingers below and behind it. The wires of the ignition system lay exposed.

I managed with little trouble to get the right wires connected and the steering wheel, which locks up when the key is taken out of the ignition, freed up. The engine came on, I fixed the panel back on, and drove off unnoticed. The fuel meter showed that the tank was half empty. Enough for a few hundred kilometres. I put the bag of weapons in the back and drove back to the hotel. I checked out of it, put my bags in the car, and drove out towards Mysore. Past the Country Club onto the highway in a light drizzle I slowed down, looking for a small road leading off the highway. I found one some five kilometres ahead, pulled off the highway and I went down it a half kilometre, found a clearing by the road, and stopped. There I fastened one of my sets of false plates on top of the genuine ones with a tube of superglue, and while waiting for the glue to dry broke the lock on the petrol tank. A couple of minutes later I was back on the highway to Mysore.

I was in Mysore by midnight, and there I checked into the Leela Palace with instructions that I was to be woken at six. I left the hotel at seven, heavy and tired from another sleepless night, heading for Hassan and on to Virajpet, which was some three bumpy hours away. At nine, with the fuel meter showing near zero, I stopped at a mechanic's shop and bought a five-gallon can for fuel. This I filled at the next petrol pump—I didn't want the attendant to see the broken lock on the tank cap—and emptied it into the tank four kilometres on.

The surface of the road was miserable and I wished I'd

taken a four-wheel drive instead of this flimsy little vehicle, because the worst was yet to come. I drove into Virajpet at half past eleven, went past the bus stand, and found a small restaurant where I stopped for a cup of tea. The man at the counter looked me up and down, then out at the car, and told me I wouldn't find a suitable hotel in the vicinity. When I told him that all I wanted was a bed and a reasonably clean toilet, he scratched his head and gave me instructions to a hotel a kilometre up the road, adding apologetically that meals would be hard to get.

I found the hotel, paid two hundred rupees at the counter and checked in. The room was small and the mattress was filthy but the toilet was usable and I could always sleep on a sheet spread on the floor. I got my bags out of the car, changed, slept for a while, and at three in the afternoon went down to the receptionist with the rack full of pigeonholes behind him. When I asked him about Youssuf's plantation he gave me directions to it, then asked why I was visiting. When I said I was looking for a steady supply of coffee beans he told me to be careful not to step onto Youssuf's land or to touch the fence. When I asked why, he told me that the fence was electrified, and there were vicious dogs running loose in the estate, except when people were actually working in it. And since there was no work to be done on the coffee at that time of the year, the dogs would be out in force.

I wished I'd had more time to talk to Youssuf about his estate, about where the diaries were kept, and so on. The receptionist had told me that the house on the estate was some three hundred metres along a driveway from the main gate in the fence, that it had two floors and hadn't been rebuilt after Youssuf bought it, and that the drying yards were just inside the gate, but that was all. At the back of my mind the thought persisted that the last two times I'd been on a raid on a place the layout of which I hadn't known, they had ended disastrously. I thrust this out of my mind and drove out towards the estate as the sun went behind the clouds. The rains in these parts were heavy and the land fertile. Nagarhole was just forty kilometres away and if I had to make a break for it I could head for the forest as I'd done earlier from Kabini. Youssuf's estate was fenced with viciously barbed wire, twelve double strands of it making a barrier eight feet high, supported on what seemed to be galvanized iron pipe instead of the usual stone fenceposts: stone posts of that height would break too easily, hence the iron. Along the four uppermost rows I saw insulators wherever the wire touched the posts, rubber strips wound around the poles. There were insulators around the bottom strands as well, but some of the ones along the bottom had come off: they must have cut off the electricity to those wires when they started losing their own dogs to it.

Within the fence an area of some five yards had been cleared of coffee bushes and all vegetation except grass. As I watched, a Dobermann loped into the five-yard strip from the coffee bushes beyond and came to a halt opposite me, its tongue hanging out, ears forward. A drizzle began but the dog didn't move. When I got into the car and drove slowly along the road, he followed, keeping the car in sight until I got to the gate, where another dog joined it.

The gate was a solid wrought-iron affair with a shed inside that served as a sort of sentrybox. There were two watchmen in there, canes in hand, uniformed—unlike other watchmen in these parts—in khakis. Inside the gates a gravelled driveway slanted upwards, curving gently past the concrete drying yards, past an orchard of mango and orange and jackfruit. All around were coffee bushes, trimmed about four or five feet high. And there was no trace of the house.

The compound was bordered on two sides by road, some four kilometres of it. I reckoned the perimeter of the three-hundred-acre estate at a bit over five kilometres, in an irregular rectangle around a hill, with two gates, both guarded. Within the estate were roads that would be used by supervisors when they did their rounds in their four-wheel drives.

There were at least six dogs inside, and at least eight men. I had no idea how many men were in the house itself, but I assumed that Youssuf wouldn't keep a standing army here—it would draw needless attention to the estate—but instead a group of reliable men to guard the diaries. Not that they'd know they were guarding the diaries, though.

I drove back to town and found a butcher's stall where I bought two kilos of fresh beef off a leg, asking the butcher to cut it into strips. Back in the hotel, I took a quarter-kilo lump of plastic—much more than necessary—out of the two-kilo block Mankekar had sent, and divided it into two.

Into the fist-sized lumps of plastic I stuffed three handfuls of nails bought from a hardware store. Each lump then got a primer, and into each primer went a cylindrical detonator, a time pencil, one set for five minutes, the other for two. I divided the beef into two parts, wrapped the strips of meat around the plastic so it was well hidden, and wrapped the whole mess in polythene wrappers. I made twelve more bombs, with much less plastic—fifty grams each—and with five-second time pencils, putting nails into half of them.

Plastic can be shaped like modelling clay. It's useful when you need a directed blast, but here there was no question of direction. I'd be tossing the bombs in the dark. All the same, I went out to buy some cans of Coke, and soon I had half-a-dozen bombs enclosed in them. By six all the bombs were ready. I packed them carefully in the car and then snoozed for an hour. At eight I went out for a light meal and coffee, returned, bought petrol in the can and topped up the tank. I drove around looking for another car to steal, preferably a Gypsy, but found only another Maruti a kilometre up the road, parked inside the compound of a darkened house with a latch on the gate. The occupants appeared to have gone out for a short while, and car thefts weren't common here. I parked my car—the first car I'd stolen—back outside the hotel and walked up to the house in the rain which had begun to fall steadily.

I opened the gate unseen, walked into the porch and stole this second car in exactly the same fashion as I'd stolen the first. By eleven, I had both cars, tanks full, in position on the road bordering Youssuf's estate: one a half-kilometre east of the main gate, the other the same distance west, both parked a little off the road so they wouldn't be conspicuous in the dark.

The rain intensified and at midnight I moved. I went to a point a quarter kilometre east of the gate, twisted the five-minute pencil to start it going, undid some of the polythene wrapping, and tossed the bomb and the meat into the compound. The first dog showed up a minute later, running full-tilt towards the smell of blood and rotting meat. I jogged off towards the gate, and a hundred yards away from the bomb I snipped through the lowest three strands of barbed wire with a pair of wire cutters.

Then I took off west, past the gate, to a point a quarter kilometre away. I picked the bomb with the two-minute fuse this time, tossed it in, and kept going to the place where I'd left the car. Here, again, I cut the bottom three strands of wire.

The first bomb went off, and there was a far-off scream of pain. The nails I'd packed into the bomb would have spread out, killing or disabling anyone within ten or fifteen metres, if not more. The dogs, certainly, would be dead. There was commotion in the house that I heard clearly. There were shouts and I heard a man running.

I waited for a while and the second bomb went off, much louder, much closer. More commotion. I pushed the wires back and crossed the cleared area, confident that between the two of them the meat-wrapped bombs I'd tossed in would have taken care of the dogs. They had, and as I ran through the coffee bushes I could hear the minders' shouts as they milled around in confusion where the bombs had gone off. Soon the compound was alive with torches, but they were all heading for the fence and under the cover of the coffee bushes I had no trouble at all moving about in the plantation.

The house appeared, about three hundred metres inside the fence where I'd broken in. It loomed sharply up in the rain, past a twenty-yard clearing. I ran towards the back, where, by the servants' quarters that normally adjoin such houses, there should have been a kitchen door.

There was. It was right next to what looked like a shed for the generator. And in the doorway, with a rifle in his hands and a bright light shining into the clearing, was a man on guard. Lights were coming on all over the house and around it, and I knew I didn't have much time. I could hear the thudding of the diesel generator now.

The man in the doorway lowered his rifle and I tossed a bomb with a five-second pencil at the generator shed. The man raised his rifle but I was back within cover by the time it came up and in line. He fired once. I heard the bullet go past my head, and then the bomb went off with a tremendous blast that shook the bushes around me. When I looked, most of the generator shed was gone, the lights were all off, and the man in the door was gone, knocked out by the blast. But two more men appeared just behind the doorway, on their way out, and I stepped out from cover and let loose with a three-second burst from the Ingram that emptied the thirty-round magazine. At the speed at which it fired, close to a thousand rounds a minute, it sounded like a gigantic zipper being zipped, and without a flash suppressor the muzzle flash destroyed my night vision.

Both the men went down and I pulled my NVGs over my eyes and charged at the door, changing magazines on the Ingram with a speed born of long and painful practice. I went through the kitchen into the dining room, stepping over one of the men who had been hit by the first burst. Others might have seen it, and must have heard the noise. Now that the generator was gone they would blunder in the dark and the fence would be dead.

I went through the dining room to what looked like the living room without slowing, caught sight of the foot of a staircase, and then a dark shape came bounding in through the front door. A dog had survived. I cut it down with another burst from the Ingram, spraying rounds all over the room, then turned and ran up the stairs, changing magazines again.

The weight landed on me silently. I made out a man's arms and legs and then I was knocked down the stairs. I landed awkwardly on my right side and rolled away, using my momentum to get back on my knees, dropping the Ingram as I went. The man who had jumped me had a knife and he knew how to use it. He must have figured I was wearing a flak-jacket. He kicked the Ingram away out of my reach. There was no time to draw the automatic or the knife I had in my pack. I'd landed next to a chair when the man knocked me down the stairs, and as he came in now

I whipped around and swept the chair at his head.

His knife hit me just below the ribs. I was wearing armour, not the flak jacket, and the knife came through easily against the thin Kevlar. Kevlar can stop a bullet, particularly a soft-nosed one, but a strong man with a sharp stiletto can pierce it. The armour gave and I felt the prick of the end of the knife and then he let go the knife and sprawled, unable to keep on his feet, thrown way off balance by the chair. I went for the Ingram in a rolling dive and he tossed the corpse of the dog at me. By the time I'd swerved out of the way he was out of sight, outside, and I changed direction again and went back up the stairs.

I paused to regain my breath, taking off the NVGs, then kept going, reckless enough now to use a torch. I saw no one on the first floor. Three doors, all shut, led from the passage above. I tried them. The second door turned out to be the one leading to a large master bedroom with a king-size double bed in the middle. I looked around for a safe, saw none. There was a painting on the wall, above the head of the bed. I pulled it off, and there was the safe, an old, solid iron box with a large keyhole and a handle.

I took out a bomb, one without nails, stuffed half the plastic through the outsize keyhole until only the primer and detonator and fuse were outside, then twisted the pencil and ducked out of the room. I was just past the door when the bomb burst, and when I went back into the bedroom I saw through the haze of dust and smoke that the door was hanging loose.

There were bits of paper still floating in the air and

inside were stacks of more paper, most singed and burnt. I rummaged amidst the blackened bits of paper and saw it. A brown paper packet with a blackened corner, about the right size to be the diaries. I ripped the packet open, and found the diaries inside. I checked that there were four volumes, then stuffed them in my pack and turned and ran.

When I got to the door two men were just starting up the stairs. I left a bomb with a five-second pencil at the top of the stairs and ran for the door at the end of the passage that seemed to lead to a terrace, taking a hook and rope out of my pack. As I reached the railing I had the hook on it and went straight down the rope to the lawn in front of the porch.

There was a dull boom from inside, and then the drumroll of a heavy machine gun. A fifty-calibre, from the sound of it. A half-inch-diameter bullet from that would penetrate anybody in armour or a flak-jacket. I dashed for the corner of the house just as another machine gun sounded, higher and faster than an AK-47—an AK-74, perhaps.

The big gun boomed again, and bullets spattered the wall behind me, the corner crumbling as the man behind the gun emptied the belt in my direction. I waited for a silence, knowing that any machine-gunner is most vulnerable while changing belts, and tossed another bomb out from behind the shelter of the wall. The big gun started again and I ran around the house, not waiting for pursuit, to what remained of the generator shed. I dropped another bomb in it and headed for the coffee bushes: the machine-gunner wasn't as mobile as I was and amongst the coffee bushes I could get away.

The rest of the shed went up behind me, and from the yellow flames that followed I guessed the diesel stored in the shed had at last caught fire. Petrol would have been better, because petrol vapour tends to explode, but a diesel fire was good enough.

Through the rows of coffee bushes and past the fruit trees and the sentrybox I went, seeing enough through the NVGs to avoid bumps and holes in the ground, ducking into cover thrice to avoid being seen, and made my way to the hole I'd made in the fence by the second car.

Just short of the edge of the coffee bushes inside the fence I saw movement by the car, and stopped. With the electricity off and the dogs down, I ran along the bushes for some thirty yards west, and made a fresh cut in the wires from where I emerged, crossing the road into the shadows and moving along their edge, approaching the car from behind. There were two men near the car, and one of them was smoking, which is the last thing you do when you want to watch out at night: the glowing end destroys night vision. I saw them clearly in the NVGs, waiting, looking at the break in the fence. One of them raised his arm to look at his watch and then I attacked.

The smoker went first. His night sight was gone and when I hit him with the butt of the Ingram he went down without a sound, dropping the cigarette in a small shower of sparks. I had the Ingram turned and the muzzle in his comrade's face a moment later. 'What are you doing here?' I asked.

'Colonel Menon?' he stuttered. 'We . . . we have your wife.'

I took a step back as the rage caught me. I held it back and stuffed the muzzle of the Ingram into his mouth. 'Where?' I asked. 'What do you want?'

He gestured to me to take the end of the gun out of his mouth. When I did, he spat to a side and wiped his mouth before answering. 'We have your wife. We have your brother. You have the diaries. An exchange. Your wife and brother for the diaries.'

I'd told Mankekar I was going after the diaries. No one else. He'd told the Committee. Who had told these men? I raised the Ingram again. He held up both hands in a gesture of surrender. 'We'll get nowhere if you kill me, Colonel,' he said. 'Take it easy.'

'Right,' I said. I made him stand spread-eagled on the side of the car, hands on the bonnet, and with my left hand frisked him. He had a knife in his pocket and nothing else. I tossed his knife away, checked his comrade, made him put the man in the back, and drove away from that blasted plantation. Had the man in the back recovered, they could have taken me. But I was past caring, only the anxiety for Sandhya and Gopi keeping me from breaking down or taking the Ingram to those men and finishing them off right there.

I drove the ten kilometres up to Virajpet, past the hotel and then the post office and a clinic, following the directions the man beside me issued. 'I hope my friend is all right, Colonel,' he said. 'We should have taken care to make a friendly approach.'

Anxiety for Sandhya and Gopi tore at me. I stopped. He gestured me to move on. There wasn't a light in the car and I could see his profile as he peered forward to see why I had stopped and when he turned to face me I punched him in the mouth as hard as I could, feeling with some satisfaction the crunch of bone, feeling the pain in my own hand. He ducked but couldn't save himself entirely, slumped in the seat, holding his mouth, moaning and swearing incomprehensibly through mashed lips. 'Get out of the car,' I said, 'stand by it. Try to run and I'll cut you up without killing you and you'll live years in misery.'

He got out, spitting. As I emerged on the driver's side a pair of headlamps swept up from the direction we had come. It was the car I'd parked to the east of the gate. I pushed the man into the glare of the headlamps and pointed the Ingram in the general direction of the windscreen.

The headlamps went off and the doors opened. Two men emerged, their hands up. 'Take it easy, Colonel,' the driver said, 'we just want to talk to you.'

'All right,' I said, 'say your bit.'

'Colonel, we have your wife and brother. Near Delhi. We have orders to accompany you to Delhi by tomorrow's afternoon flight there from Bangalore.'

'And if I say no?'

'We are unarmed. Not quite unarmed, but we have nothing with which to deal with a man like you. You would have found my friends unarmed.'

'Yes.'

'Like I said, we will accompany you. We have our own vehicles parked further up, two of them. Come with us in comfort, meet our chief and work out an exchange. The diaries in exchange for your wife and brother.'

'I have things in these cars that I need to take along.'

'Feel free, Colonel. Take what you like. We'll come along. You can search our cars, and one of us will drive you to a hotel in Bangalore. We'll leave you free, except that you must take that flight and come with us from the airport.'

'Before we go, prove that you have them.'

He smiled. 'I thought you'd never ask . . . your wife asked me to tell you that the only time your stepson pissed on you was in a tent in Madras. And your brother said, if you want a wet-nurse you can get someone else because he's tired of the job.'

Their cars, two Gypsies, were parked five kilometres from where I'd stopped to talk to them. I put my bags in the rear Gypsy, and the leader of the four, a short, stumpy man, took the wheel with me sitting in the back. I had the Ingram in my hands, finger hooked around the trigger, and the diaries in my pack. He drove fast, much faster than I had, and with the light traffic we reached Bangalore at dawn. He drove straight on to the Oberoi.

They checked me in, the weaponry and the NVGs and armour and gloves tucked away into innocuous bags. When I demanded a separate room they agreed without demur.

The short man who'd driven me here joined me in my room minutes after I went in, and said, 'Colonel, we're going to leave you alone. If you could be ready by noon, well take you along to the airport.'

'Right,' I said. Six hours to go. After he left I went to the bathroom, taking the Ingram and the pack with the diaries in with me. I washed and changed, then called the receptionist to ask for a photocopier. 'When do you need it, sir?' she asked.

'Right away,' I said, 'I have about eight hundred sheets in four books to be photocopied before eleven.'

'Give me a minute to check, sir,' she said.

She called back in a minute. 'You could use one in our business centre,' she said.

'Can you get me one in this room?' I asked. 'I can pay for it. I'll even buy the dam' copier if you like.'

There was silence. Then, 'I'll put you onto our business services people, sir.'

The business services people hemmed and hawed and finally agreed, for an outrageous price, to have a working copier and two thousand sheets of paper delivered to my room in fifteen minutes. 'But we can't put it on your bill,' they said, 'you'll have to pay for it.'

'Sure,' I said, 'do you take cash?'

My minders would notice all this, of course, but I was fairly certain they wouldn't interfere. They'd let me be till now. They had orders to bring me to Delhi and that was precisely what they would do. While waiting for the copier to arrive I used a crocodile clip and bits of plastic to make a bomb that would go off via a battery-powered electrical circuit the moment the jaws of the clip touched. I stuck a bit of plastic broken off a coaster between the jaws to hold them apart and put the bomb in my pack, with the diaries.

The copier arrived and I set to work copying the diaries. At first glance they looked like innocuous business documents but as I made the copies I glanced at the contents and found in them names, names of politicians, ministers, and beside the names figures, fractions. From what Youssuf had told me the figures were in hundreds of thousands . . . If they were, these books told of a total of well over a thousand crores paid out as bribes over three years, not just three hundred as Youssuf had said.

By ten past eleven I'd finished the copying and my chest was hurting once again. I called the receptionist to have the machine taken away and paid off the business services people with a wad of five-hundred rupee notes that they accepted with smiles and bobbing heads. I went downstairs, packed the copies in envelopes, gave them to reception to take to a courier service to be delivered to my father-in-law for safekeeping. Then, exhausted, I lay down for a nap.

Now that I had the diaries I could call Mankekar. Or even Kelkar. If my minders had bugged the room . . . They must have, to follow my phone calls. I slept.

The short man returned at twelve, as I was putting on a fresh shirt. I finished dressing, picked up my bags, and accompanied him to the Gypsy waiting downstairs. At the airport, I demanded to check in separately, and he agreed. I checked my bags in and wandered out into the corridor where there was a public telephone to call Mankekar.

No one picked up. I let it ring until the connection was cut off, and then tried Kelkar. He was home. 'This is Raja,' I said.

'Where are you, Raja?' he asked warily. 'Where have you been?'

'I've got the diaries,' I said, 'I'm on my way to Delhi. They've got Sandhya. And my brother, Gopi. They want to swap them for the diaries.'

He recovered quickly. 'Do you want back-up?' he asked.

'Yes,' I said, 'I've checked in on the flight from Bangalore to Delhi. Get someone to leave a transmitter at Delhi airport. In the first stall in the toilets by the exit. I'll pick it up.' I described my appearance to him. 'Have someone verify that I walk out of the toilet. Then follow . . . Have Hari and a company in place. I'll try to get you the address as we go along. At this number . . .'

'I'll have it manned.'

'There are four men minding me, so expect lots of resistance.'

'We'll be prepared.'

'Don't tell anyone . . . Someone on the Committee's feeding the opposition.'

'Don't worry,' he said, 'I'll run this on my own. We'll get them out . . . You can explain after that.'

I heard the ring of concern in his voice and felt close to tears. I walked out of the booth carrying the diaries, picked up some coffee at a stall and went out into the departure area. The flight was called on time, and when I went out on the tarmac my stumpy minder was right behind.

On the flight I slept again, waking up only as the craft began its descent into Delhi. At the airport I picked up the radio transmitter in the toilet. The four men had arranged for a car. I sat in the back with one man on either side. Ten minutes out of the airport, on the way to the Ring Road, I said, 'I want to talk to my wife. Make sure she's still all right.'

'Sure,' the leader replied, 'we'll stop at a phone booth. I'll call my friends and when they get your wife to the phone you can come out of the car and speak to her.'

We stopped five minutes later and I waited with stretched nerves while he dialled. He spoke briefly, then signalled me. I went into the stuffy booth, picked up the phone, and said, 'Hello.'

'Raja?' asked a tentative female voice. Sandhya.

'Yes,' I said. 'Sandhya, what did your mother cook for me the first time I had lunch at your place?'

There was silence for a while, then she caught on. She told me, then waited.

'Hang on,' I said, 'I'm on my way. Be there in a short while. Are you all right?'

'Raja,' she said, beginning to cry, 'they shot Gopi. They killed Ahmed and they shot Gopi in the knee and now he can't walk.'

I went cold inside. 'Did they take him to a doctor?' I asked, trying to keep my voice level. She continued to cry. 'Sandhya, love, this is no time for tears.'

I heard her sniff a couple of times. 'They showed him

to a doctor but he just tied up the wound and cleaned it up. The doctor stopped the bleeding and bandaged him, and gave him a couple of shots . . . They've got him on a stretcher here, Raja, he's asleep. He was in pain and they gave him something to knock him out. Raja . . . Please get here fast.'

'I will,' I replied, and she told me to hold.

A male voice came on the line, breezy and relaxed, educated and smooth, with a touch of an accent . . . Arabic? Mahmoud. The man in black. The one whom Urmila had liked, the gentle kidnapper. 'I'm sorry, Colonel,' he said, 'your brother was foolish. As your wife just told you, he suffered some injuries in transit. We got him to a doctor but the wound is in the knee and requires some major surgery soon . . . Our doctor couldn't handle it with the facilities we have.'

'What's the damage?' I asked.

'A .38 in the kneecap. Right leg. The bullet exited but pieces of bone have to be extracted. If you don't take too long you might be able to get him into a hospital in time to save the leg. But it'll be stiff all the rest of his life.'

'How about Sandhya?' I asked.

'Your wife? If you behave yourself you'll get her back safe. Otherwise . . .'

'You're Mahmoud,' I said levelly. 'Lay a finger on her and I'll kill you, Mahmoud. There's too much blood on your hands.'

He laughed pleasantly. 'I'm glad you know me, it'll be a pleasure to meet you . . . again. You do remember our previous meetings, don't you? Adios.'

As we resumed the journey, I began to make sense of the landmarks. We went round on the Ring Road, out to Punjabi Bagh, on the road to Bahadurgarh and Gurgaon, on the way to Rohtak. The late-afternoon traffic thickened and slowed, and we were stuck behind a convoy of lorries, sweating in the sultry air after a bout of rain. We pushed on slowly, past the dusty dhabas, past trans-shipment agents and truckers' offices, past workshops and garages, the usual shops and businesses along any highway.

Some eight kilometres short of Bahadurgarh we turned off the highway onto a bumpy secondary road, and in the deepening twilight rattled dustily towards a farm some four kilometres off the highway. We were in farm country now, buffaloes and fields aplenty, and mynahs in the trees. The rains had just arrived here and the earth was fresher for it.

We stopped outside a pair of large iron gates set into a high wall that ran at least a hundred yards to either side of the gates, and continued thereafter as a barbed-wire fence. The gates opened and I saw two men inside, both armed with sub-machine guns, waving us on inwards. Ahead was a straight driveway, bordered with henna, leading up to a farmhouse with a well-lit porch where I could see more men, a white Ambassador, and behind that a blue Sierra.

'Stop,' I said, playing for time to allow Kelkar to get into position. 'I want to talk to my wife. Right now. From here.' I reached into the pack, brought out the crocodile clip, removed the bit of plastic holding them apart. Now it was only my thumb and forefinger preventing the bomb from going up.

'You spoke to her an hour ago,' the short, stumpy man said, eyeing the clip nervously.

'That was an hour ago. I want to confirm they're all right before I hand over the diaries. Talk to Mahmoud . . . You know what'll happen if I let go this clip?'

He nodded shakily, then stepped out of the car and spoke to one of the men at the gate. He got a walkie-talkie from him and spoke into it at length, then brought it over to me. 'Speak here,' he said.

'This is Menon,' I said into the mike.

'Yes, Colonel, what seems to be the problem?' The same pleasant, educated, smooth voice with just that trace of an accent.

'I want to see my wife and brother,' I told him. 'Now, before we work out the exchange.'

'Don't you trust me, Colonel?' Surprise. He was mocking me.

'Trust doesn't come into it,' I said, 'I want to see them alive. Then we talk.'

'I'd like to agree, Colonel, but your brother's asleep. Our medicine man gave him a shot. He's sound asleep.' Still mocking. He had the organization on his side, and, as he thought, the time.

Please let's stretch this out, I thought. 'Check with your medic whether he can wake him up without further damage.'

'Hang on.' There was a silence and I heard him speak to

someone else. 'It'll take a few minutes, Colonel.'

'Don't hurt him.'

'We won't. Not as long as you're going to give us the diaries. Why don't we work that out now?'

'No,' I said, 'only after I confirm visually. We can wait.' I handed the walkie-talkie back to the minder.

Three terrible minutes passed before the walkie-talkie buzzed again. 'Your wife will be on the porch in a moment, Colonel, also your brother. He'll be in a wheelchair.'

'Can he talk?'

'He might not be fully awake . . . That'll take more time.' His voice hardened. 'And I am not willing to waste much more time to satisfy your whims.'

'I have to confirm that they are alive, just as you have to confirm that I have the diaries.'

The pleasantness was back in his voice. 'That's no problem,' he said, 'give us one volume, any one.'

'All right,' I said, 'put my wife on.' I put my handout and the minder gave me a pair of binoculars which I focussed on the porch.

'Give me one of the diaries when you see your wife.'

'Nothing doing,' I said, 'I'll do it after I talk to her. Otherwise the whole lot goes up in flames. I've wired it up.'

The pleasantness receded and was gone as if it had never been. 'I was sure you would . . . That's why I asked my men to take it easy with you. Some other man and we wouldn't have wasted so much time, my men would have snatched the diaries in Virajpet. You're a hard bastard, Menon. I wish you were on my side. Think on it, Menon. Join us and you'll have your wife, your brother will get the best of treatment on this earth and you yourself will have more money than you imagined . . . Name your figure, and don't worry about a few zeroes here and there. Are you game?'

'I'll consider it, Mahmoud,' I said, 'but one of these days I'd like to take you. Head to head.'

He laughed, a hard edge to his voice. 'You and who else, Colonel? I'll break you into little pieces and make you eat them. But enough of this. The exchange. I won't wait any more.'

There was a finality in his voice I couldn't ignore. 'All right,' I said, 'I give one of the diaries to the minder here. He verifies it for you. He gives it back to me, and when I've spoken to my wife and brother I start walking up the drive towards the house. You put them in a car and they drive out of here when I'm in the middle of the driveway. We all wait until she gets to Bahadurgarh and calls me. Then I give you the diaries and walk away.'

'Not asking for guarantees for your own life?' he asked.

'No. Now that the diaries are practically in your hands, I don't see what I can do to you.'

'Being sensible, are we?' he said. 'All right.'

The front door opened and Sandhya came out, a man behind her. Then a wheelchair emerged, with Gopi slumped in it. His head lolled to one side. I didn't like his looks. Another man emerged from the door and handed Sandhya a walkie-talkie. The last of the light had faded from the sky and the clouds above covered the moon and the stars and I hoped Kelkar was in position. If I knew Hari at all he'd be there. I hoped he'd be there. He'd have the sense to keep us out of the crossfire

The seconds plodded heavily past. Sandhya, my love, Gopi, my blood. Please stay alive. I prayed. My hands trembled.

The walkie-talkie hissed. 'Raja?' Her voice was lifeless defeated.

I swallowed hard, and the words came out hoarse. 'Sandhya. I'm here. I can see you. Can you see me?'

'No. It's too dark. Raja . . .'

'No panic. You're on your way out. Have they told you what to do? Are you clear?'

'Yes . . . I drive out of here when they give me the signal. Raja, what will you do after we leave?'

'Wait for your call. Give them the diaries. Leave.'

'Raja, they'll kill you.'

'They don't need to . . . get your act together. Give it to Gopi now.'

She handed the walkie-talkie to Gopi and seconds later I heard him speak with a forced liveliness that brought the prick of tears to my eyes. 'Raja, you cretin! You need a bloody wet-nurse. We should never have left you.'

'Right,' I said, 'as soon as this is over I'll get a battle-axe to take care of me.' My voice thickened until it was barely audible 'Little brother, take care.'

'I knew you would come,' he replied, 'you always did.' he sounded tired. 'See you around.'

I gave the walkie-talkie back to the minder, took the diary from him. A Maruti drew up to the porch. Sandhya climbed in, and two men lifted Gopi off the wheelchair and put him in the rear seat. I put the diary back in my pack, adjusted the flak-jacket around me, and stepped out onto the dark driveway.

The car came slowly along at walking speed. They must have told her to take it easy along the driveway. I stepped off onto the grass and the car came closer, ten yards from the house, then twenty, thirty . . . I ripped the wires off the clip to disable the bomb.

With a roar and a flash that nearly blinded me, the eastern corner of the building exploded. Kelkar had timed it perfectly.

I ran for the car, ducking and weaving through the barrage of fire, head down, pulling the Ingram out of the pack as I went. I got to the driver's side, got Sandhya out and onto the ground, rolled over her. Then I got up and went around to the rear seat where Gopi had managed to get the door open. I got my hands under his arms and then there was the familiar sound of a sub-machine gun. Two hammer blows on my side knocked me down and I rolled over.

Two dark shapes loomed up, black-clad, helmeted, Ingrams at the ready. SOF men. I could see the outline of a spade across one's shoulders. Hari. At this range the Ingrams were not much use because they couldn't be aimed. Another man joined them, giving Hari and his buddy cover as they raced up to cover Gopi, who was now half out of the car. I got up and out of the corner of my eyes saw a figure run away from the house, directly towards the car.

Mahmoud. He flung away the empty sub-machine gun

in his hands, pulled a long, gleaming knife out of his trouser leg, and came on. Hari had seen him, too. He rose to face the Libyan but I pushed him back and drew the spade off his harness. Mahmoud slowed, saw me rise, and kept coming on. Instead of waiting for him I ran out to meet him and just eight feet away I hurled the spade at his unprotected head. It took him completely by surprise and I heard the impact as it hit him in the face, but his momentum carried him on until he went past me and collapsed on the grass at my side, knocking me down again.

I got to my knees, saw Mahmoud lying motionless on the grass, and turned around. Sandhya had come up on her knees and Gopi was on the ground, a SOF man bending over him. Suddenly I realized that the gunfire had stopped. It was over. I looked at Gopi lying by the car. He was sprawled shapelessly on the ground and there were two splotches on his chest. I got to my feet and pushed aside the SOF man kneeling by him. Even as I reached for his wrist to check his pulse I knew he was gone. I let his wrist fall to the grass and dropped on my knees beside him. There was a great weight in my chest that bent me down until I felt the wetness of his blood on my forehead. As I knelt on the damp grass there was a roaring in my ears and a great, searing emptiness in my heart.

chapter sixteen

I lit Gopi's pyre on a grey, wet August morning, as I had lit my father's many years ago. The stacked firewood on the riverbank sparked briefly, then, helped by the kerosene the attendants poured on it, crackled into flame. Kelkar and Hari and Alok were there, hard-faced and bleak-eyed as soldiers are on these occasions. Sandhya stood by me all the time, worry knotting her forehead.

The mourners came. They came to the cremation, in the rain, from far away. Urmila came, with her father, the lone uninhibited mourner there. She stood in front of me intending to say something comforting but only managed instead to burst into tears. She hugged me briefly and her father pulled her away, giving my hand a hard squeeze.

Mankekar came, despite his illness, despite the distance, despite the weather. He leant on his cane and raised his hand in benediction and excused himself early. His words as I saw him back to his car seemed out of place. 'Find it in yourself to forgive,' he said.

And there were the VIPs. They came because they knew now about the photocopies. They came with grief on their faces and condolences on their lips but calculation in their eyes. They all spoke a few words and moved on and I watched with a great coldness in my heart, for one of them had killed Gopi.

'You don't have to meet them, son,' Kelkar whispered soothingly in my ear, 'I'll take care of them.' But I insisted because I wanted to look in their eyes and try to find out which one.

Patil came first, the lean and hungry lawyer. He shook his head in synthetic sorrow, said, 'It's a great loss. If there is anything I can do to help . . .'

Then came Pravin Kumar, the humbler, bleary-eyed, gripping my hand in both of his for long enough for me to see his insincerity. 'We are all grieved,' he said. 'A bright young man . . .'

A little behind him, his hardness a little softened today, came his junior, Varma. 'We grieve with you,' he said. 'A fine young man. His best was yet to come.'

Kewal Ram limped up. He did a namaste, muttered something in Sanskrit that I didn't understand. I nodded and he moved on.

At the end came Shankar Pai, short and tubby, jolly eyes now carefully blank. He shook my hand, did a namaste to Sandhya, made as if to say something, then changed his mind and joined the others waiting for him.

The forty sleepless hours after Gopi died on the grass had been the hardest of my life. Kelkar had dragged me off home, postponing with Mankekar's help the bright lights and loud questions that follow such occasions.

In the hours after the battle at the farmhouse, many things had become clear.

The Orphan had thought up the diaries years ago. Mehta had created them. The Orphan had then begun to set up a network of bagmen and frighteners to enforce his blackmail but then Mehta had been arrested and the diaries taken by the CBI.

The Orphan organized the kidnapping to get back the diaries. He had taken it one step further: since the Prime Minister was the only senior politician not directly implicated by the diaries the Orphan arranged for the murder of the granddaughter to grieve the PM into retirement. After that, with the diaries in his hands, he and his group wouldn't have cared who was in power.

He hired Rawat and Mahmoud, a Libyan mercenary who had fought in Afghanistan, to run it for him. Only Mahmoud—Hairy Face—knew that the hostages were to be killed: everyone else on the kidnap team thought they would be returned when the ransom was paid.

When the Orphan and Mahmoud discovered that they needed two more men, Rawat got in touch with Youssuf, who provided them. Mahmoud survived the raid and got away in the dark, as did Youssuf's nephew, the man with the bugs. Mahmoud was supposed to have the diaries but I got to them first. Youssuf's man took them from me before he got away, and left them with Youssuf.

Mahmoud, always suspicious, had thought I'd hidden

the diaries away somewhere. He had me watched in hospital. They knew when I got away, and followed me to Kabini. There Mahmoud killed Basappa because he knew that the cook would only lead me to him, and not to whoever had the diaries. Mahmoud lost us in the forest but found me when I went after Rawat. He lost us again when we took the train south, but my abortive raid on Ahmed in Kochi alerted him again. They had used the bugs extensively. They'd bugged our room at Kabini, and figured out that I didn't have the diaries. With their strategy falling apart, Mahmoud had persuaded the Orphan to let me continue after the diaries: the idea was to use me as a lightning rod. After Mahmoud caught up with me at Ahmed's flat in Bombay he never lost track. He and the Orphan listened to all my conversations in the hotels after that. Mahmoud's minders had bugged my room in Bangalore after Mahmoud took Sandhya and Gopi captive, but they had missed the chat I had with General Kelkar from the airport.

I gave Kelkar the diaries. He had delivered them to the Supreme Court, where they would once again be the basis of further investigations.

Mahmoud had been the knife man. He enjoyed it. A psychopath, apparently, but so many terrorists are. The spade had hit him just below his nose, and the sharp edge had broken through and driven splinters of bone into his brain, killing him.

No great loss. But I would have gladly let him live if he had let Gopi live. In the last minute of his life he had extracted from me a price that was too great.

And the Orphan . . . He could have been any one of those five men on the Committee. I'd told Mankekar, he'd told the Committee, and hours later Gopi and Sandhya were in Mahmoud's hands while Ahmed was dead. It had to be one of these five, and I had no idea who.

A sharp, moist wind sprang up. I needed to be alone. For a few minutes, just to gather myself. I walked unnoticed, past the VIPs standing around, to the toilets beyond. I went in, washed my face and hands, dried them with a kerchief. Felt the desolate salt taste of grief at the back of my mouth. Sagged against the white-tiled wall, trembling with weariness.

Why was I alive and Gopi dead?

After a minute or two I went quietly back out, and stood beside Sandhya next to the group of VIPs. There was a little group of them, talking to General Kelkar. Bits of their conversation floated out to me. 'Bad day . . . My arthritis is bad.' 'My grandson refuses to go to school.' Then, some talk about Gopi. 'A brave young man . . . Only a little over thirty.' Another voice said, 'Very active . . . Brilliant. He would have loved this weather.' I looked at the speaker, recognized him from his broad back.

The flames leapt high and I felt Sandhya's fingers tighten on my arm. I put my hand on hers and she in turn covered mine. Far above, a kite soared and banked and made circles in the sky. It saw something on the ground and came swooping down. And the coldness lifted from my heart.

I knew.

The flames crackled on. The VIPs stirred, preparing to

leave. I took Sandhya's hand off my arm and turned to Hari. 'Call Kelkar,' I told him. 'Alone. Now.' Hari took one look at my face and ran, and behind us the SOF detachment came watchfully alive.

'I know who it is,' I whispered in Kelkar's ear when he came.

'Who?' he asked, and I explained. 'How?' he asked.

'That man, sir,' I said, almost numb with anger and pain, 'he knows Gopi loved the rain—Gopi said that to me in Kabini . . . the lodge. Our room was bugged . . .'

'We'll stop him,' he said, and walked quickly on to where the VIPs' vehicles were parked. He stopped by the white Contessa as its owner reached its side. 'One moment,' he said.

I stepped up to the man. 'How did you know,' I asked him flatly, 'that Gopi would have loved this weather?'

Rage flashed in his amber eyes. His bodyguard stepped up, the sub-machine gun no longer pointed upwards but at me. I heard footsteps behind and when I turned Hari was there, his sidearm drawn, and behind him the SOF detachment spreading out to encircle the group.

'Come on, Mr Varma,' Kelkar said, 'I heard you say that. We'd really like to know.'

His features twisted into a mask of fury. 'Not Varma,' he said hoarsely, 'Niazi. Humayun Khan Niazi. I took on myself the name of the Indian dog who raised me, but only for convenience.'

I wanted to kill him where he stood but Mankekar's parting words held me back. I turned away from the hatred in those eyes and stumbled back towards the pyre, unseeing, wet-eyed. Sandhya ran up, a white blur. She put her arm around me and pulled my head down until my forehead rested on hers. Out of a corner of my eyes I saw the flames of the pyre beginning to subside. There was a great flash of lightning above, and a crack of thunder ahead of the rain. It came down in great white sheets, the water mixing with the tears on my cheeks as I wept, and then there was only the memory of a little boy dancing in the rain.